The New Zealand Bed and Breakfast Book

Homes Farms Guest Houses

Compiled by J. and J. Thomas

PELICAN PUBLISHING COMPANY
GRETNA 1990

Published in New Zealand by Moonshine Press, 1989
Pelican edition, January 1990

Library of Congress Cataloging-in-Publication Data

Thomas, J. (James)
    The New Zealand bed and breakfast book : homes, farms,
guest houses / compiled by J. and J. Thomas. – Pelican ed.
      p.   cm.
    "Published in New Zealand by Moonshine Press, 1989."
    ISBN 0-88289-791-8
    1. Bed and Breakfast accommodations – New Zealand –
Guide-books. 2. New Zealand – Description and travel –
1981- – Guide-books. I. Thomas, J. (Janete) II. Title.
TX907.5.N45T48   1990
647.949303 – dc20   89-70962
                                       CIP

Cover sketch: Cannobie-Lee, Amberley

The information in this guidebook is based on authoritative data available at the time of printing. Prices and other information of businesses listed are subject to change without notice. Readers are asked to take this into account when consulting this guide.

Manufactured in the United States of America
Published by Pelican Publishing Company, Inc.
1101 Monroe Street, Gretna, Louisiana 70053

From letters on our file

"I congratulate you on your book, its format and the very nice people you were successful in listing in your publication. They truly made our trip to New Zealand memorable."
MONTREAL, CANADA

"I would certainly use the book again if I am lucky enough to return to New Zealand and will recommend it to friends. My only criticism — all the people were so hospitable that I chatted for hours and got very tired."
BROCKENHURST, HAMPSHIRE, ENGLAND

"We were delighted with your publication and the high standard of accommodation."
ASHFORD, KENT, ENGLAND

"Your book helped make our holiday brilliant. All of our hosts were lovely and we wouldn't have found them without your help."
DETROIT, MICHIGAN, USA

"Our farmstay holiday was tremendously successful. The hospitality extended to us was outstanding. All in all it was a wonderful experience and we are looking forward to planning another."
TAUPO, NEW ZEALAND

"I would like to say how much better your kind of accommodation is than motels."
KINGS LYNN, NORFOLK, ENGLAND

"Since discovering the New Zealand Bed and Breakfast Book my husband and I have used it regularly on our trips away from New Plymouth and we have been really pleased with both the accommodation and great hospitality offered."
NEW PLYMOUTH, NEW ZEALAND

New Zealand Regions

Northland

Auckland

Gisborne and District

Waikato, Coromandel Peninsula, King Country

Bay of Plenty

Hawkes Bay

Taranaki, Wanganui

Manawatu

Wairarapa

Wellington

Nelson, Marlborough

Christchurch and District

Westland

Timaru, Oamaru District

Dunedin and District

Southland

Contents

Introduction

New Zealand has several travel and accommodation guides but this is the first time that a book listing Bed and Breakfast accommodation available in private homes has been published. The 280 hosts who are listed here are homeowners who want to share their love of the country with travellers. Each listing has been written by the host, and you will discover the warmth and personality of the host is obvious in their writing. Ours is not simply an accommodation guide but an introduction to a uniquely New Zealand holiday experience.

Any holiday is remembered primarily by the people one meets. How many of us have loved a country simply because of one or two especially memorable individuals encountered there? Bed and Breakfast offers the traveller who wants to experience the feel of the real country and get to know the people to do just that.

Bed and Breakfast in New Zealand means a warm welcome into someone's home. Most of the places listed are homes, with a sprinkling of private hotels and guesthouses.

Please remember that Bed and Breakfast hosts cannot offer hotel facilities and that many have occupations outside of their homes. Therefore please telephone ahead to book your accommodation, give ample notice if you require dinner, and be prepared to leave by 10 a.m. on the morning of departure.

Tariff
Most hosts will charge a tariff which is fairly consistent throughout the country. A few have chosen to ask different tariffs because of facilities or location and these are shown in each listing. In most cases the prices listed will apply for the year 1990. There will be no extra costs to pay unless you request extra services. However there may have been a reason to change the tariff, so always check.

Self-Contained Accommodation
Many homes in towns and on farms can offer separate self-contained accommodation. In almost every case linen and food will be provided if required. The tariff will vary depending on your requirements, so check when booking.

Campervans
For those who get to know the country by camping or campervan, Bed and Breakfast offers wonderful advantages. You will see in many listings the word 'campervans'. These homes have suitable facilities available such as laundry, bathroom, electricity and meals if necessary. The charge usually for up to four people is modest and is shown in each listing.

Finding Your Way Around

A satisfying part of compiling *The New Zealand Bed and Breakfast Book* is that we have been able to change an irritating aspect of most New Zealand guide books. Usually towns are listed alphabetically so that we hop about the country from such places as Ashley to Auckland to Balclutha for example. This is infuriating to a reasonably well-travelled native like myself, so I imagine the despair of a visitor unfamiliar with place names and local geography.

New Zealand is long and narrow. It makes more sense to me to travel southwards down the islands listing the homes as we come to them. We have divided New Zealand into geographical regions using the same boundaries as used by the New Zealand Post Office, and have included a map of each region. We have simply listed the homes as they occur on our southward journey. In areas such as Southland where we travel across more than down, the route we have taken should be quite obvious.

I picked up a young Japanese hitch-hiker near Wellington and asked him if I should include a list of problems which might arise for a traveller in New Zealand. He emphatically replied, "No. Because New Zealanders are so friendly they make everything OK!"

Whether you are from overseas or a fellow New Zealander, please take the opportunity to stay with New Zealanders in their homes. Chat with your hosts. Enjoy their company. Each host will be your additional personal travel agent and guide. They want to make everything in your holiday OK.

We wish you an enjoyable holiday and welcome comments from guests. Please write after you have spoken to your hosts with compliments or suggestions to:

The New Zealand Bed and Breakfast Book
Pelican Publishing Company, Inc.
P.O. Box 189
1101 Monroe Street
Gretna, Louisiana 70053

All telephone numbers in New Zealand are being changed during 1990 so the numbers listed may not be current. Ring 018 for directory assistance if you cannot contact your hosts.

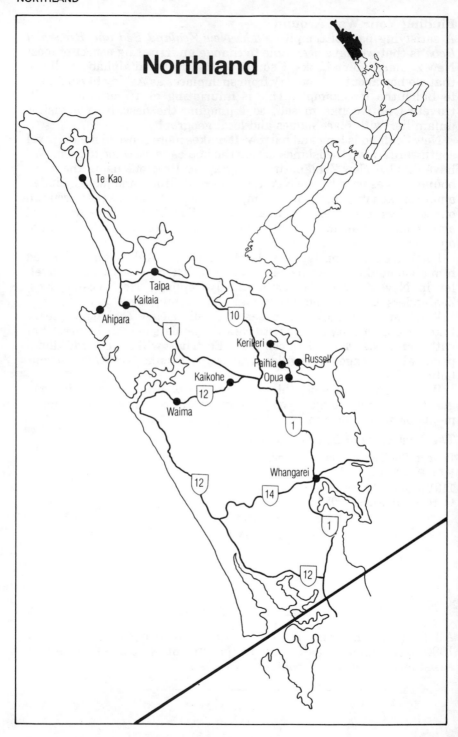

Northland

Te Kao

Taipa
Kaitaia

Ahipara

10

Kerikeri

Paihia
Kaikohe
Opua

Russell

12

Waima

12

Whangarei

14

1

12

Te Kao, Kaitaia

Guest House
Address: Te Kao Guest House, Far North Road, RD4, Kaitaia
Name: Maurice Loveday
Telephone: 088957 826
Beds: 3 Double, 4 Single (4 bedrooms, all ensuite)
Tariff: Accommodation only. Double $32, Single $20, Stay of
3 or more days $15 per person per day, Children ½ price; Dinner $12,
Breakfast (cooked) $4.50, (Continental) $3.50
Nearest Town: 72 km north of Kaitaia

Explore and fish the winterless far north from my modern accom-
modation. Over 40 world game fish records have been broken by my
guests during the last three years.
The Guest House is situated in a lovely bush area just across the road
from a tidal stream at the south end of Parengarenga Harbour. It is
10 km from the west coast (90 mile beach), 3 km from the east coast and
40 km from Cape Reinga.
Guests may cook their own meals in my large, modern kitchen which
has both microwave and conventional cooking facilities. TV in lounge
and dining room. Pool table and excellent library.
Directions: *Continue 72 km north from Kaitaia. I am about 2 km*
north of the Te Kao District High School and the local general store.
Watch for my sign on the right just before a one-way bridge over the Te
Kao stream.

Taipa

Homestay
Address: "The Bean Farm", Oruru Road, Taipa
(PO Box 202, Mangonui)
Name: Agnes Hauptli and Peter Meier
Telephone: (0889) 72-893
Beds: 2 Double Rooms
Tariff: B&B Double $50, Single $30; Dinner $12
Nearest Town: 8 km from Taipa, 14 km from Mangonui,
40 km from Kaitaia

We are a couple originally from Switzerland, well experienced in
tourism, and are now experimenting 'to live in harmony with nature' in
this beautiful Oruru Valley.
Our cooking is Continental and International.
Home: *A 100-year-old former schoolhouse. 3 acres of land, trees and*
two glasshouses. Six sheep, chooks for fresh eggs and two cats.
Land: *Horticulture, lots of veges, lemon, orange, peach, apple, fig,*
avocado and plum trees. Grapes.
Doubtless Bay offers beautiful beaches, Tokerau and Whatuwhiwhi
Beach to the west, Taipa, Cable Bay, Coopers Beach and Mangonui to

continued over

the south. The local yachting club is in Taipa. The beaches are all safe and windsurfing equipment can be rented. The Ninety-Mile Beach and Cape Reinga can be visited by regular bus excursions.

Mangonui, once the gateway to the Far North, is a quiet township offering a popular restaurant, an aquarium of salt-water fish, good boating facilities and arts and crafts shops.

Directions: *Turn off from Highway 10 at Taipa, follow the AA sign Oruru, after 8 km after passing the old dairy factory on the right you will see the house and glasshouses on your left. Guests arriving by the N.Z. Rail Bus are picked up in Taipa.*

NZ phone numbers are being changed. Ring 018 for directory.

Taipa, Kaitaia

Farmhouse
Address: Cnr Back River Road and
    Oruru Road, RD3, Kaitaia
Name: John and Jeannie Kennedy
Telephone: (0889 72) 859
Beds: 1 Double, 3 Single (2 bedrooms, self-contained unit)
Tariff: B&B Double $55, Single $35; Dinner $15;
Children under 12 years ½ price
Nearest Town: Manganui 12 km, Kaitaia, 38 km to the northwest

I would like to invite you to stay with my wife, two teenage children and myself.

We live in a beautiful valley 6 km inland by tarseal road from Taipa on Northland's east coast. Our 45-year-old home is set in a lovely, well established, large country garden with in-ground swimming pool and full-size billiards room.

All the local buses pick up passengers for the Cape Reinga trips from Taipa. Our beautiful beaches which stretch as far as the eye can see, are some of the most appealing that I have ever seen.

We trust that everyone who stays with us will wish to return for a second visit.

My wife's interests are family, gardening and handcrafts and I enjoy my billiards and all things mechanical.

So come and spend some time with us and discover the joys of simple country living.

Directions: *After crossing one way bridge at Taipa going north, turn left and travel 6 km inland. Take 2nd turn to the left and we are the first house on Back River Road. Free transport from Taipa as required.*

Ahipara

Guesthouse
Address: Siesta Guest House,
Tasman Heights Road,
P.O. Box 67,
Ahipara
Name: Rolf and Hanna Stump
Telephone: (0889) 74-565
Beds: 2 Double (2 bedrooms, guest bathrooms)
Tariff: B&B Double $90, Single $50; Dinner $25
Nearest Town: Kaitaia 15 km

We are a family of four with two teenage girls, emigrated from Switzerland some 10 years ago to this beautiful country. As well as English we speak perfect German. Our home is especially designed and build as a guest house with the comfort and privacy of our guests in mind. It is situated on a large hillside section, 50 m above sea level. You have a fantastic panoramic view, overlooking the famous Ninety Mile Beach, Ahipara Bay and rocky shore with sandhills to the left. The setting is very peaceful, framed by pine trees and the gentle rolling ocean beyond. The European-style house is solidly built with concrete to offer maximum quietness, faces north and receives all day sun.

Each of the large double guest rooms has natural timber ceilings, comfortable queen-size beds, colour TV, radio and writing desk, has its own bathroom, tea- and coffee-making facilities and sheltered balcony with uninterrupted sea views; even a sea view out of your bed.

Our house is most ideal for couples or anybody wanting to get away from it all and enjoy a clean environment with plenty of outdoor activities. As we will host no more than four people at any one time, we can provide you with the best of service in all aspects. Also we can offer you full board with a first class evening meal, served in our spacious family dining room.

Directions: *Take the road to the west coast from Kaitaia approx. 15 km.*

Kerikeri

Homestay
Address: Bulls Road, RD3, Highway 10
Name: Jetty Zijderveld
Telephone: (0887) 79-220
Beds: 2 Double, 3 Single (3 bedrooms, guests bathroom)
Tariff: B&B Double $50, Single $30
Nearest Town: Kerikeri 5 minutes, Paihia 15 minutes
Our house is warm and sunny. It is nearly new with 3 double bedrooms

11

continued over

*for guests (one with twin beds) and one small room with a single bed.
The house has 2 bathrooms, so you have your own for your use.*

*We are on a 16 acre farmlet with beautiful rural views on all sides
overlooking Waimate North.*

*Kerikeri is situated in the Bay of Islands and is ideally situated to
explore the area. Our house is 5 minutes drive from Kerikeri and 15
minutes from Paihia.*

Directions: *On State Highway 10 with a Bed and Breakfast sign
outside so it is easy to find. Please phone for further details.*

Paihia

Homestay
Address: 31 Selwyn Road,
 Paihia, Bay of Islands
Name: Bill and Bunny Lind
Telephone: (0885) 27-182
Beds: 3 Single (2 bedrooms)
Tariff: B&B Double $50, Single $30,
Children half price; Continental breakfast only

*We are a retired couple who enjoy meeting people from all walks of life.
Our family are grown up and we now have only one daughter here who
is a hostess on the cruise ships in our lovely bay. Our special interests
are outdoor bowling and china painting.*

*We are only a two minute walk from the beach and a five minute walk
from all the shops and restaurants. The departure points for all tours
and cruises are within the five minute walk.*

*Our home is a modern 2-storey townhouse with a spacious open plan
living area and a sea and bush outlook. We have one single bedroom
downstairs and one twin room upstairs. The bathroom is on a shared
basis, with one toilet and washing facilities downstairs and one
upstairs.*

*Although we have Continental breakfast only it is of a very generous
proportion and variety.*

*Paihia can also offer many lovely walks in bush and beach. We love our
town and enjoy sharing it with others.*

Directions: *Turn left at the Post Office, then the first turn right which
is Selwyn Road. We are the last house on the right with our name on
the wooden fence. If travelling south turn right at Paihia Post Office,
then follow same as above.*

12

Russell

Homestay
Address: Brown Lodge, Ashby Street, Russell
Name: Roly and Joan Brown
Telephone: (0885) 37-693
Beds: 1 Double, 1 Single (1 bedroom, guest bathroom)
Tariff: B&B Double $80, Single $60

Our home is in central Russell with beautiful sea views. Personal and friendly attention in one of the interesting new homes built in keeping with the historic nature of Russell. NZ timbers and old world charm of yesterday combine pleasing harmony with your hosts conscious of good living environment. We have airconditioning and heating for year-round comfort.

Deep sea and light tackle fishing, island cruising, sailing, diving can be arranged, also historic places, beaches, bush walks and restaurants are handy.

One guest room twin/double with private bathroom, TV and tea-making facilities.

Russell

Homestay
Address: Jacks Bay, No. 1 RD, Russell, Bay of Islands
Name: Marie C. Graham
Telephone: (0885) 37-322 (Before 9 am and after 5.30 pm)
Beds: 4 Single (2 bedrooms, guest bathroom)
Tariff: B&B Double $65, Single $35; Campervans $20
(no more than 4 people); Dinner $15 per person
Nearest Town: Russell 16 km

My house is situated approximately 16 km from Russell on a metal road, just above the Jack and Jill Resort. Near the beach with lovely views of the sea and islands. A quiet situation and very peaceful.
I am a farmer's widow and live alone with one corgi dog who is very gentle and loving and lives inside.
Guests have separate bathroom and toilet facilities. I work part time for social welfare so some days I am out during the middle of the day.
Directions: *To reach my place you turn off the Opua–Russell road at Oronga Bay onto a metal road, follow the road to Jacks Bay. It is well signposted. I am on the left side of the road just after the entrance to the camp — a 1½ storey house painted green and white.*

Russell

Homestay
Address: Robertson Street,
Russell (PO Box 203)
Name: Dudley and Sharyn Smith
Telephone: (0885) 37-200 (Fax 37-537)
Beds: Private facilities in self-contained unit. Sleeps 4
Tariff: B&B Double $55, Single $35,
Children $15; Campervan Facilities $25

Our new home is situated on an elevated section in the historic town of Russell. We have magnificent views of the town and Russell Harbour. Our home has a large basement flat with its own shower, toilet and coffee-making facilities. This area has excellent views and good parking. As our kitchen, dining area and lounge is all open living it becomes very easy for guests to make themselves at home.
We operate an 11·5 metre charter boat for big game and light tackle fishing and would imagine our guests to be people who like the sea and perhaps intend to go fishing with us.
Directions: *Please phone when you arrive.*

Russell

Homestay
Address: Major Bridge Drive,
Te Wahapu, Russell
Name: Eva and Denis Brown
Telephone: (0885) 37-431
Beds: 1 Double, 1 Single (1 Bedroom, guest bathroom)
Tariff: B&B Double $50, Single $28, Child $15; Dinner $16
Nearest Town: Russell, 7 km by car or 20 minutes rowing
in our dinghy

Our wooden house is near a quiet beach in a sheltered bay. We recommend walking shoes to our guests because our parking area is on the top of the hill and our house is by the water. A footpath leads down through a tunnel of native ferns, kanukas and manukas.

We provide a dinghy free for fishing or rowing to Russell, the historic first capital of New Zealand. It is a small village with a museum and historic buildings, tourist boats, yacht charters, gourmet restaurants and the visitors' centre of the Bay of Islands Maritime and Historic Park.

Beach walks start from our front door, and it takes days to see, but some of the bays, Maori pas, kauri forests and historic sites are only a short drive, walk or sail away from our house.

Optional dinners may be arranged (with or without meat — special diets are catered for). Breakfasts range from homemade muesli, fresh fruit and wholemeal bread to bacon and eggs to order.

Please phone ahead as we only have one guest room. We can pick up guests at the ferry on the Russell wharf or at the nearby stop of Clark's Northliner bus.

Opua, Bay of Islands

Address: Please phone
Name: Pat and Dan Jansen
Telephone: (0885) 28-099
Beds: 1 Double, 2 Single (2 bedrooms)
Tariff: B&B Double $55, Single $30; Dinner $12 by arrangement; Children ½ price
Nearest Town: Paihia 6 km

We are a family of four though our children are grown up and living away. We have a Burmese cat, very spoilt. Our home is modern but very comfortable with lovely sea and rural views. We are close to beaches, golf course, bush walks, boat and bus tours and many other attractions. Handy to bus stop.
Our interests include sailing, walking, reading, music and travel.

Kaikohe

Homestay + Campervan Park
Address: Waima Lodge,
Main Road, Waima,
South Hokianga.
Postal: Private Bag,
Taheke, Kaikohe

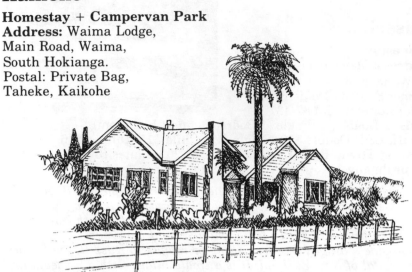

Name: Dennis and Pearl Horne
Telephone: (0887) 53-836 (evenings preferred). Fax (0887) 53-836
Beds: 1 Double, 1 Twin (guest bathroom)
Tariff: B&B Double $60, Single $40; Dinner $20
Nearest Town: Kaikohe 26 km, Opononi 26 km, Rawene 17 km

We have a lovely old kauri homestead set in 4½ acres of orchards and gardens by the Waima river and mountains. We enjoy cooking and will be serving all our home-grown fruit and vegetables. We enjoy meeting people from all over the world and to show them the beauty and local history of the area. We are situated within a short distance of most of Northland's attractions, such as the Waipoua kauri forest, Opononi beaches, Kaitaia and the Bay of Islands. We are ideal as a touring base. We have two private bathrooms recently added to guest bedrooms, to give our guests the highest standard of comfort.
We have no children but 2 friendly dogs, 2 cats and 8 sheep.
Directions: *Our house is on State Highway 12 about midway between Kaikohe and Opononi. Look for signs and tall palms, also marae across the road.*

Always telephone ahead to enquire about a
B&B. It is a nuisance for you if you simply
arrive to find someone is already staying there.
And besides, hosts need a little time to
prepare.

Kamo, Whangarei

Self-Contained Accommodation
Address: Dip Road, Kamo, Whangarei (PO Box 4041, Kamo)
Name: Jock and Corin Elliot
Telephone: (089) 51-427
Beds: 1 Double, 1 Single in self-contained unit
Tariff: B&B Double $50, Single $30, Children half-price
Nearest Town: 8 km north from Whangarei City Centre

Our home is situated on the outskirts of the city of Whangarei amidst two acres of ground. We have a large garden which provides us with a plentiful supply of fresh, organically grown vegetables and fruit. We share the property with three sheep, a dozen free-range hens — their handsome lord and master and a hive of bees. A native bush reserve runs along our eastern boundary.
Guests are accommodated in a self-contained unit which has a double and single bed, its own bathroom and cooking facilities and opens through glass doors directly onto a private area of the garden.
If you play golf the nearest course is five minutes' walk away and a thirty minute drive will take you to a variety of beaches and the deep sea fishing base at Tutukaka. And, if you enjoy sailing we can arrange to take you out on the harbour — weather and tides permitting!
Directions: *Travel north via State Highway 1 to the Kamo traffic lights at the intersection of Kamo Road and Three Mile Bush Road. Take the left turn into Three Mile Bush Road and after 1.1 km turn right into Dip Road. A further 1.1 km and you will see our name on the right at the entranceway.*

Whangarei

Farmhouse
Address: 59 Pukenui Road, Whangarei
Name: Patricia and Owen Flower
Telephone: (089) 488-080 or 487-464
Beds: 4 Single (2 bedrooms, guest bathrooms)
Tariff: B&B Double $50, Single $35; Dinner $15
Nearest Town: Whangarei

We are five minutes by car from the centre of town. Our home is situated on a twelve-acre block with views of the town and countryside. Our animals include sheep, cows, hens, ducks, etc.
Recreational facilities include tramping through native bush, swimming and surfing within half an hours travelling.
The two guest rooms have two single beds in each and you have your own bathroom and toilet.
Cooked or Continental breakfast is available and you are welcome to join us for dinner.

17

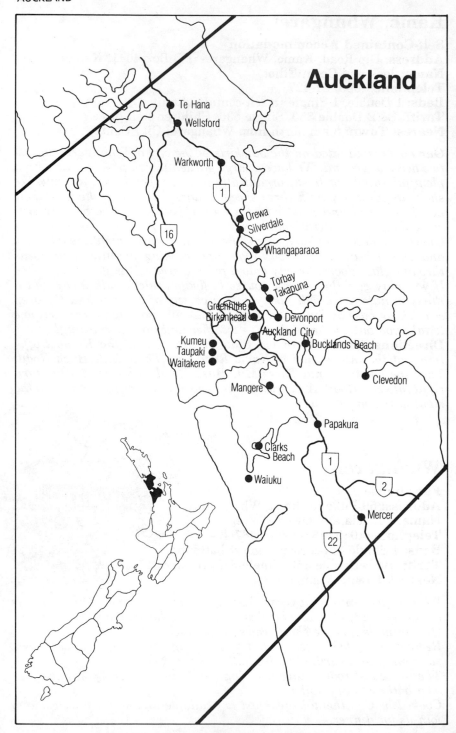

Auckland

Te Hana, Wellsford

Farmhouse
Address: 'The Retreat', Te Hana, RD5, Wellsford
Name: Tony and Colleen Moore
Telephone: (08463) 8547
Beds: 1 Double, 2 Single (2 bedrooms, guest bathroom)
Tariff: B&B Double $48, Single $25; Dinner $15

'The Retreat' is a kauri homestead built in 1867 for a family with 12 children. It faces north and we look out over farmland including the eight acres where we graze black and white sheep. Colleen is a spinner and weaver and produces goods from the wool which are sold from the house.

Guests have a choice of twin or double bedrooms and use of their own bathroom.
Creating a garden to compliment the house is an ongoing source of enjoyment and a large herb garden and perennial borders are features that visitors can appreciate.
We have travelled extensively overseas and in New Zealand and are keen to promote our scenic and historic places — especially local ones.
Directions: *'The Retreat' is on State Highway 1, 6·5 km north of the Wellsford Post Office. You will see the weaving sign by our entrance.*

All telephone numbers in New Zealand are being changed during 1990 so the numbers listed may not be current. Ring 018 for directory assistance if you cannot contact your hosts.

Te Hana, Wellsford

Farmhouse
Address: Te Hana, RD5, Wellsford
Name: George and Olga Yuretich
Telephone: (08463) 7237
Beds: 1 Double, 2 Single (2 bedrooms)
Tariff: B&B Double $55, Single $35; Dinner $15; Children half price
Nearest Town: 8 km north of Wellsford, 1 hour north of Auckland and 1 hour south of Whangarei.

We are a farming family with four teenage daughters, two of whom now work in Auckland. We enjoy meeting people and sharing what we have to offer with others.
Our home is a large, modern open-plan farmhouse set in two acres of garden with 20 acres of native bush as a backdrop.
Enjoy a touch of rural New Zealand in our area. We offer a variety of bush walks. A beautiful coastal walk along the cliff-tops of Mangawhai and back along the seashore. Ocean surf beaches 30 minutes away offer swimming, fishing, surfing, and lazing. Lake Tomarata (fresh water) 20 minutes away for swimming or trout fishing. Matakohe Northland Pioneer and Kauri Gum Museum is 45 minutes away. Dargaville Waipoua State Forest with its magnificent kauri trees — 1 hour away. Forty minutes to the Kauwau Island ferry.
Pottery and crafts.
Directions: *Please phone.*

Warkworth

Farmhouse
Address: Aurelia Farm, 416 Mahurangi East Road, Snells Beach, Warkworth, North Auckland
Name: Aurelia Farm (Jim and June Simons)
Telephone: (0846) 55-465
Beds: 2 Double, 2 Single (3 bedrooms, guest bathroom)
Tariff: B&B Double $50, Single $30, Children ½ price

We have a lovely colonial style home one hour north of Auckland on the Mahurangi peninsular. Our family of three sons and one daughter have grown up and left home so that the entire upper floor of three bedrooms plus a bathroom is available for our guests.
Our home has sweeping views of Snells beach to the east and the Mahurangi Harbour to the south and is a few minutes walk to safe swimming at Snells beach. Day trips to Kawau Island leave from the sandspit and we recommend our guests visit the home of New Zealand's first Governor, Sir George Grey.
We offer warm and friendly hospitality and enjoy a chat with our guests over supper.

Orewa

Homestay +
Self-Contained Accommodation
Address: The Pines,
244 Main Road, Orewa
Name: Trudi and Bernie Cooper
Telephone: (0942) 66-699
Beds: 2 Double, 1 Single (3 bedrooms, guest bathroom)
Tariff: B&B Double $55, Single $35; Children half price; Tariff for self-contained accommodation available on request
Nearest Town: Auckland

Orewa is a popular holiday resort on the beautiful Hibiscus Coast, 30 minutes north of Auckland and five minutes from Waiwera thermal hot pools.
Our area has much to offer visitors of all ages, cruise the many islands of our Hauraki Gulf, visit our many parks and beaches or just relax in a thermal hot pool.
Orewa's shopping centre, attractions and restaurants are all within easy walking distance, off-street parking is available with buses at the door.
Our home is opposite the beach overlooking the Hauraki Gulf and Whangaparaoa peninsula. The house is tudor style with large glass gables to let in the sun, high-beamed ceilings and natural timber walls. A fireplace, electric blankets and duvets ensure a warm winter's night. Complimentary tea and coffee are always available. Guests have their own entrance, en-suite and lounge.

continued over

21

A two-bedroom, self-contained flat is also available on a weekly basis.
As we are non-smokers, please no smoking in our home.
Let us spoil you with some 'kiwi' hospitality which includes a generous,
wholesome breakfast.
We are yachting folk with a grown up family and are presently fitting-
out our 13 metre yacht for cruising.
Meeting people, especially from overseas, is always a pleasure, and we
are happy to help with local knowledge and itinerary.

Red Beach, Orewa

Homestay
Address: 54 Walton Street, Red Beach
Name: Helen and John Bassett
Telephone: (0942) 66-963
Beds: 1 Double, 2 Single (guest bathroom)
Tariff: B&B Double $50; Dinner $15
Nearest Town: Orewa

Recently retired, we live 2 km from State Highway 1 and 100 metres
from a good beach. Orewa 5 km, Auckland 30 km and Waiwera
thermal pools 10 km.
We have a recently-built house on a large, private section, peaceful and
quiet. It will be possible to give guests the use of separate bedroom and
bathroom suite if required.
We are happy to help with local sightseeing and to share our local
knowledge.

Silverdale

Farmhouse +
Self-Contained
Accommodation
Address: Manuel Rd, RD2,
Silverdale
Name: Don and Ute Wyatt
Telephone: (0942) 66-175
Beds: 1 Double, 4 Single (3 bedrooms, guest bathroom)
Tariff: B&B Double $60, Single $40, Children $20; Dinner $15
Self-contained, semi-detached flat $300 per week
Nearest Town: Orewa 6 km, 40 km north of Auckland

If you wish to experience the peace and tranquility of New Zealand
country living, then our home is for you. We are situated in rolling
farmland country, 2 km off the main highway.

Our wooden home is cosy and inviting and we pride ourselves in providing an atmosphere of friendliness and warmth.
Farm attractions include coloured sheep, goats, ducks, chickens —
some of them pets. Wool spinning and shearing demonstrations are
available on request.
We also offer home-grown meat, fruit and vegetables and delicious
home cooking.
It is our pleasure to provide details of local attractions — beaches,
boating, scuba diving, fishing, bushwalks, horse-riding, ice-skating,
hot pools, clubs (golf, bowling), berry picking.
Hire cars are available in Orewa or you can use our bicycles.
I speak fluent German and some French. We welcome all nationalities.
Directions: *Please ring before 9 am or after 4 pm.*

Whangaparaoa Peninsula

Homestay
Address: 1249 Whangaparaoa Road, Fisherman's Rock,
Whangaparaoa, Auckland
Name: David and Audrey Eades
Telephone: (0942) 45-316
Beds: 1 Double, 2 Single (2 bedrooms, guest bathroom)
Tariff: B&B Double $55, Single $28
Nearest Town: Orewa 10 km

Our home is situated towards the end of beautiful Whangaparaoa
Pensinsula — 50 km north of Auckland.
We can be reached from the airport via Auckland by buses which pass
our door. (More information given on request.)
Close at hand is the 'Gulf Harbour Marina' and a choice of ocean
beaches, headland walks, shops, churches, restaurants and golf course
are all within easy reach. A 20 minute drive away are the Waiwera
thermal pools.
Our children are now overseas and we have room to offer you a comfort-
able stay. The double room which is upstairs has separate bathroom
facilities, the single room (2 beds) is on the ground floor.
We really enjoy meeting people and will do all we can to make your stay
with us a happy time. Visitors from abroad are very welcome. Guests
may have dinner with us by arrangement.

Some homes share the bathroom, others have
bathrooms exclusively for guests — they are
indicated in the listing.

Torbay

Homestay
Address: 23 Auld Street, Torbay, North Shore, Auckland
Name: Colleen and Maurie Gray   **Telephone:** (09) 403-9558
Beds: 1 Double, 2 Single (2 bedrooms, guest bathroom)
Tariff: B&B Double $70, Single $35, Children half price; Dinner $15
Nearest Town: Browns Bay

Our spacious modern home has been designed with guests' comfort in mind. We enjoy sharing the beautiful sea views, luxurious living and rambling garden. We have created a restful atmosphere and plenty of outdoor living area for the warmer days. A grand-piano graces the large lounge and we have a huge open-fireplace. We enjoy the outdoors, swimming, sailing, barbecues and are located within a few minutes walk of a beautiful beach. Torbay offers sandy beaches, safe swimming, cliff-top walks, a choice of restaurants. Easy bus-ride to Auckland city. I enjoy preparing attractive, wholesome meals so you're welcome to dine with us. We have two Persian cats who will love to meet you too! A smoke-free home.
Directions: *Turn right as you leave the motorway at East Coast Bays exit. Turn left into East Coast Road. Proceed to Browns Bay turnoff and turn right. Pass Browns Bay, travel along Beach Road, past picturesque Wiaka Beach. Turn right at Torbay Service Station and you're in Auld Street.*

Takapuna

Homestay
Address: 3 Bay View Road, Takapuna
Name: Eleanor J. Benton   **Telephone:** (09) 463-746
Beds: 1 Double, 2 Single (1 bedroom)
Tariff: B&B Double $60, Single $30, Children $10; Dinner $15

Ours is a very nice home in a desirable suburb on the North Shore in Auckland. Buses to city and ferry at the end of our road. Five minutes to Auckland's loveliest beach, fifteen minutes by bus to city, fifteen minutes walk to Takapuna city shops. Close to restaurants of all types. We treat our guests as our friends and make them welcome in our home and do our best to see that they are happy and comfortable. There are a variety of activities available close at hand for all ages.
A full cooked breakfast will be served in our 'Ridgeway' dining room and the rest of the house is available for guests' comfort at all times. We have our own private spa available to guests also.
Directions: *By ferry to Devonport, bus to Hauraki Corner, stop at end of Bay View Road. By bus from city to Bayswater, ask for Hauraki Corner bus stop. By car, take Devonport/Takapuna turnoff from motorway, turn right toward Devonport at T-intersection, first road on right past next set of lights.*

24

Devonport

Homestay
Address: 2 Grove Road, Devonport
Name: Joyce and Harry Mossman
Telephone: (09) 459-437
Beds: 5 Single (3 bedrooms, guest bathroom)
Tariff: B&B Double $55, Single $35; Meals by arrangement;
Children are welcome
Nearest Town: Devonport — 20 minutes across harbour
from Auckland city
Transport: Available by "Super" Shuttle Bus direct from airport

Adjacent to lovely Cheltenham Beach. Twenty minutes by road or relaxing ferry ride across harbour to city. Fifty minutes to International Airport.

Large, clean, comfortable home in quiet area with a sea view, shade trees and spacious lawn.

Facilities have private shower, toilet and handbasin and own entrance. One minute walk onto beautiful, safe beach (swimming/sailing/ walking). Two minutes' walk to shops and bus stops. Short walk to golf course, bowling and croquet club, squash, rugby, soccer and sailing. Pleasant walks to North Head Maritime Park and Mt Victoria with unexcelled extensive views of Waitemata Harbour, city and Auckland Harbour Bridge and Hauraki Gulf.

Other meals in addition to bed and breakfast by arrangement. Complimentary tea and coffee is provided. Restaurants handy.

We supply an escort service by private car for business, sightseeing, pleasure and places of interest. Mobile mini-camper available.

Our interests and activities are people, travel, tourism, family, swimming, camping, boating and fishing, photography and we have a background of farming, navy and building.

There is no other marine suburb which offers so much in such a small picturesque area.

A warm welcome is assured by your hosts. We regret no animals. Reservations are advisable to avoid disappointment.

Devonport

Guest House
Address: Devonport Manor, 7 Cambridge Terrace, Devonport
Name: Jackie Cozby
Telephone: (09) 452-529
Beds: 5 Double (Queen size), 2 Single (5 bedrooms, guest bathrooms)
Tariff: B&B Double $77–$110, Single $55–$88
Nearest Town: Devonport. Auckland's inner city is just 7 minutes
by ferry or 15 minutes by car.

continued over

25

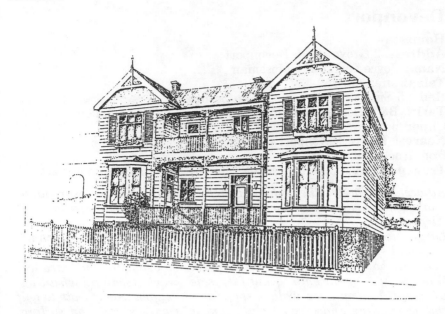

Devonport Manor is a lovely old 1874 colonial villa and offers you comfortable charm and delightful harbour views.

Jackie came to Devonport recently by way of Boston, Massachusetts and Carmel, California and has established this new guest house along the lines of California and New England bed and breakfast inns with antiques, fluffy comforters, and fresh flowers. There are teddy bears to cuddle and cocker spaniels to welcome you.

Our tariff includes a delicious full breakfast of fresh orange juice, fresh fruit salad, muesli and yoghurt, homemade muffins and eggs from guest comments in our guest book, breakfast is a favorite part of their experience. The comfortable, friendly atmosphere is another.

Guest rooms all have queen size beds, some singles, and either shared or private baths.

Devonport is a peaceful old-world village just across the harbour from downtown Auckland. It is a special place offering the best of both worlds, being so close to inner city excitement yet having its own excellent variety of restaurants and shops, lovely beaches, and fine harbour and gulf views.

We're happy to help you with your travel plans, and have bicycles and picnic baskets available to you and a courtesy car to and from the Devonport ferry.

Directions: *From the International Airport take the Downtown Airport Bus to the Devonport ferry. or drive north across the harbour bridge to the Takapuna–Devonport turnoff, follow Devonport signs past the town shops, turning left along the harbour to Cambridge Terrace and our two-storey, pink and white villa.*

Devonport

Homestay
Address: 14 Sinclair Street, Devonport
Name: Tony and Karin Loesch
Telephone: (09) 458-689
Beds: 1 Double (guest bathroom), 2 Single (shared bathroom) (2 bedrooms)
Tariff: B&B Double $52, Single $29, Children negotiable; Dinner $15
Nearest Town: 15 minutes by ferry from central Auckland or 20 minutes over the harbour bridge by car on State Highway 1. Take the Takapuna–Devonport turnoff

Our old villa shares half an acre of lawn with some ancient fruit trees. The renovated interior is airy, light and comfortable. At the end of a sunny cul-de-sac, the location is very peaceful. Local attractions include a golf course (2 minutes' walk) and a charming tree-lined beach (5 minutes' walk). Local shops, garage and bus stops around the corner.

Three minutes' drive away is the picturesque centre of Devonport with a choice of restaurants and take-aways, its parks, beaches, marine promenade, city and harbour views overlooked by Mt Victoria.

We enjoy this historic seaside suburb because of its variety and year-round holiday atmosphere.

Tony is a native Kiwi and Karin comes from Hamburg, so our household is bilingual. We have two school-age children. Having all lived overseas and travelled widely, we enjoy meeting people on the move.

You will love your breakfast on the balcony in the sun which include homemade muesli and jams. You can help yourself to real coffee and tea anytime. We also invite you to join the family barbecue if you wish. Guests are welcome to use the kitchen and laundry.

Directions: *From Auckland Airport take the airport bus to the Downtown City Terminal. Ferries to Devonport depart regularly from Queens Wharf opposite. We will be pleased to meet your from the ferry.*

Birkenhead

Homestay
Address: 13 Miraka Place, Birkenhead, Auckland 10
Name: Robert and Jo Paine
Telephone: (09) 480-9646
Beds: 1 Double, 1 Single (1 bedroom, guest bathroom)
Tariff: B&B Double $60, Single $30, Children half price; Dinner $12
Nearest Town: Auckland

continued over

We are a family of five with three young children, one at school and the other two pre-schoolers.
Our house is on a very quiet section with lovely views over the bush reserve to Rangitoto Island.
The guest bedroom and bathroom is on the ground floor with the family living area upstairs. Guests would be very welcome to join the family. As we have young children ourselves we obviously have facilities and equipment for them and would be pleased to babysit for guests.
We are English and after having lived in New Zealand and Hong Kong we decided to return to New Zealand permanently and have settled well into the suburb of Birkenhead, which is just north of the Harbour Bridge. From here we have easy access to the city or the motorway which makes it an ideal touring base for the area.

Greenhithe

Homestay
Address: 177 Upper Harbour Drive, Greenhithe
Name: Ned and Therese Jujnovich
Telephone: (09) 413-9270
Beds: 4 Single (2 bedrooms, guest bathroom)
Tariff: B&B $25 per person; Dinner $15
Nearest Town: Glenfield 5 km, Auckland city 15 km
(about 15 minutes)

Ranch-style home nestling above the Upper Harbour set in 10 acres of pasture and native bush to the water's edge. On the opposite shores trees reflect their shadows in the silver water of the sea. Wooden balconies are draped with clematis and jasmine, tall kauri trees lean over the decks. Early morning sun streams into the bedrooms — the air is alive with bird song.
An early morning cup of tea (if you wish), cosy breakfasts viewing the mangroves and the harbour. Warm wood fires in the winter, swimming pool in the summer months.
You can look at our Angora goat herd, walk among the ferns and tall trees to the water below, swim in the pool in the summer, do a spot of native birdwatching, relax in the tranquil surroundings. And you can take in the sights of Auckland city too.
Your hosts Ned and Therese Jujnovich have travelled extensively in New Zealand and overseas. With their family of five, all grown up — they especially welcome overseas guests.
Sightseeing in Auckland city and surroundings can easily be arranged. Greenhithe is also a handy starting-off place to the Bay of Islands being about 4 km north of the Harbour Bridge.
Directions: *From Auckland — over the Harbour Bridge — turn left at Tristram Avenue. Turn right at Wairau Road. Proceed to Greenhithe turnoff (left turn). Continue 2 km to 177 Upper Harbour Drive — (4 letterboxes — 177 is at the end of right of way). Transport from city terminal available on request.*

Kumeu

Farmhouse
Address: Nor-West Greenlands, Riverhead Road, RD2, Kumeu
Name: Kerry and Kay Hamilton
Telephone: (09) 412-8167
Beds: 1 Double, 1 Single (2 bedrooms, guest bathrooms)
Tariff: B&B Double $55, Single $35; Dinner $15; Campervans $20
Nearest Town: Kumeu 3½ km, Auckland city 26 km

Our 20 acre farmlet with its backdrop of native bush, pond and stream is home to cashgora goats, black and white sheep, beef cattle, two cats and a dog. We grow cut flowers, mainly cymbidium orchids.
While in the centre of an extensive horticultural area growing grapes, kiwifruit, vegetables and fruit, we are only 20 minutes from the centre of Auckland.
We are available to meet your plane, train, or coach at minimum rates. Guests have a choice of twin or double bedrooms with their own bathrooms.

Facilities available include a separate guest lounge with coloured TV and coffee/tea making, a spa pool, swimming pool and barbecue.
Breakfast is of your choice and you are most welcome to join us for dinner of homegrown meat, vegetables and fruit.
Within 10 km of our home there are 13 wineries, three with their own first class restaurants. We are only 2 km from an 18-hole golf course and 7 km from a riding school. Travel 20 km east and you can swim on the suburban east coast beaches with their white sand and 20 km west to ruggest west coast black sand beaches.
All this and only 20 minutes to Auckland.
Directions: *Take the north-western motorway, continue north on State Highway 16, turn right onto State Highway 18 and Riverhead Road is the second road on the left.*

Taupaki, Henderson

Homestay
Address: Hunters Road,
  Taupaki, RD2, Henderson
Name: 'Connaught Lodge'
Telephone: (09) 810-9732
Beds: 1 Double, 2 Single (2 bedrooms)
Tariff: B&B Double $65, Single $45;
Dinner $15; Children under 12 half price;
Nearest Town: Kumeu

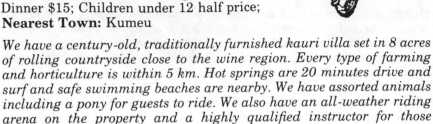

We have a century-old, traditionally furnished kauri villa set in 8 acres of rolling countryside close to the wine region. Every type of farming and horticulture is within 5 km. Hot springs are 20 minutes drive and surf and safe swimming beaches are nearby. We have assorted animals including a pony for guests to ride. We also have an all-weather riding arena on the property and a highly qualified instructor for those wanting riding lessons.

Your host is an accountant and your hostess a professional cook (Cordon Bleu) and musician (singer/harpist). Two teenage sons are proficient in German, French and Japanese. Interests are many and include all sports, especially soccer, rowing, cricket and shooting.

We hope you will join us for dinner (any special requirements catered for) but if you prefer to dine out we can provide bed and breakfast only — farm-style or Continental breakfast to suit.

All major credit cards accepted.

Directions: *Taupaki is a peaceful rural retreat only 30 minutes' drive from central Auckland — follow the north west motorway (Highway 16) towards Helensville, past the junction with Highway 18 and opposite Selaks Vineyard turn left into Taupaki Road. Follow signs to Taupaki. Cross railway lines then left at Y-fork. Hunters Road is the first on the right and Connaught Lodge is well signposted.*

NZ phone numbers are being changed. Ring 018 for directory.

Many homes have facilities for campervans.
The ideal camping spot with electricity,
bathroom, laundry and friendly hospitality. Tell
campervanners about this when you see them.

Waitakere

Farm/Self-Contained Accommodation
Address: Greenmead Farm, Bethells Beach Road, Waitakere
(RD1 Henderson, Auckland)
Name: Averil and Jon Bateman
Telephone: (09) 8109-363
Beds: 4 Single (2 bedrooms,
guest bathroom)
Tariff: Self-contained
cottage —
Double $55, $10 for
each extra guest; Meals
available with the
family if required
— Dinner $20, Breakfast $7
Nearest Town: Henderson
16 km, Auckland central
30 minutes by car

We live in a 100-year-old homestead in the Waitakere Ranges, a mile from the sea and half an hour by car from central Auckland. We breed Simmental cattle and grow globe artichokes commercially. This area has much to offer those who enjoy country life with an exciting west coast beach at the end of the road.

There are good walking tracks along the coast and through the bush. Horse-riding and golf are available and we are close to a wine-growing district.

The self-contained guest cottage is across the courtyard from the main house. It has two bedrooms (linen provided), bathroom, a kitchen/living room and a small parlour with a colour TV. You are welcome to eat with us if you wish or you may prefer to cook for yourselves.

The main house and guest cottage are surrounded by a large garden and home orchard. We grow our own vegetables and herbs, raise our own beef, handmilk a housecow and keep chickens and bees to provide fresh eggs and honey.

The standard of accommodation in *The New Zealand Bed and Breakfast Book* ranges from homely to luxurious but you can always be sure of superior hospitality.

Parnell, Auckland City

Guest House
Address: 36 St Stephens Avenue, Parnell, Auckland 1
Name: Ascot Parnell
Telephone: (09) 399-012
Beds: 6 Double, 3 Single (9 bedrooms, all with phone and private facilities)
Tariff: B&B Double $79 plus GST, Single $58 plus GST; No meals provided, about 20 restaurants in walking distance

The Ascot Parnell is an historic home restored to its former elegance, yet combined with modern comfort. It is handy to the city and offers reasonable rates.

The Ascot Parnell only has nine guest rooms. This intimacy makes it possible for the guests to enjoy a friendly service and personal attention. A delightful gourmet breakfast with a variety to please all palates is served in a dining room which shows the beauty of this lovely home. Throughout the day free tea, coffee and juice are served in the lounge. Upon request a minibus from the airport stops in front of the house. The tidy, comfortable guest rooms are individual in character. Beautifully maintained old world charm is combined with tasteful furniture and modern facilities. Each room has its own bathroom, direct dial telephone, heating and electric blankets.

The lovely garden of the Ascot Parnell displays many of the trees, bushes and flowers native to New Zealand.

Although the Ascot Parnell is a quiet place to stay in, it is nevertheless very close to the city centre (2·5 km) and within walking distance to many tourist attractions such as Parnell Village, the Auckland Museum or the Rose Gardens.

Freemans Bay, Auckland City

Guest House
Address: 65 Wellington Street, Freemans Bay, Auckland
Name: Freeman's Travellers' Hotel
Telephone: (09) 765-046
Beds: 2 Double, 17 Single (12 bedrooms)
Tariff: B&B Double $50, Single $35, Triple $60
Nearest Town: Auckland

Freeman's is a small, completely redecorated bed and breakfast hotel in a convenient Auckland city location. It is run by Megan Holmes and Richard Quartermass who, between them, have travelled, studied and worked in Britain, Europe, Asia, North America, Africa, the South Pacific and of course, in New Zealand.

Their aim is to create a haven for travellers in an inner city environment and to this end are assisted by a garden with a small swimming pool, a barbecue and a conservatory. In the guest lounge are a telephone, a fridge, complimentary tea, coffee and chocolate and a piano. The atmosphere is of a well-run house where independence is valued as much as friendliness.

Megan and Richard are able to assist in getting the best out of a stay in Auckland and New Zealand and in particular will undertake to book cars and campervans at the cheapest possible rates.

By keeping their prices low, Megan and Richard intend that Freeman's will become known as offering the best value in a place to start and end a tour of New Zealand. Their most prized compliments from guests returning from touring or even a from a day out? "It's like coming home!"

Ponsonby, Auckland City

Homestay
Address: 33 Summer Street, Ponsonby
Name: Louise Simich
Telephone: (09) 784-963
Beds: 1 Double, 1 Single (1 bedroom)
Tariff: B&B Double $55, Single $28, Children half price;
Dinner $12
Nearest Town: 3 km from downtown Auckland

Our home, built in 1882, has been lovingly restored around the beautiful woods used in the building of the house. Our guest room is private, huge and comfortably furnished. The atmosphere in our home has been described by our friends as peaceful, healing, warm . . . in our garden it is hard to believe that we are in the city.

My skills include good Cancerian ones as a home-manager and excellent cook. I enjoy and have a lot of experience in sharing my home with people. My first profession was nursing and I currently work as a community worker with a number of local groups on a number of issues. My interests are diverse and include travelling anywhere, knitting, jogging, yoga, working out at the gym, trying out new recipes and eating them, caring for kids, running a business, veteran cars, etc. My 11-year-old daughter's interests are jazz dancing, reading, meeting other kids, computer games, television, netball, touch rugby, swimming and sprinting.

Our local area is famous for a wide range of excellent cafes and restaurants. We are within easy and pleasant walking distance of beaches and central Auckland.

Many homes have facilities for campervans.
The ideal camping spot with electricity,
bathroom, laundry and friendly hospitality. Tell
campervanners about this when you see them.

Can't contact your host? Ring 018 for directory assistance.

Epsom, Auckland City

Homestay
Address: 82 St Andrews Road, Epsom, Auckland
Name: Kay and Bill Foley
Telephone: (09) 688-628
Beds: 1 Double (1 bedroom, guest bathroom)
Tariff: B&B Double $55, Single $35, Children half price;
Dinner by arrangement $15
Nearest Town: Auckland city centre 5 km

Our 80-year-old villa is centrally located only 10 minutes from the city centre by car and is served by the Waikowhai bus route with stops to and from town outside our gate. The Airporter bus route is 10 minutes walk to the house from the stop at Greenlane Road intersection. We are close to many of Auckland's attractions — One Tree Hill, trotting and racing tracks and the Domain and there is a variety of shops and restaurants close at hand.

Our self-contained guest accommodation consists of a bedroom with double bed, private bathroom with laundry facilities and a lounge with a kitchen corner and TV. Family groups can be catered for in the lounge as we can supply additional beds.
Our three children in their twenties still live at home but have many plans for future travel. Our dog and two cats are very much part of our family and we have a house rule of no smoking indoors.
Our swimming pool, garden and big comfortable family home are here for you to enjoy.

Epsom, Auckland City

Homestay
Address: 27 Shipherds Avenue,
 Epsom, Auckland 1003
Name: John and Sheila Rose
Telephone: (09) 603-542
Beds: 1 Double, 1 Single, Rollaway available (2 bedrooms, guest bathroom)
Tariff: B&B Double $60, Single $36, Children under 12 half price, under 4 free; Dinner $20
Nearest Town: Auckland — at city end of Epsom, 5 km from C.P.O. (10 minutes car/taxi) on good bus routes from city. Write for map/brochure/transport details

Your hosts are a senior retired couple who have travelled very exten-sively and have lived in Asia. They have married sons in London, Washington D.C., and in Milan, Italy. Their home is new, well heated and attractively furnished reflecting their wide travels. Most con-veniently situated to central Auckland, to four central bus routes, to airport and motorway transport, for sightseeing and to restaurants.
The guest wing is self-contained, off the breakfast room, but please use our sitting room.
The area is particularly quiet and restful with a backdrop of attractive trees.
The hosts have a holiday home at Pauanui Beach (2 hours south) on the historical and beautiful Coromandel Peninsula which guests can use by arrangement. Guests are welcome to use our laundry facilities.
No pets and non-smokers please.
Auckland is the gateway city into New Zealand and has much to offer. Allow time to recover from overseas flights and to see Auckland. Your hosts would be happy to advise on travel throughout New Zealand from their own detailed knowledge.
Directions: *From Gillies Avenue into Brightside Road into Shipherds Ave. Bus routes — Waikowhai, National Women's Hospital, Airport City, Three Kings, or phone.*

If you find something missing that you are
accustomed to, simply ask you hosts for it.

Epsom, Auckland City

Homestay
Address: 10 Ngaroma Road, Epsom, Auckland 3
Name: Janet and Jim Millar
Telephone: (09) 657-336
Beds: 1 Double, 2 Single (2 bedrooms, guest bathrooms)
Tariff: B&B Double $55, Single $35, Children $10; Dinner $15
Nearest Town: Auckland 5 km

Our 69-year-old home is on the lower slopes of One Tree Hill (Maunga-kiekie), and has walking access to its Domain, one of Auckland's love-liest parks with glorious views.

We are 200 metres off the direct airport-downtown Auckland route in a quiet tree-lined street. Close by are several good restaurants and the bus stop to the City.

Our two guest bedrooms both have their own private bathrooms and the one downstairs has a sun lounge opening onto a patio. There are laundry facilities and off-street parking. It takes 10 minutes by car to downtown.

We have three grown-up children no longer living at home, and four lively grandchildren. We enjoy meeting people and making them feel at home. We have travelled extensively ourselves, both overseas and in N.Z. and we enjoy exchanging experiences.

A self-catering cottage is available in Paeroa — a good centre from which to explore the Coromandel Peninsula, a unique area which many overseas visitors don't have the opportunity to visit.

Directions: *Exit motorway at Greenlane, travel west to Manukau Road which our street runs off at Greenwoods Corner.*

Remuera, Auckland City

Guest House
Address: 39 Market Road,
Remuera, Auckland 5
Name: Aachen House –
Jean and Don Goldschmidt
Telephone: (09) 520-2329
Beds: 5 Double rooms, 2 Single rooms (7 bedrooms,
3 guest bathrooms)
Tariff: B&B Double $67.50, Single $45, Children $12,
under 3 free; Dinner $16
Nearest Town: 4 km from central city

Ours is a large Victorian house set in half an acre of garden. We overlook a large park and back on to Mt Hobson, one of Auckland's many extinct volcanos. We are close to the museum, showgrounds, hospitals and race tracks. The motorway off-ramp is nearby and there is an excellent bus service two minutes walk away. Our car will collect guests from the Railway Station while the shuttle buses have a door-to-door service from the airport. Off-street parking is available.

We have created a friendly, homely atmosphere in our large, beautiful home and people feel relaxed and comfortable. Our seven bedrooms comprise singles, doubles, triples and quads. Each room has a hand-basin and there are three shared bathrooms.

Our one rule is NO SMOKING and this seems to please the overseas guests as well as New Zealanders.

Directions: *Take Market Road turnoff from the motorway, phone from the railway or bus stations, or come by minibus from the airport.*

Remuera, Auckland City

Homestay
Address: 37A Kelvin Road, Remuera, Auckland 5
Name: Jocelyn and Don Ross
Telephone: (09) 549-909
Beds: 1 Double, 2 Single (2 bedrooms, guest bathroom)
Tariff: B&B Double $60, Single $45, Children half price;
Dinner by arrangement
Nearest Town: Auckland — 5 km from C.P.O., 10 minutes by car, on good bus route

We are a semi-retired couple with a large, two-storey brick home situated on 1/3 acre consisting of gardens and orchard, which overlook a valley of native bush. Three of our four children have left home.

Our guest accommodation consists of two bedrooms and separate lounge with private bathroom facilities, which opens onto a large, private patio area and heated spa pool. Laundry facilities are available.

There are several good restaurants and shopping complexes in the surrounding area. Tennis courts are within two minutes walk.
Directions: *From north or southern motorways take Greenlane Intersection Off-ramp. Proceed northwards to end of Greenlane Road and at intersection with Remuera Road turn right. Kelvin Road is fifth on left (at bottom of dip). From airport upon reaching Manukau Road turn right into Greenlane Road and at Greenlane Motorway Intersection proceed as aforegoing.*

Bucklands Beach

Homestay
Address: 152D Bucklands Beach Road, Bucklands Beach, Auckland
Name: Gloria Duncan (Mrs)
Telephone: (09) 534-7173
Beds: 2 Single (1 bedroom, guest bathroom)
Tariff: B&B Double $50, Single $30, Children half price
Nearest Town: Howick 4 km, Pakuranga 7 km, Auckland 20 km

I live in a townhouse with a separate guest bedroom complete with its own bathroom and toilet. The bedroom leads out onto a very sunny patio set in a courtyard and quite private. I am fortunate to live on the peninsula at Bucklands Beach, within four minutes walking to either Eastern Beach or Bucklands Beach. There are many pleasant walks in the vicinity and my unit is close to the Howick Golf Club and the Halfmoon Bay Marina and close to the Waiheke vehicular ferry. The bus stop to Auckland is on the corner.
There are a wide range of restaurants within a few kilometres. I can provide breakfast either Continental or cooked to suit.
Airport/train/bus transfers by arrangement.
Directions: *Take the highway to Howick from Pakuranga or Panmure and just past Pakuranga College take the next road left into Bucklands Beach Road, following the highway all the way until it turns back down the peninsular. Turn right into Vivien Wilson Drive. Unit on corner.*

Mangere East

Homestay
Address: 81 Raglan Street, Mangere East
Name: Enid and Terry Cripps
Telephone: (09) 275-5448
Beds: 1 Double (1 bedroom, en-suite bathroom, private lounge, tea/coffee facilities)
Tariff: B&B Double $50, Single $25;
Dinner $20 per person; Children ½ price; Campervans $15 (laundry/kitchen/bathroom facilities)
Nearest Town: 12 km south from Auckland city on State Highway 1

Enid and Terry Cripps offer you a warm welcome to our home. We live

39

continued over

in an area known for its ethnic diversity, considered by some to reflect the true multi-cultural nature of Auckland. Our comfortable home is within easy travelling distance to all our city has to offer, as well as to other points of interest in the surrounding areas. We offer a relaxing atmosphere and such comforts as a heated spa pool.

In addition to a cooked breakfast of your choice you are invited to join us for dinner and we would be happy to provide a picnic lunch on request.

A courtesy car to and from the airport which is 10 minutes away is provided.

Phone numbers may have changed. Ring 018 for directory.

Clevedon

Farmhouse + Self-Contained Accommodation
Address: North Road, PO Box 72, Clevedon
Name: John and Annette Hodge
Telephone: (09) 292-8707
Beds: 1 Double, 2 Single (3 bedrooms, guest bathroom)
Tariff: B&B Double $55, Single $35; Dinner $15; Children half price; Campervans $15; Self-contained 2 bedroom unit with 1 double bed and 2 single beds tariff negotiable
Nearest Town: 40 km from Auckland, 23 km from Papakura

Longer stays welcome, including light midday meals.
Our family of three (now adults), have moved away from home. Our 270-acre property is only 35 minutes from the Auckland International Airport in a farming community. We offer a perfect environment in which to relax from the effects of prolonged travel before moving on, or a resting place to unwind.
We are available, by prior arrangement, at any time to meet your plane, train or coach at minimum rates.
Ours is a beef fattening farm, stretching from a native tree-clad hillside, across the flats to the coastal waters of the Waitemata Harbour. Views from our comfortable home include the lower reaches of the Wairoa River valley from Clevedon, parts of Waiheke Island and other smaller islands to the distant range of the Coromandel Peninsula.
Amenities available or nearby include: sheep shearing, native bush, farm or waterfront walks; horse riding; boat trips; fishing; visits to kiwifruit, dairy, rabbit or goat farms; Auckland Polo Club; Ardmore Airport, golf; Clevedon village and Maraetai Beach craft shops, service stations and other shopping facilities.
Directions: *Clevedon is 14 km east of Papakura. Our home is on the left on North Road, 9 km from Clevedon.*

Tell other travellers about your favourite homes.

Clevedon

Farmhouse
Address: "Willowgrove", Kawakawa Bay Road, Clevedon, RD5, Papakura
Name: Brian and Eileen Wallace
Telephone: (09) 292-8456
Beds: 1 Double, additional beds if required (1 bedroom, guest bathroom)
Tariff: B&B Double $60, Single $30, Children half price; Dinner $15
Nearest Town: Auckland

Clevedon is a village in a rural area with craft shops, restaurants and all services. Eileen and I live and work on our property of about 11 acres. An adult daughter also lives with us.

We produce summer fruit, nectarines and peaches and have sheep, goats, calves and chickens. We produce our own vegetables.

The house is set in a delightful garden which has a very restful atmosphere. We enjoy the special atmosphere and peaceful surroundings and are pleased to share it with others.

We are close enough for visitors to take in any of the Auckland attractions and numerous boating, fishing and swimming beaches are within 15 minutes drive.

The guest room is a large upstairs room with its own sitting area, toilet and shower. You may share our family room and lounge or relax in your room as you please. We also have a games room including a pool table.

Directions: *Exit motorway at Takanini. Travel south on Great South Road towards Papakura, follow signs to Clevedon through Manuroa Road and Airfield Road. From Clevedon take the Clevedon–Kawakawa Bay Road and travel for 8 km to our house (not visible from road) on left past Linkfield Horse Training Centre. Look for this sign and our "Willowgrove" sign. If required we can collect from airport or public transport for a small charge (negotiable).*

Papakura

Homestay
Address: 8 Mill End, Papakura, South Auckland
Name: Jack and Lillian Heathfield
Telephone: (09) 299-6243
Beds: 1 Double, 1 Single (2 bedrooms)
Tariff: B&B $25 per person; Dinner $15; Children half price

We enjoy meeting people and welcome to our home visitors from home and overseas. We are a retired couple with a corgi dog, living in a cul-de-sac in a quiet, attractive area. We have a small private garden with mature trees and shrubs with a restful view over the inlet from our relaxing terrace. We are situated conveniently twenty-five minutes drive to Auckland, the same to Auckland airport and two minutes from the National Bloodstock Sales.
Local shopping and restaurants are a short distance away but I am a keen cook and we would enjoy learning of your lifestyle over a relaxed dinner or breakfast. You are most welcome to help yourself to tea or coffee any time. We look forward to meeting you.
Directions: *Please phone.*

NZ phone numbers are being changed. Ring 018 for directory.

Clarks Beach, South Auckland

Homestay
Address: 123 Torkar Road, Clarks Beach
Name: Ray and Elaine Golding
Telephone: (085) 21-756
Beds: 1 Double, 2 Single (2 bedrooms, guest bathroom)
Tariff: B&B Double $55, Single $30, Children half price; Dinner $14
Nearest Town: Papakura, 30 minutes south of Auckland

We are a family of four, one daughter and one son both living away. We have a home on the water's edge of the Manukau Harbour. From the lounge we overlook the water across to the lights of Auckland city. Ray is a keen gardener so we have a lovely garden and the floral arrangements indoors are also done by Ray.
There is a 9-hole golf course across the road. Clarks Beach is a popular place with fishing, golf, bowls, yachting all very popular and a short distance by car there is the popular Glenbrook vintage railway.
You may share an evening meal with the family and a light lunch can be provided at a nominal charge if required.
Transport to and from the airport also available on request at a nominal charge. We are only 45 minutes from the Auckland airport.
Directions: *30 minutes south from Auckland on the motorway to Papakura then 20 minutes west from Papakura. Signposted.*

Waiuku

Homestay
Address: 96 Kitchener Road, Waiuku, Franklin West
Name: Mrs Julia Smith   **Telephone:** (085) 57-151
Beds: 1 Double, 1 Single (1 bedroom)
Tariff: B&B Double $40, Single $25, Children half price;
Dinner $12
Nearest Town: Pukekohe 20 km, Papakura 30 km

*Children and disabled people are welcome in my home. I live on the
main road going into the township of Waiuku. My concrete block and
tile roof house was built 20 years ago by the Glenbrook Steel Mill.*
*The guest room has one single and one double bed, the bathroom is a
shared one.*
*An evening meal can be provided, however there are three very good
eating places in Waiuku. Breakfast is of your choice.*
*The Glenbrook Steel Mill is worth a visit with tour guides to show you
around. There is a well-stocked museum, many lovely harbour and
surf beaches to visit with the Waikato River not far away.*
*Waiuku is 20 km from the market gardening township of Pukekohe.
Forestry, golf courses, tennis and squash courts are close at hand plus a
scenic drive up the Manukau peninsular.*
Directions: *Travel on the motorway until the Drury Pukekohe turnoff.
Turn west and follow the Pukekohe signposts until the golf course,
approximately 5 km. Take the right hand turning and continue.
Travelling time from the Drury turnoff ½ an hour.*

Mercer

Farmhouse + Self-Contained Accommodation
Address: Koheroa Road, Mercer, Pokeno
Name: Alan and Dorothy McGuire   **Telephone:** (085) 26-837
Beds: 2 Double (2 bedroom, guest bathroom)
Tariff: B&B Double $55, Single $30, Children negotiable; Dinner $15
Nearest Town: Papakura 25 km, Pukekohe 22 km,
Auckland Airport 40 minutes

*We live on a 550 acre sheep and cattle farm with a modern brick home
which has a self-contained unit attached. We have a large swimming
pool and barbecue facilities. We are 3 km off the main
Auckland–Hamilton highway. Our house site gives wide panoramic
views of the countryside from Bombay to Thames.*
*We are very happy to provide dinner but there are three restaurants
within 5 km.*
*The farm provides ample opportunity for taking walks and viewing
farm animals plus turkeys, pheasants, ducks and quail.*
Directions: *Travel State Highway 1 to Mercer, cross railway lines,
travel 3 km up Koheroa Road, house is on left right near road just past
Kellyville Road junction. Name clearly visible.*

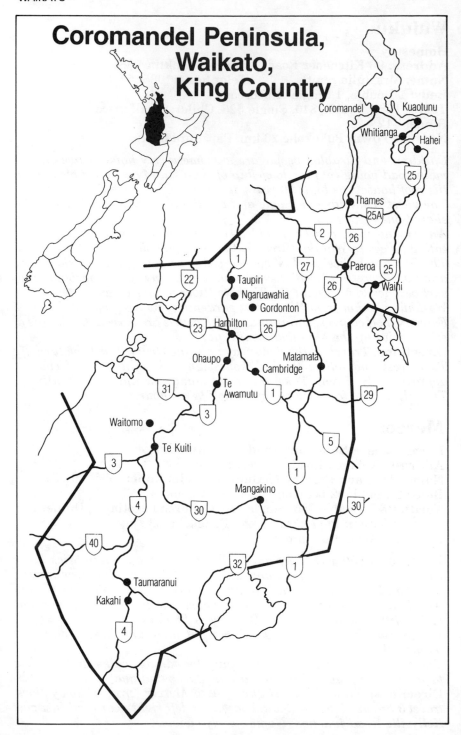

Coromandel Peninsula, Waikato, King Country

Coromandel

Farmhouse + Self-Contained Accommodation
Address: Te Kouma Harbour Farms, State Highway 25, Coromandel.
Postal: PO Box 110, Coromandel
Name: Ron and Megan Cameron
Telephone: (0843) 58-747
Beds: 1 Double, 4 Single (2 bedrooms, guest bathroom)
Tariff: B&B Double $60, Single $40, Children under 12 years
half price; Dinner $22; Budget caravan and cabin accommodation $15;
Breakfast $5; Campervans $20
Nearest Town: Coromandel 12 km, Thames 44 km

*Our property is one of the largest and most beautiful farms on the
Coromandel Peninsula. It is located around the shores of Te Kouma
Harbour on the western side of the Peninsula.*
*The harbour is one of the "jewels" of the area and a yachtman's haven.
We raise beef cattle (including a Simmental Cattle Stud), deer, goats
and a few sheep. Geese, turkeys, peacocks, pheasant, quail and many
other fowl roam free over the farm.*
*Large bush areas offer wild pig hunting. We also offer other shooting in
season. We have a small fleet of canoes, rowing boats, small sailing
boats as well as a large yacht for day or overnight cruising, fishing and
diving. Secluded areas around the harbour provide great camping or
picnic areas. Many on-farm bush, coastal and scenic walks are available, also rockhounding and 4-wheel-drive safaris. Prices for these on
application. In fact we cater for a full range of outdoor activities. Our
facilities are modern and can be self-contained if required. They
include separate accommodation around the homestead, swimming
pool, airstrip, 9-hole putting course and within 15 minutes from the
property golf, tennis, bowls, crafts and potteries, places of historic
interest, etc.*
We are a family of five with diverse interests.
Directions: *Located on State Highway 25 (Western side), 44 km north
of Thames, 2 km north of Manaia Village, ½-way up the next hill on
left. Name on letterbox.*

45

Kuaotunu

Homestay
Address: Main Road, Kuaotunu,
Coromandel Peninsula
Name: John and Robin Twemlow
Telephone: (0843) 65-735
Beds: 2 Single (1 bedroom, guest bathroom)
Tariff: B&B Double $35, Single $20, Children half price; Dinner $12;
Campervans $15
Nearest Town: Whitianga 18 km on State Highway 25

*We are a Christian family of five with two adult sons (both left the nest)
and one 11-year-old daughter. Our house is by the beach. We enjoy
fishing, walking and spending time on the beach — in fact just plain
relaxing. For the more energetic this area offers bushwalks and
exploring of old goldmines.*
*If you are looking for a stopover on your way round the Coromandel
Peninsula, our home could well be the place you're looking for. We're a
very relaxed household — no frills but food to fill. Vegetarian meals
prepared on request.*
*We also have a very comfortable sofa that folds down to a double bed in
the library for extra sleeping if needed.*
Directions: *Please phone.*

Can't contact your host? Ring 018 for directory assistance.

Whitianga

Homestay/Tourist Lodge
Address: Main Road, Coroglen, RD1, Whitianga
Name: Glenn and Rennie Leach
Telephone: (084363) 808
Beds: 8 Single (4 bedrooms, guest bathroom)
Tariff: B&B Double $68, Single $37, Children half price; Dinner $16

*We invite you to share our home, Aotearoa Lodge and discover the
Coromandel Peninsula. We operate an outdoor adventure business and
can take you on a mini coach tour to the northernmost point of the
Peninsula, or to old goldmine sites, private beaches, to kauri groves, on
a scenic rafting trip, visit Hot Water Beach, see local craftsmen and
potters and historic places. All this can be included while staying with
us or simply relax and enjoy a quiet time in our garden or on one of the
beautiful beaches here. Guests have their own toilet facilities, lounge
and self-contained kitchen. Breakfast and dinner is shared with our
family.*
*We have two sons, our eldest son is a keen rower and lives in Hamilton
and our younger son lives at home and works locally.*
We enjoy entertaining and look forward to having you to stay.

Hahei Beach, Whitianga

Homestay
Address: Grange Road, Hahei Beach, RD1, Whitianga
Name: Barbara and Alan Lucas
Telephone: (0843) 63-543
Beds: 1 Double, 1 Single, extra beds available (2 bedrooms, guest bathroom)
Tariff: B&B Double $50, Single $25, Children under 10 half price; Dinner $15, Packed lunches by prior arrangement; Campervans $20 (for 2 people)
Nearest Town: Tairua 36 km, Whitianga 38 km

My wife and I are semi-retired and live in a Lockwood home over-looking the sea with panoramic views from the Alderman Islands to the Mercury Islands.
We are five minutes walk from Hahei Beach and are on the road to Cathedral Cove and its beaches, a must when visiting this area. Hot Water Beach is just a short distance away where you can enjoy a warm soak at any time of the year.
The area offers bush walks, surf beaches, fishing and spectacular views for photography.
Our interests are meeting people and gardening.
We enjoy our own vegetables and can assure you of excellent meals, my wife is a first class cook, at least, I think so.
Please give us a telephone call when you wish to come and we can promise you a most enjoyable, relaxed stay.
We look forward to hearing from you.
Directions: *Turn off at Whenuakite.*

Whitianga

Homestay
Address: Cosy Cat Cottage,
    41 South Highway, Whitianga
Name: Gordon and Janet Pearce
Telephone: (0843) 64-488
Beds: 1 Double, 4 Single (3 bedrooms, guest bathroom)
Tariff: B&B Double $60, Single $40, Children half price; Dinner $15; (During peak season 24 Dec. to 31 Jan. and Public Holidays add $5 per person)
Nearest Town: 1 km from Whitianga Post Office; Thames 93 km via State Highway 25

At Cosy Cat Cottage your comfort is our aim. The house is two-storey and 12 years old. It is carpeted throughout and has exposed beams.
The guest bathroom is large, modern and well appointed. We hope you will have a good night's rest in the comfortable beds, then enjoy a

continued over

hearty breakfast. Delicious home cooked dinners are available. Special diets and vegetarians are gladly catered for. Please ask.
Relax in the guest lounge with T.V., library or board games.
Have complimentary tea or coffee on the large shaded deck with pleasant garden and rural views.
If you like cats you'll love our decor — all on a cat theme. We also breed Tonkinese cats.
A courtesy car is available and sightseeing trips can be arranged. Whitianga, Mercury Bay, is famous for its safe, beautiful beaches, magnificent scenery, historic sites, boating, fishing and pleasant climate. Whitianga is also the home of the Mercury Bay Boating Club, of AMERICAS CUP fame.
It is the perfect central location from which to explore the fascinating and lovely Coromandel Peninsula.
We look forward to meeting you.
Directions: *When entering Whitianga from the South on State Highway 25, look for our sign on your left, before the school.*

Phone numbers may have changed. Ring 018 for directory.

Thames

Farmhouse
Address: 'Thorold', Kopu, RD1, Thames
Name: Helen and Tony Smith
Telephone: (0843) 88-480
Beds: 1 Double, 2 Single (2 bedrooms, guest bathroom)
Tariff: B&B Double $66, Single $36, Children $15; Dinner $20
Nearest Town: Thames 6 km to the north on State Highway 26

Our spacious home is set in 30 acres of garden and farmland where we graze sheep, cattle and pigs. The guest wing is luxurious, separate, peaceful and private. There are two bedrooms — one double with queensize bed and a twin room. All with electric blankets. Bathroom adjoins bedrooms. There are coffee and tea making facilities with a fridge. The guest sitting room has comfortable chairs, television and billiard table. All rooms open out to a swimming pool.
Two of our three sons are at university and one son lives at home and works in Thames. My husband is very involved in the farming industry and we both enjoy gardening, boating, fishing, tramping and many sports. The local golf course is five minutes away.
Dinner is available on request. Across the road is a hotel and a shop selling takeaways and in Thames which is 10 minutes from our home there is a wider choice of restaurants.
Thames and the Coromandel Peninsula have so much to offer and we would be pleased to be part of your stay.
Directions: *Please phone.*

Thames

Homestay
Address: Please phone
Name: Glenys and Russell Rutherford
Telephone: (0843) 87-788
Beds: 1 Double, 2 Single (2 bedrooms, guest bathroom)
Tariff: B&B Double $55, Single $35, Children half price; Dinner $15
Nearest Town: Thames 1 km

We have a spacious and comfortable home with sweeping views of the Firth of Thames.
Our interests include gardening, golf, music and entertaining family and friends.

We offer a double room opening onto a games/lounge area with private adjoining shower and toilet facilities, also a twin room upstairs.
We have a swimming pool for a cool swim after a day's driving.
Being an historic goldmining settlement, museums and gold prospectors diggings are of particular interest. Due to its natural beauty the Coromandel has attracted many potters and painters, some of world renown. Their galleries can be visited on a scenic day trip up the coast to Coromandel village, and continuing back through the popular beach resorts of Whitianga, Pauanui and Tairua. This drive takes the traveller through some of the most beautiful native bush in New Zealand.
Our intention is for you to enjoy some of these features and we welcome your visit.
You may care to join us for dinner or simply enjoy a comfortable night's rest and a satisfying breakfast to set you off on your day's journey.

Let the phone ring for a long time when telephoning.

Paeroa

Homestay
Address: 17 Hill Street, Paeroa
Name: Maria and Axie Macfarlane
Telephone: (0816) 7770
Beds: 2 Double, 1 Single (2 bedrooms)
Tariff: B&B $25 per person; Dinner $15
Nearest Town: Thames 20 minutes, Waihi 15 minutes,
Te Aroha 10 minutes

Paeroa is situated approximately halfway between Auckland and Tauranga. Our home is clean and comfortable with lovely views over the Hauraki plains.
Our family is grown up and away from home. We have travelled and love meeting people.
You are welcome to have dinner with us or just bed and breakfast. You are welcome for one night or several.
There are many interesting places to visit from Paeroa. Thames, just 20 minutes away, overlooks the Hauraki Gulf and offers a scenic drive up the coast. Waihi is a 15 minute drive away through the famous Karangahake Gorge which is very picturesque and also offers some lovely walking tracks taking you along the Ohinemuri River and through the old train tunnel which goes through Karangahake Mountain. If you are a trout fishing enthusiast you can also while away a few hours trying your luck.
Waihi, once a booming gold-mining town, has once again opened gold mines and there are tours available. You can also take a ride on their old steam train on certain days of the week. We would be only too pleased to tell you about the places of interest in this area.
We will collect you from the bus depot if required although that is only a ten minute walk from our home. We both look forward to meeting you.
Directions: *As you arrive in Paeroa from Auckland, go over the railway lines and turn sharp left (Taylors Ave) then 1st turn on right (Hill St). We are number seventeen.*

Waihi

Homestay + Self-Contained Accommodation
Address: 17 Riverbank Terrace, Waihi
Name: Thea Mosch
Telephone: (08163) 8780
Beds: 1 Double, 4 Single (3 bedrooms)
Tariff: B&B Double $45, Single $25, Children $15; Dinner $15
Nearest Town: Tauranga ¾ hour drive, Thames ½ hour drive,
Hamilton 1 hour drive

Waihi is an old goldmining town that offers a lot for people who are interested in history and outdoor life.

We built our house on the outskirts of town, overlooking the rural area and still only a five minute walk from the town centre.
Waihi has an easy gateway to the Coromandel Peninsula, Bay of Plenty and the Waikato.
Waihi Beach is only a ten minute drive and is one of the safest beaches on the east coast. Ideal for swimming and surfing. The Karangahake Gorge has some nice walks and historic tracks.
My teenage son, daughter and I have travelled a lot in New Zealand as well as overseas and love to exchange experiences. Tours and transport can be arranged and children are more than welcome.
Directions: *Before you leave Waihi (going to Waihi Beach or Tauranga) you take the last turn right at the panelbeater's into Adam Street. Take the first turn on your left and the first turn on your left again into Riverbank Terrace. Our house is the last one at the end of the drive.*

Waihi

Homestay
Address: "Chez Nous",
41 Seddon Avenue, Waihi
Name: Sara and David Parish
Telephone: (08163) 7538
Beds: 1 Double, 1 Single (2 bedrooms, guest bathroom)
Tariff: B&B Double $45, Single $35; Dinner by
prior arrangement $10

Waihi is the southern gateway to the beautiful Coromandel Peninsula and a mere fifteen minute drive from the spectacular expanse of Waihi Beach. The latter is a favourite with surfers and is also very safe for bathing.
The Bay of Plenty seaside resort of Mt Maunganui is a comfortable sixty minute drive to the south. Waihi is steeped in history, particularly with respect to goldmining and it is a mecca for small craft industries. With a superb golf course, salt and freshwater fishing and challenging bush walks it is an outdoor sportsperson's paradise.
We have a large, modern house situated within easy walking distance of Waihi's shops, restaurants and hotels. We are interested in travel and enjoy meeting people both from within New Zealand and from overseas. Guests have their own shower and toilet facilities.
Directions: *Seddon Avenue is the main road leading out of Waihi towards Paeroa.*

51

Taupiri

Farmhouse
Address: Catley Road, RD2, Taupiri
Name: Roy and Carolle Smith
Telephone: (071) 244-723
Beds: 1 Double, 2 Single (2 bedrooms)
Tariff: B&B Double $55, Single $35, Children $20;
Dinner $15; Campervans $20
Nearest Town: 35 km from Hamilton, 18 km from Ngaruawahia,
15 km from Huntly, 115 km from Auckland.

A typical Waikato dairy farm, off the beaten track but not far from Highway 1.
We have a comfortable family home and garden with swimming pool. You are one of the family during your stay, children are very welcome. Learn a little about N.Z. farming, try our hospitality.
Only one hour's run to Auckland.

Ngaruawahia

Homestay
Address: 43 Havelock Road, Ngaruawahia
Name: Ged and Ngaire Sampson
Telephone: (024) 8420
Beds: 2 Single (1 bedroom)
Tariff: B&B Double $50, Single $30, Children
under 10 half price; Dinner $20
Nearest Town: 19 km from Hamilton city, 1 km from
Ngaruawahi township

Our three bedroom home is very comfortable, set amid mature trees on a spacious section and within easy walking distance from our village. A large inground pool enhances a very pleasant and restful area which is the source of a lot of fun for family and friends during the summer months.
We have three married daughters — two residing in New Zealand, our other in Australia — plus Buddy, a white persian cat.
Ngaruawahia is situated on the main highway, 19 km north of Hamilton city, just 1½ hours drive to Auckland and ½ an hour to Raglan Beach on the West Coast. It is the ancestoral home of the Maori Queen, steeped in history and within easy access to many attractions, including Waingaro Hot Pools, Hereford Fine China and Hilldale Game Park.
Over the years we have been fortunate enough to enjoy travelling in New Zealand and overseas. We love meeting people, have many interests and can offer genuine, warm, Kiwi hospitality.

Gordonton, Hamilton

Homestay
Address: Gordonton Road, RD1, Hamilton
Name: Tim and Nan Thorrold
Telephone: (071) 56-742, 395-219 (bus)
Beds: 4 Single (2 bedrooms, guest bathroom)
Tariff: B&B Double $55, Single $35, Children $20; Dinner $15
Nearest Town: 11 km N.E. of Hamilton P.O.

*We have a lovely new home with extensive rural views that we would
love to share with you. Situated in the centre of the Waikato dairying
district we are involved with farming and will be happy to arrange
farm visits.*
We are handy to golf courses.
*Catch up on your washing if you wish — auto washing machine and
drier available.*
Directions: *Hamilton East–Taupiri bypass via Gordonton, 6 km from
city boundary.*

Hamilton

Homestay
Address: 2 Ruakiwi Road, Hamilton
Name: Richard and Pamela Harington
Telephone: (071) 82-328
Beds: 4 Single (2 bedrooms, guest bathrooms)
Tariff: B&B Double $65, Single $45; Dinner by arrangement

*Our superior home is right on the edge of the inner city within 1 km of
the bus terminal, railway station and C.P.O. We are opposite the
Hamilton Lake with its surrounding park which is skirted by beautiful
residential properties. There is a 9-hole golf course, miniature railway,
children's playground as well as sailing at the lake.*
*Hamilton, a university city, bestriding the Waikato river, offers beauti-
ful river walks and gardens and there are river cruises as well.*
*The city has many arts and craft studios, galleries and excellent golf,
squash, swimming and other recreational facilities. It is within easy
motoring of natural mineral pools, world-famous Waitomo Caves,
beaches, lakes and mountains.*
*The area is famous for its grassland farming where beef, dairy, sheep
and stud farms flourish. An agricultural museum and "Farmworld"
exhibit fascinating examples of the diversity of the rural environment.
As your hosts we'd be happy to take you places or help you arrange an
itinerary.*
*You may have family dinner with us or patronise the many attractive
restaurants within walking distance (including one on a river cruise in
a paddle-steamer).*
The guest rooms convert to self-contained accommodation if preferred.

Hamilton

Self-Contained Accommodation
Address: 45 St Andrews Terrace, Hamilton
Name: Niel and Betty Andersen
Telephone: (071) 493-258
Beds: 1 Double Settee, 2 Single (1 bedroom, guest bathroom)
Tariff: B&B Double $50, Single $40, $10 each extra person
reasonable weekly rates on request

My husband and I are of retirement age and live in a quiet location of Hamilton about 4 km from the Central Post Office. Our home overlooks the Hamilton Golf Course (better known as St Andrews) and we are within close proximity of twelve other courses.

We have a self-contained flat at the back of our home, which consists of one twin bedroom, bathroom, large lounge with billiard table, plus kitchenette and lounge area. The six foot settee opens up to sleep two, if required. We let this on a motel basis of clean towels each day, etc.
Our aim is to give travellers time to relax and do as they wish and it is with this in mind that we supply a Continental Breakfast in the flat to have at leisure.
Through business and pleasure we have travelled extensively throughout New Zealand and overseas, so have been able to assist our guests in making further travel plans.
Hamilton is only one and a half hours driving time from Auckland Airport and is centrally located for making day trips to Rotorua, Waitomo Caves and many other interesting places. Guided trips by arrangement.

Please let the hosts know if you have to cancel.
They will have spent time preparing for you.

54

Hamilton

Homestay
Address: 7 Delamare Road, Bryant Park, Hamilton
Name: Mrs Esther Kelly
Telephone: (071) 492-070
Beds: 2 Single (1 bedroom, guest bathroom)
Tariff: B&B Double $55, Single $30; Dinner $15
Nearest Town: Hamilton

I have travelled in many countries and would welcome tourists and would be happy to advise you on travel in New Zealand.

I live in the suburb of Bryant Park, close to the Waikato River with its tranquil river walks and I am within walking distance of St Andrews Golf Course. Hamilton is a picturesque city with rose gardens, a new museum, Ruakura Animal Research Farm and an agricultural museum called "Farmworld". Hamilton is in the centre of the dairy industry.

My interests are cooking, gardening, tramping, boating, trout fishing, playing golf, art and also Mah Jong. I am a member of Business and Professional Women's Club.

I look forward to offering you friendly hospitality.

Directions: *If approaching from Auckland — leave main highway just after passing Te Rapa Air Force Station on right. Turn left at Pukete Road, turn right at Sandwich Road and Delamare Road is 1 km on left. If approaching from Hamilton — travel north 1·5 km on Ulster Street until you reach four cross-roads with lights. Just after lights, turn right to Beerescourt Road. Travel 2 km to Braid Road shops on right and after shops turn left to Sandwich Road and Delamare Road is on right. (4·5 km from Hamilton city)*

Hamilton

Self-Contained Accommodation
Address: 182 Tramway Road, Hamilton
Name: P. and M. Gutmann
Telephone: (071) 556-260
Beds: 2 Single (1 bedrooms, guest bathroom and kitchen)
Tariff: B&B Double $50, Single $25
Nearest Town: Hamilton

We both speak German and are interested in gardening, herbs, beekeeping and antiques.
You can go on walks along the Waikato River, enjoy the rose garden, roller skating (if young at heart) or book one of the popular cruise boats. World famous Ruakura Agriculture Research Station is nearby. We are in the centre of the rich Waikato dairying area.
Directions: *We live 2 km from the main post office in Victoria Street, Hamilton. Tramway Road is on the other side of the Waikato River, east side.*

Hamilton

Homestay
Address: 530 Grey Street, Hamilton
Name: Norman and Frances Wills
Telephone: (071) 382-120
Beds: 1 Twin Room, 1 Single Room (guest bathroom)
Tariff: B&B Double $55, Single $35, Children half price; Dinner $15
Nearest Town: Hamilton

Pleasant family home away from traffic noise but very handy to city — 12 minutes walk to Chief Post Office.

Grey Street is the main north–south street on the east side of the Waikato River running through Hamilton East shopping centre to Claudelands Showgrounds.
We have travelled overseas and are accustomed to entertaining visitors — American, Asian and European. We can assist with local and district sightseeing information.
No smoking in house please, but we are a friendly home and enjoy guests.

Frankton, Hamilton

Farmhouse
Address: "Farndale",
RD10, Frankton
Name: Sylvia and Rod Smith
Telephone: (071) 298-511
Beds: 1 Double, 3 Single (3 bedrooms, guest bathroom)
Tariff: B&B Double $50, Single $30, Children under 10
half price; Dinner with wine $20

Our home is roomy and comfortable with good views in every direction.
We offer a generous three-course meal with New Zealand wines.
Local attractions include tramping, horse riding, golf, beach at Raglan
(½ hour drive), Waitomo caves (1 hour drive).
Our interests include horticulture and animal farming, music, arts and
crafts and travel.
Directions: *Please phone.*

NZ phone numbers are being changed. Ring 018 for directory.

Raglan

Farmhouse + Self-Contained Accommodation
Address: "Matawha", RD2, Raglan
Name: Peter and Jenny Thomson
Telephone: (071) 256-709
Beds: 2 Single; 1 Double + 2 Singles in self-contained unit
Tariff: B&B Double $30, Single $20, Children half price,
Babies free; Dinner $15; Campervans $20 (laundry and
bathroom facilities available)
Nearest Town: Raglan 30 minutes, Hamilton 1 hour

We are a family of four with two boys aged 10 and 13 years. We are
fortunate to farm right on the west coast with panoramic views from the
house.
Our beach is very private with good fishing and hang gliding.
Our farm has been in the family for over 100 years and we take great
pride in breeding top class Romney sheep, and stud and commercial
Hereford cattle. We also do some riding and have a large area of flower
garden. We have a large garden, and all vegetables and meat are
supplied by the farm.
We have excellent scenic drives and bush walks available. Our visitors
enjoy participating in all our farm activities.
Directions: *Take Hamilton–Raglan road and travel to the Kauroa*
and Te Mata Bridal Veil Falls (signposted) and turn right. Take the
first turn to the right through Te Mata (Waimaori Road) and follow for
7 miles. Our place is named on letterbox at a "T" junction marked
Ruapuke Road and Waimaori Rd, no exit.

Ohaupo

Homestay
Address: "Grandview", No 15 State Highway 3, Ohaupo
Postal: RD3 Ohaupo
Name: Peter and Bernie van Kempen
Telephone: (071) 296-564
Beds: 1 Double, 2 Single (2 bedrooms)
Tariff: B&B Double $45, Single $25, Children half price,
Cot available; Dinner $12
Nearest Town: Hamilton 17 km north, Te Awamutu 10 km south

Our family has flown the coop. As we are a semi-retired business couple we miss the contact with people which we enjoyed very much. We live in a rural district with great lake views to the east and Mt Pirongia to the west. Many major tourist attractions are within easy distance for day trips, as well as varied and interesting local sights. We offer a courtesy car to and from Hamilton airport (5 minutes) to our guests.

Can't contact your host? Ring 018 for directory assistance.

Ohaupo

Farmhouse
Address: Mill Road, RD1, Ohaupo, Waikato
Name: Joyce and Robert Snodgrass
Telephone: (071) 296-794
Beds: 1 Double, 2 Single (2 bedrooms, guest bathroom)
Tariff: B&B Double $50, Single $25, Children half price; Dinner $15
Nearest Town: Ohaupo 5 km

We are a dairy farming couple with three grown children. Our fifteen-year-old home is built to catch the sun and is ideal for a relaxing stay. We have one large bedroom with double bed and one small room with single beds for guests.
Our farm is situated on a quiet country road within easy reach of Te Awamutu, Cambridge and Hamilton and their well known attractions. We are 5 km from our local village (approx 400 population) with its country store, restaurant and tavern.
Directions: *Take State Highway 3 to the Ohaupo school. Opposite turn into West Road then second turn right into Mill Road. We are 1 km down on the left.*

If you find something missing that you are
accustomed to, simply ask you hosts for it.

58

Ohaupo

Homestay
Address: Main Road
(State Highway 3),
RD3 Ohaupo
(near Hamilton)
Name: "Hillside House" — Norm and Pamela Powell
Telephone: (07) 871-5070
Beds: 1 Double, 4 Single
Tariff: Accommodation only Double $40, Single $20; Breakfast (cooked) $5, (Continental) $3, Dinner by arrangement $10

Our brick home appears deceptively small from the main road entrance, as the main area is built out on a hillside overlooking panoramic views of lush Waikato farmland.
We live two hours drive south of Auckland airport and are on the main route to Waitomo Caves and Otorohanga Kiwi House in an area of sheep, goat, dairy and deer farms.
Te Awamutu is a pleasant town with beautiful rose gardens and a good shopping area.
We have a vareity of interests, have travelled widely, and especially enjoyed the variety of friendly hospitality at bed and breakfast homes in the U.K. which we endeavour to extend to our visitors.
Directions: *From Hamilton, take the main road (State Highway 3) to Te Awamutu for 22 km. Watch for large Caltex Service Station on left. Our house is signposted about 500 metres further on, also on the left.*

Matamata

Farmhouse
Address: "Denson Dale",
  RD3, Matamata
Name: Betty and Chas Wilson
Telephone: (0818) 26-719
Beds: 1 Double, 2 Single plus small single extra if required (2 bedrooms, guest bathroom)
Tariff: B&B Double $54, Single $27, Small extra single
if required $20; Campervans $20 (parking space and all facilities)
Nearest Town: Matamata 8 km

We live on a dairy farm, situated on Taihoa South road, 100 metres from State Highway 27 and 2 km from State Highway 29. We are less than an hour's drive from Hamilton, Tauranga and Rotorua — two

continued over

59

hours' drive to Auckland. Several beaches are all approximately 1 hour's drive away.

Beach accommodation right on the water's edge can be arranged if requested. As we are very centrally situated, those wishing to make our home their holiday base for a longer stay will have the benefit of cheaper rates.

Guests will enjoy family meals and hospitality, a spacious home and every convenience.

We enjoy travelling and meeting people of all ages. Our interests are many, including stud Jersey cattle and the growing of roses.

Directions: *Please write or phone.*

Tell other travellers about your favourite homes.

Cambridge

Homestay/Farmhouse
Address: Cambridge Te Awamutu Main Highway
Name: Withdrawn
Telephone: Withdrawn
Beds: 4 Single (2 bedrooms, guest bathroom)
Tariff: B&B Double $55, Single $35

We are semi-retired farmers living in a gracious old home in the central Waikato midway between Auckland and Rotorua. There is a small farmlet attached on which we graze our pedigree Jersey heifers — the replacements for our dairy farm.

Cambridge, which is 4 km away, is the centre of intensive dairying and thoroughbred horse studs. Lake Karapiro is 10 km and Mystery Creek and airport 6 km. Cambridge is New Zealand's largest craft centre.

Our home was built in 1912 and is a landmark in the area. It has a feeling of warmth and comfort as you enter and we enjoy hosting visitors. The guest rooms are upstairs with beautiful pastoral views and you will have private facilities.

We welcome you to have dinner with us or bed and breakfast if you wish. A warm welcome will await you.

Directions: *4 km on the main highway from Cambridge to Te Awamutu. A lamppost with 'Monavale Homestead' is at the gate.*

Waitomo, Te Kuiti

Farmhouse
Address: Glenview Station, RD4, Te Kuiti
Name: Warren and Cindy Clayton-Greene
Telephone: (0813) 87-705
Beds: 1 Double, 2 Single (2 bedrooms)
Tariff: B&B Double $40, Single $25, Children $10 each; Dinner $10

We would like to invite you to stay on a New Zealand sheep and cattle station. Enjoy the comfort and hospitality that rural life has to offer. Relax amongst the quiet and beautiful countryside while enjoying the farm's bush, trout streams and unique limestone formations. Our farm is run in the traditional way by horse and dog. The farm carries approximately 5,000 sheep and 600 cattle on 2,200 acres.

We will share with you our attractive home set in lovely gardens. You will find us nestled in the hills above Waitomo Caves with a panoramic view of the King Country region.

Directions: *Follow the road west from Waitomo Caves towards Marakopa for approximately 6 km. We're on the right, just look for our name on the mailbox.*

Waitomo, Te Kuiti

Farmhouse
Address: Te Toko Station, Putaki-Hauturu Road,
Name: Bob and Judy Osborne
Telephone: (0813) 88-372
Beds: 4 Single (2 bedrooms)
Tariff: B&B Double $52, Single $32; Dinner $10
Nearest Town: Waitomo Caves Village 14 km, Otorohanga 29 km,
Te Kuiti approximately 40 minutes

*We are a family of four, with our son working on the station and our
daughter at university.*
*Our sheep and cattle station consists of 2,500 acres carrying 3,500
sheep and 300 head of cattle plus 150 goats.*
*We have a generous proportion of native bush (birdlife galore) and
limestone formations seldom seen elsewhere. This is a pocket of New
Zealand scenery that you will have little trouble falling in love with.*
*Our homestead is a 4-bedroom Lockwood, six years old and the
grounds are shaping up nicely with rhododendrons in the foreground
covering an embankment which enhances the entrance to our home.*
*We are very happy for our guests to take part in or be shown the activi-
ties on the station. We have farm hacks on the station and people with
previous riding experience are welcome to come on a three hour trail
ride at $10 per hour.*
*Stay a night or two with us — others say it is a great way to get to know
New Zealand.*
Directions: *Second turn on right, 10 km from Waitomo Caves. First
house on left, 5 km up the road.*

Waitomo, Te Kuiti

Farmhouse
Address: Gadsby Road, Te Kuiti
Postal: Box 307, Te Kuiti
Name: Merv and Lola Anderson
Telephone: (0813) 87-023
Beds: 2 Single (1 bedroom)
Tariff: Double $30, Single $20; Dinner $10
Nearest Town: 1·2 km north of Te Kuiti

*We enjoy a country lifestyle just minutes from Te Kuiti on a 14-acre
self-sufficiency-style farmlet which produces all our meat, milk, eggs
and most of our vegetables. We run a small flock of pedigree Suffolk
sheep and enjoy a large informal garden. As we are situated on a hill
our views are panoramic.*
We have two dogs who live inside.

Visitors would be welcome to view and perhaps handle or photograph the farm animals, most of which are very quiet.

We enjoy meeting other people and learning about other people's backgrounds and way of life.

We are handy to Waitomo Caves with black water rafting and caves viewing, Otorohanga Kiwi House and deer farm, Pureora Forest, which is a recreational hunting area and the good fishing which the west coast at Marakopa and Kiritehere provides.

We have friends who have deer farms, goat farms and sheep and cattle farms. We could arrange visits and/or hunting or fishing trips.

Please, as we are outside a lot, let the phone ring for long periods or just come up. We would be delighted to see you. We are seldom away for very long and there is always someone here from 4 pm onwards.

All telephone numbers in New Zealand are being changed during 1990 so the numbers listed may not be current. Ring 018 for directory assistance if you cannot contact your hosts.

Kakahi, Taumarunui

Farmhouse
Address: "Rawhide", PO Kakahi via Taumarunui
Name: Rex and Barbara Taylor
Telephone: (0812) 26-550
Beds: 4 Single (2 bedrooms)
Tariff: B&B, Lunch and Dinner — Double $110, Single $60;
B&B Double $60, Single $35; Dinner $15; Campervans $12
Nearest Town: Taumarunui 20 km

Be our guest in a modern home on 20 acres at Kakahi which is 20 km south of Taumarunui, one of the country's best, yet least-used vacation spots in New Zealand.

Our property is next to bush reserve and the Wanganui river. Good country-style cooking with 90% of the food being home produced on the property. We have a quarter horse stud, western saddlery and leather craft workshop.

Attractions include trout fishing, tramping, swimming, glow worms, handy to jet boat tours, canoeing, top golf course. Three-quarter hour drive to ski fields. Large gun collection short drive away. Guided horseback treks available, half-day, full day or four-day-wilderness camping and trout fishing trips by horseback, tramping or helicopter.

Packed lunch available for day trips away. Special diets can be catered for. Extra charge for liquor or bring your own.

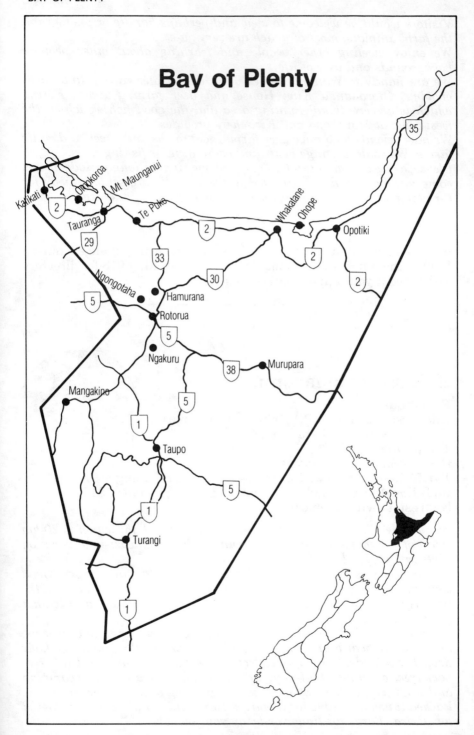

Katikati

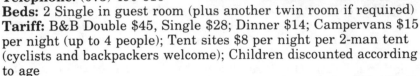

Farmstay
Address: Jacaranda Cottage,
Thompson's Track,
RD2, Katikati
Name: Lynlie and Rick Watson
Telephone: (075) 490 616
Beds: 2 Single in guest room (plus another twin room if required)
Tariff: B&B Double $45, Single $28; Dinner $14; Campervans $15
per night (up to 4 people); Tent sites $8 per night per 2-man tent
(cyclists and backpackers welcome); Children discounted according
to age
Nearest Town: 40 km north of Tauranga, 8 km south of Katikati

*Jacaranda Cottage, on a 5-acre farmlet, enjoys magnificent views in
every direction — from sea to mountains, from rolling farmlands to
native forests.*
*Our aim is to provide you with a taste of simple country life at an
affordable cost. We offer friendly hospitality; clean, warm accommodation; and plenty of wholesome farmhouse food — fresh farm eggs and
milk, home-made bread, organically reared meat, etc. Most of our
guests enjoy living "as family" at Jacaranda Cottage, or, if you would
prefer it, we can supply just the basic necessities. We prefer guests who
smoke to do so outside.*
*Enjoy the variety of animals on our farmlet. Try things you may not
have done before — hand-milk a cow or goat, collect warm, freshly-laid
eggs, spin wool, scratch a pig's back, ride a pony, cuddle a cow.*
*We also sell beautiful, antique clocks, handmade from NZ kauri
recovered from swamps and carbon-dated 23,600 years old!*
*Transport can be arranged to any nearby places of interest — or you can
simply relax in the tranquil surroundings of Jacaranda Cottage. You
are welcome to extend your stay with us if you wish.*
Directions: *Thompson's Track is 6 km south of Katikati, on the
Tauranga side of the Forta Leza Restaurant. Jacaranda Cottage is
2.4 km up Thompson's Track — there is a small sign on the mailbox
opposite the gateway.*

Omokoroa, Tauranga

Homestay
Address: 12 Walnut Grove, Omokoroa, RD2, Tauranga
Name: Jane and Jim Russell   **Telephone:** (075) 480-577
Beds: 1 Double, 2 Single (2 bedrooms, guest bathroom)
Tariff: B&B Double $30, Single $15; Dinner $15
Nearest Town: 13 km from Tauranga

*We are retired Scots/New Zealanders eager to show hospitality to
overseas travellers. Our home is in a quiet village ideally placed for*
continued over

anyone wishing to see the Bay of Plenty/Waikato area and only an hour's drive from Rotorua and its tourist attractions. Or to recover from that long plane trip and plan the rest of a holiday in N.Z. — we would be happy to help on both counts.

A 2½ hour drive from Auckland on the main highway to Tauranga, the Omokoroa turnoff is well signposted.

We have a small, self-contained area of sitting room, bedroom with two single beds, separate shower/toilet, all opening on to our secluded garden with beach access. Also a double bedroom upstairs, sharing the family bathroom with shower and separate loo.

We keep a well-stocked larder and would provide breakfast of your choice, as well as dinner in the evening if required (with a few hours advance warning!).

Directions: *Follow Omokoroa Beach Road into Harbour View Road: Walnut Grove is cul-de-sac on left at top of hill.*

Phone numbers may have changed. Ring 018 for directory.

Te Puna, Tauranga

Farmhouse
Address:
Name: Withdrawn
Telephone: Withdrawn
Beds: 1 Double, 2 Single (2 bedrooms)
Tariff: B&B Double $50, Single $30, Children $12.50;
Campervans $15; Dinner $15;
Nearest Town: 10 km north of Tauranga on State Highway 2

We have a modern family home on a fifteen-acre kiwifruit and citrus orchard, and as our family has left home we now have two spare bedrooms which we like to share with tourists.

We live in a lovely area of the Bay of Plenty with many facilities being only a short distance away.

Tauranga has many beautiful parks and gardens and is well known for its fishing. Mt Maunganui with its beautiful open beaches is only a 15 minutes drive over the new harbour bridge.

Stan is a very keen sportsman and finds it very easy to make time for a round of golf.

We can offer a traditional N.Z. dinner in our own home or we can recommend the bistro meal which is served between 6–8 pm at the Te Puna Tavern only 2 km away, either preceded or followed by a dip in the large thermal swimming pool only 4 km away.

On arrival at our place you will be given a rousing welcome by our pair of friendly corgi dogs.

Directions: *10 km north of Tauranga or 20 km south of Katikati on State Highway 2. Easily found behind Parklands roadside stall.*

Tauranga

Homestay
Address: 2A Tenth Avenue (at end of drive), Tauranga
Name: Gordon and Christine Ross
Telephone: (075) 784-826
Beds: 2 Single (1 bedroom, guest bathroom)
Tariff: B&B $30 per person

Our home is a very attractive townhouse, easily located and handy to town. Easy walking distance to shops and restaurants. We enjoy extensive views over the park and water.
The guest room is large with every comfort, plus own bathroom. Breakfast of your choice. Any other meals by arrangement.
Off-street parking.

Tauranga

Homestay
Address:
75 Manuwai Drive,
Matua, Tauranga
Name: Trevor and Gloria Shepherd
Telephone: (075) 62-791
Beds: 1 Double, 2 Single (2 bedrooms, guest bathroom)
Tariff: B&B $25 per person, Children half price;
Dinner $15; Campervans $20 for 4 persons

We are a retired couple in our mid 60's with a family of three who are now married and we have eight grandchildren. We have travelled extensively overseas and within New Zealand and enjoy meeting people from places around the world, also fellow New Zealanders.
We offer hospitality in a modern home, close to the sea (harbour) in a very quiet location 6 km from the centre of Tauranga town. There are pleasant walks and scenic drives within close proximity and it is only 12 km to Mt Maunganui beach and hot salt-water baths.
Our special interests include Church, travel and nursing.
We can offer two bedrooms, one with a double bed and one with two single beds and a guest bathroom. You may have family dinner with us, or if you prefer, only bed and breakfast. We can provide the breakfast of your choice.
We will meet the plane or bus.
Directions: *Travel out to the Matua Peninsular. Proceed along Levers Road to Matua Road. This runs into Manuwai Drive.*

Tauranga

Homestay
Address: 85 Forrester Drive, Welcome Bay, Tauranga
Name: Ray and Yvonne Mead
Telephone: (075) 441-021
Beds: 4 Single (2 are divans in living area)
(1 bedroom, guest bathroom)
Tariff: B&B Double $60, Single $35, Children ½ price;
Campervans $15 or $20 for 3 or more; Dinner $20, Breakfast $5
Nearest Town: Tauranga 7 km, Mount Maunganui 14 km

Our home is spacious and comfortable with wooden interior and high ceilings. We have tranquil views of the harbour, city and country. Accommodation opens on to a living/kitchen area with private adjoining shower and toilet facilities and this opens on to a pleasant and private barbecue area. A few steps leads to the edge of a park and 30 feet to the water, where, at high tide, we can swim. Canoes and dinghy are available. We enjoy trout fishing on the Rotorua lakes from our boat and this is available to guests with a charge to cover costs and lunch.

There are many interesting places and/or towns to visit near here and if you so wish we can transport you and act as a guide. The area provides many good restaurants, some ethnic and we are only 20 km from Te Puke, the kiwifruit capital of the world. Mount Maunganui is one of the best surf beaches in the country and Matamata, about half-an-hour's drive away, has many horse racing studs. Natural and salt water hot pools are also close at hand.
We have travelled in numerous countries and would be happy to assist in further travel arrangements etc. Our 13-year-old granddaughter lives with us, so children in that age group would be especially welcome. New Zealand cuisine of a high standard is our specialty.
Directions: *Take the Welcome Bay Road until the· Welcome Bay Village Shops. Forrester Drive is opposite.*

Mount Maunganui

Address: 36 Rita Street, Mount Maunganui
Name: Margaret and Lloyd Seed
Telephone: (075) 55-250 evenings
Beds: 2 Single (1 bedroom)
Tariff: B&B Double $60, Single $40, Children $15; 3 Course
Dinner $20, we also offer (1) Campervan site with power,
shared bathroom and laundry $12; (2) 2-berth caravan with power
and gas on site $28; Breakfast for campervan and caravanners $8
Nearest Town: ½ km downtown The Mount, 6 km Tauranga city

We are a retired couple who have travelled, so we have an interest in people, especially from overseas. We have chosen Mount Maunganui for our place of retirement and live just five minutes' walk from the ocean, harbour and downtown. There are delightful walks in close proximity e.g. therapeutic hot salt pools 1 km away at the foot of the Mount, Mount Drury Leisure Island and Blowhole all ½ km away, the walk around or part way up and around the Mount, or even to the top, all commanding glorious views. We are blessed with magnificent views, both harbour and ocean, from our home.
We are 6 km from Tauranga now that the new harbour bridge is opened thus bringing us very close to the historical village rose gardens and all sports. For the fisherman the wharf where boats leave for Mayor Island and fishing trips is in easy walking distance.
Directions: *Upon reaching downtown Mount, turn right at roundabout at Coronation Park then take the second turn left into Rita Street. We live fourth on the left. Our name and number 36 is on the box. We look forward to meeting you.*

Mount Maunganui

Homestay + Self-Contained Accommodation
Address: 7 Percy Road, Papamoa
Name: Joan and Jim Francis
Telephone: (075) 420-815
Beds: 1 Double, 4 Single (3 bedrooms, guest bathroom)
Tariff: B&B Double $50, Single $30, Children half price; Dinner $8;
Self-contained bedsit flat Double $35, $5 each extra
Nearest Town: Mount Maunganui or Te Puke

We are an informal, middle aged couple with four children out in the world, three grandchildren (two are in England) and friends in many countries. Our interests are gardening, travel, meeting people — our home is full of souvenirs, antiques, sunshine, books and we hope — welcome!
All beds have electric blankets, there are two toilets/bathrooms and a separate shower. You can soak in our spa; sit and admire the sea and

continued over

69

rural views — walk/swim at the beach 250 m away or eat at the top class restaurant.

The self-contained flat at the rear of our house has a double bed, two fold-up singles, TV, automatic washing machine etc. and linen is available at additional cost.

We are only 10–15 minutes from local tourist attractions and we will meet public transport or take you sightseeing.

Directions: *We are about 2 km from State Highway 2 (Rotorua–Te Puke–Tauranga) turning at the Garden Centre signpost 'Papamoa Domain', Percy Road is the first left after the Papamoa Tavern. Joan and I look forward to welcoming you to our house.*

Can't contact your host? Ring 018 for directory assistance.

Te Puke

Self-Contained Accommodation
Address: Rangiuru Road, RD8, Te Puke
Name: Margaret and Barry Waite
Telephone: (075) 738-534
Beds: 4 Single (2 bedrooms, guest bathroom)
Tariff: B&B $30 per person, Children half price
Nearest Town: Te Puke 18 km

We have a hill farm of 650 acres with about 500 acres in grass and the remainder in native bush. We keep sheep, cattle and deer and have a few acres of kiwifruit.

The flat, which is nextdoor to our house, in a large garden, has two bedrooms and living/dining area with two-ring stove, microwave oven, fridge and TV.

Outside is a large swimming pool for summer and a spa pool.

Directions: *2 km east of Te Puke turn right into Te Matai Road. Keep going for about 15 km then turn left into Rangiuru Road, 1½ km and we are on the right hand side. Please phone for booking.*

Whakatane

Farmhouse
Address: State Highway 2,
  RD2, Whakatane
  (7 km west of Whakatane)
Name: Jim and Kathleen Law
Telephone: (076) 87-955
Beds: 1 Double (1 bedroom)
Tariff: B&B $30 per person; Dinner $15; Campervans $15
Nearest Town: Whakatane 7 km

Whakatane is the centre of the Sunshine Coast. It is off the beaten tourist track, but it has many attractions. We have both lived here all our lives and although our four sons have all left home — one still at University — we have chosen to remain.

Two 50/50 sharemilkers manage our farms — one on town supply, the other on factory supply. We breed black and coloured and spotted sheep and also operate a craft shop called The Red Barn, promoting local craftspeople. This is an outlet for fruit grown in our commercial orchard of citrus, apples and feijoas.

We have travelled extensively overseas and enjoy meeting people of all ages.

Bowls, genealogy and organic gardening are some of our interests outside of farming.

There is one double bed in our guest room that shares some bathroom facilities. Large recreation room with pool table and extensive library. You are invited to join in any of our activities, we can arrange sight-seeing trips or you may just relax in peaceful surroundings.

Directions: *State Highway 2, 7 km west of Whakatane, near Powdrell Road look for The Red Barn sign.*

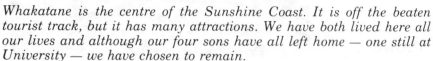

Opotiki

Guest House
Address: 112 Ford Street,
Name: Patiti Lodge
Telephone: (076) 56-834
Beds: 2 Double, 10 Single (9 bedrooms)
Tariff: B&B Double $38.50, Single $24; Continental Breakfast $5.50, Cooked Breakfast $9.90, Children meals half price

Robyn and Jim Towersey welcome you to Patiti Lodge. It is quiet and comfortable — off the main roads, and only two minutes walk to the main road. We have spacious single, double and twin rooms with electric blankets on the beds. There are two colour TV lounges with tea and coffee making facilities. We have a first class fully licenced dining room. Laundry facilities are available.   Off-street parking.

View of
White Island
from
The Rafters

Ohope

Homestay + Self-Contained Accommodation
Address: The Rafters, 261a Pohutukawa
Avenue, Box 3101, Ohope
Name: Mavis and Pat Rafter
Telephone: (076) 24-856
Beds: 1 Double, 5 Single (3 bedrooms, guest bathrooms)
Tariff: B&B Double $60, $10 each extra person (limit 2), Single $50,
School-age Children Free; Dinner $30, Children $10 (includes
premium wines, pre-dinner drinks, full menu, top rate cuisine);
Lunches are available (including packed) $5.00
Nearest Town: Whakatane 8 km, Rotorua 85 km

*Mavis, an experienced cook, has a background in nursing, keenly
interested in art; Pat, Senior Tutor at Whakatane High School, keen on
golf, music and literature.*
*Guest rooms occupy two wings of the house, each has its own en-suite,
lounge with colour TV, panoramic views of Ohope Beach. Kitchenette
with fridge and full cooking facilities plus microwave oven is in each
guest unit so as to offer guests the choice of cooking their own lunch and
evening meal or sharing with us. The lounge of host home opens onto a
solar heated swimming pool and enclosed spa pool. There is an extensive library. B.B.Q.'s etc. are provided.*
Safe swimming and surfing on beachfront.
*Facilities (5 mins by car) include International Golf course, tennis,
bowling, fishing and bush walks.*
*Windsurfing on the inner harbour (5 mins away), lessons are available
in summer. Three bicycles are available at the Rafters for rides on the
beach. Ohope Chartered Club with dining and bar facilities is one
minute's walk away and temporary holiday membership is available.*
*Jet boat trips and deep sea fishing can be arranged. Courtesy car
available.*
Dogs welcomed if guaranteed house trained.
Directions: *Take the road from Whakatane to Ohope, turn right along
Pohutukawa Avenue and 261a is on your left on the beach side.*

Hamurana Rotorua

Farmhouse
Address: Te Waerenga Road, RD2, Ngongotaha
Name: Rod and Dianne Daniel
Telephone: (073) 23-560
Beds: 4 Single (2 bedrooms, guest bathroom)
Tariff: B&B Double $55, Single $35; Dinner $18
Nearest Town: 20 km north of Rotorua, 12 km to Ngongotaha

We have a new spacious home situated north of Rotorua with panoramic views of the lake and city. Although only a short distance from Rotorua's major tourist attractions we maintain a rural lifestyle on our 70 acre deer farm. Hamurana Park and 9-hole golf course are 2 km away.
The main guest room, upstairs adjacent to the games room, has two single beds, private bathroom facilities and a balcony overlooking Rotorua lake and city. There is also a twin room downstairs with separate toilet facilities.
We have travelled widely in the last 5 years, enjoy meeting people and would like to extend our hospitality to visitors to Rotorua and the Bay of Plenty.
Directions: *Please phone after 5 pm for bookings and directions.*

Ngongotaha

Farmhouse
Address: Please phone for booking and address
Name: Rex and Ann Wells
Telephone: (073) 72-014
Beds: 1 Double, 1 Single (2 bedrooms, guest bathroom)
Tariff: B&B Double $60, Single $35; Dinner $20
Nearest Town: Ngongotaha 3 km, Rotorua city 8 km

Rex and Ann live in a new brick home of 3500 sq ft and both have travelled overseas, Ann being born in England. We have no family at home but get enjoyment showing our 50 acre farm to other travellers. Being the nearest Farmstay hosts to the world famous Agrodome (1 km) we are very easy to find.
Our interests in life, other than farming red deer, English Leicester stud sheep, Appaloosa horses and a few cattle include table tennis, tennis, photography, dogs, travel, rugby and thoroughbred horses. We are Mercedes-Benz Car Club members. Our home also includes a full-sized billiard table room and inside spa pool. Rex is always ready to learn new tricks with a cue and ball!
Our home is close to an 18-hole golf course, trout hatchery and fishing, horse riding, 5 km to Rainbow and Fairy Springs and 12 km to Whaka thermal area.
We also operate our paddocks and stables as a horse motel — horses staying for races and nearby shows.

Ngongotaha, Rotorua

Farmhouse + Self-Contained Accommodation
Address: Jackson Road, Kaharoa (PO Box 22, Ngongotaha), Rotorua
Name: Deer Pine Lodge, Hosts John and Betty Insch
Telephone: (073) 23-458
Beds: 1 Double, 2 Single (2 bedrooms, guest bathroom)
Tariff: B&B Double $55, Single $35; Dinner with glass
of house wine $15; Campervans welcome

*We have a deer farm approximately 16 km from Rotorua. The property
is surrounded with trees and has a panoramic view of Lake Rotorua.
Guests are welcome to observe the farming of deer where possible.*
*The deer are grazing approximately 6 m from the house. We also have
sheep, a cat, dog and a couple of horses plus pony which visitors can
ride if they so wish.*
*There is a golf course just 7 km from home, and Taniwha Springs is
nearby, also the Agrodome (3 shows a day, sheep shearing, etc).*
*The nearby city of Rotorua offers fishing, bush walks, hot mineral
pools, orchid gardens, Skyline gondala rides (up Mount Ngongotaha),
Fairy Springs and herb garden complex, everything for the visitor to
enjoy.*

*Our home offers a self-contained unit — coffee making facilities, your
own bathroom, shower, etc. You can also eat your meals there.*
*Campervans are welcome — we have parking and washing facilities
available.*
Directions: *Please phone.* _____

Our B&Bs are mostly private homes. Most do
not accept credit cards.
_____

Ngongotaha, Rotorua

Homestay
Address: RD1, Ngongotaha
Name: Mrs Roslyn Livingstone
Telephone: (073)25-829, 27-723
Beds: 1 Double, 2 Single
(2 bedrooms, guest bathroom)
Tariff: B&B $22 per person; Dinner $10
Nearest Town: Rotorua 19 km

Use my farmhouse as the base for your Rotorua holiday. The homestead is modern and centrally heated. Guests have own bathroom.
The nearby city of Rotorua offers trout fishing, lake trips, Whakarewarewa village (geysers, boiling mud, hot mineral pools, Maori village, ethnic arts and crafts), the Agrodome (sheep, shearing and sheepdogs!), Fairy Springs (huge trout, Kiwihouse, native flora and fauna), the Skyline gondola ride (up Mount Ngongotaha), the Herb Garden complex, tropical and temperate orchid gardens, sophisticated shopping and restaurants ranging from the simple through ethnic to haute cuisine.
Directions: *Please phone.*

Rotorua

Farmhouse
Name: Maureen and John
Telephone: (073) 481-352
Beds: 1 Double, 2 Single (3 bedrooms)
Tariff: B&B Double $60, Single $35, Children half price;
Dinner by arrangement $20
Nearest Town: Rotorua 4 km (10 minutes by car)

Guests will be warmly welcomed at our large, modern home on the city outskirts. Superb views of the lake, city, forest and surrounding countryside. Enjoy our garden and solar heated swimming pool.
We farm 150 acres running deer, beef and sheep. Scenic farm tours available.
Our adult family of five have now sought pastures new allowing us to offer an attractive suite of rooms consisting of one double bedroom, two singles bedrooms, a small sunroom and a toilet and handbasin. Shower and bath in adjoining family area; guests having top priority. Underfloor heating, innersprung mattresses, plenty of room for cars, campervans and luggage storage. Non-smokers preferred.
Be sure and allow a few days stay so you have time to rest as well as enjoy the many nearby world renowned attractions.
We enjoy gardening, water-skiing, tramping and travelling and look forward to sharing our home and farm with you.

Rotorua

Homestay
Address: Please phone
Name: Ursula and Lindsay Prince
Telephone: (073) 470-140
Beds: 1 Double, 3 Single (2 bedrooms, guest bathrooms)
Tariff: B&B Double $60, Single $40, Children half price;
Dinner with complimentary NZ wine $15

You can be sure of a warm welcome when you decide to stay with us at our beautiful new home right at the lakefront in Rotorua. Quiet and secluded, yet only five minutes by car from the centre of our busy city with its many attractions, our house is an ideal situation.

Two spacious guest rooms, each with private bathrooms, well-cooked meals in a relaxed and informal atmosphere — the feeling to be amongst friends is what we offer you.
Relax on the deck, enjoy the tranquil lake and mountain scene, watch the waterbirds or explore the lake by Canadian canoe.
We are an active, middle-aged couple, enjoying life with all its challenges. We take an interest in world affairs, have travelled and lived overseas, love the outdoors and enjoy meeting people from all walks of life.
Being non-smokers ourselves, we thank you for not smoking in the house.
We will be happy to advise you on how to make the most of your stay in Rotorua, a city that has much to offer.

Westbrook, Rotorua

Homestay
Address: Please phone
Name: David and Vene Jones
Telephone: (073) 479-194
Beds: 1 Double, 2 Single (2 bedrooms, guest bathroom)
Tariff: B&B Double $50, Single $30, Children half price;
Dinner $15 (24 hours notice required)
Nearest Town: Rotorua 4 km, 10 minutes by car

We live in a quiet cul-de-sac down a right of way overlooking several parks — the city green belt, international stadium, Springfield golf course, Smallbone park. We have views of lake, forest and the city and also of Mt Ngongotaha. We are ten minutes from the central city and close to all the world-renowned tourist sights — Whakarewarewa thermal area, Agrodome, Blue and Green lakes and Skyline rides on Mt Ngongotaha are all close by.
We are not far from good fishing spots at the lakes and Bay of Plenty beaches. It is only one hour to Ohope and Mt Maunganui. All these are within the tourist diamond the Bay of Plenty.
We are both retired with family all married. Our hobbies are the great outdoors, hiking, bush walks, gardening, arts and crafts and painting (time allowing). We love meeting people and have travelled overseas several times the language barrier proving no problem.
I guess you would class our home as a "humble comfortable" quality home.
You have your own toilet, bathroom and shower.
No campervans, no smokers please.

Rotorua

Homestay
Address: 9 Duncan Street, Rotorua
Name: Tim and Pauline Mossman
Telephone: (073) 479-697
Beds: 1 Double, 2 Single (2 bedrooms, guest bathroom)
Tariff: B&B Double $55, Single $35, Children half price;
Dinner by arrangement
Nearest Town: 5 minutes by car to town centre

Welcome to Rotorua and to our comfortable, thermally heated home with plunge pool, handy to all Rotorua can offer including thermal activity, lakes, forestry, white water rafting, trout fishing, golfing. Famous Arikikapakapa golf course borders at the end of our quiet street. One hour to Taupo and Tauranga.
We are retired farmers having many interests. Our family of boys have left home, two living overseas and one at university.

Rotorua

Homestay
Address: 11 Upland Road, Western Heights, Rotorua
Name: Mrs May Parker
Telephone: (073) 486-754 (morning and evenings)
Beds: 4 Single (2 bedrooms)
Tariff: B&B Double $50, Single $25, Children ½ price;
Dinner $12; Campervans $15 (4 people)
Nearest Town: 5 km from Rotorua shopping centre

I have a homely three bedroom house in a quiet suburb of Rotorua —
5 km from the city centre.
Ample off-street parking available.
I have a grown-up family of three — all married and living away from
Rotorua. I work part time in a retail shop selling light fittings. I enjoy
meeting and talking to people.
Directions: *Turn off Hamilton–Rotorua State Highway 5 into Clayton*
Road at traffic lights. Travel approximately 1¼ km, turn right into
Roosevelt Road then first left into Upland Road.

Rotorua

Homestay
Address: 88 Otonga Road,
Rotorua
Name: Brian and Kate Gore
Telephone: (073) 479-385
Beds: 3 Single (2 bedrooms)
Tariff: B&B $25 per person, Children half price; Dinner $15;
Nearest Town: Rotorua

We are an adult 'young-at-heart' family of three living only 4 km from
the city centre, but close enough to forests, lakes, golf courses and rural
scenes to benefit from the best of both worlds. We love the outdoors and
have travelled extensively throughout New Zealand so we are happy to
share our local knowledge with you.
Our large comfortable home is set amongst trees and bush and you are
free to join us in our usual activities, explore for yourselves or just
simply relax. Rotorua, being the heart of the tourist industry, has so
much to offer but we like to think we can share that little bit more to
make your New Zealand experience more memorable.
Directions: *From either south or north, proceed along Old Taupo*
Road until you reach the roundabout with the garage, shops and St
Andrews Church. Turn up into Otonga Road and proceed to the next
intersection. We are on the south-west corner of the Otonga/Springfield
intersection.

Rotorua

Guest House
Address: 39 Hinemaru Street,
Rotorua
Name: Eaton Hall
Telephone: (073) 470-366
Beds: 1 Double, 4 Single, 3 Twin
(8 bedrooms)

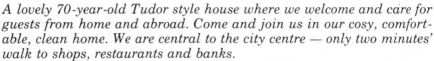

Tariff: B&B Double $55, Single $35; Dinner $12;
Children rates on application
Nearest Town: Rotorua

A lovely 70-year-old Tudor style house where we welcome and care for guests from home and abroad. Come and join us in our cosy, comfortable, clean home. We are central to the city centre — only two minutes' walk to shops, restaurants and banks.

Tea and coffee making facilities, colour TV, guest lounge, thermal central heating, a quiet, restful atmosphere.

Excellent Continental or cooked breakfast. Try our home-made muesli — it's delicious! Tasty N.Z.-style home-cooked dinner by arrangement! We are a few minutes' walk to the wonderful relaxing waters of the famous thermal Polynesian pools.

Walk through the adjacent lovely government gardens and view spectacular flowers, magnificent shrubs and trees. Browse in the nearby art gallery and museum. Watch the creation of a unique and rare spectacle, the making of a giant canoe.

See the beautiful orchid gardens and view the splendid electronic musical water fountain. Just across the street, enjoy a traditional Maori hangi (feast) followed by captivating poi dances, stirring haka, haunting melodies, truly a night to remember.

There is so much to see and do in the nation's leading tourist centre. Be prepared to stay three to four nights to enjoy the unique experiences this city has to offer.

We will organise and book half and full day tours, with guests collected from and returned to Eaton Hall. Twenty years' involvement in the hospitality industry at home and abroad enables us to say, "Service is our motto, your comfort our goal."

One of the differences between staying at a
hotel and staying at a B&B is that you don't
hug the hotel staff when you leave.

Rotorua

Farmhouse
Address: Te Kopia Road, RD1, Rotorua
Name: Brian and Barbara Hunt
Telephone: (073) 31-578
Beds: 2 Single (1 bedroom)
Tariff: B&B Double $50, Single $25;
Dinner $15; Campervans $15; Children half price
Nearest Town: Rotorua

We are farmers who have 193 hectares on which we farm sheep, bulls and deer. We have a two small children and an assorted backyard menagerie.
We have a large home and garden which we are slowly restoring with panoramic farm and thermal views — the house is adjacent to thermal activity.
Our location is very central to many attractions — within a forty minute drive you can reach Orakikorako, Taupo, Rotorua, Waiotapu, Waimangu Valley and many others. Just 10 km up the road are the lovely Waikite thermal bathing pools — not to be missed.
We enjoy visitors and look forward to sharing our home and any farm experiences.
Directions: *Mid-way between Rotorua and Taupo on Highway 5 is Waiotapu. Turn onto Waikite Valley Road adjacent to the Waiotapu Tavern and travel for approximately 10 km. Look for Te Kopia Road on your left — a gravel road on which you travel exactly 10 km to reach our front gate. We are on the right — our name is on the letterbox.*

Ngakuru, Rotorua

Farmhouse
Address: "Te Ana", Poutakataka Road, Ngakuru, RD1, Rotorua
Name: Heather and Brian Oberer
Telephone: (073) 32-720
Beds: 2 Double, 4 Single (3 bedrooms, guest bathroom)
Tariff: B&B Double $85, Single $60, Children 12 and under $35;
Dinner $20
Nearest Town: Rotorua 20 miles

"Te Ana" is a 500 acre dairy, beef, sheep, goat and deer farm situated 20 miles south of Rotorua and bounded for 1½ miles by Lake Ohakuri, with its rainbow and brown trout.
Our homestead is a clinker brick ranch-style with full length verandah at front and views of farm or garden from each of its large windows. Triple bedroom has private bathroom and two double rooms share. Electric blankets on all beds with featherdown duvets and heater in each room.

We have a daughter aged 17 and two sons aged 20 and 21 and have been hosting for the past eight years.

A canoe and fishing rod are available for use, a pony to ride, four-wheel-drive tour of farm and viewing of cows being milked. Families are most welcome.

Transfers to and from Rotorua can be provided at additional cost.

We serve wine with dinner of lamb, venison, beef, chicken or trout and plenty of iced spring water. Breakfasts include fruit juice, fruit, cereals, toast, bacon and eggs, etc, percolated coffee.

Family interests include waterskiing, hunting, snow skiing, music, art, gardening, farming, reading, tennis, swimming, rugby, knitting, cross stitch and Zonta Club.

We are only a short distance from thermal mineral swimming pool.
Directions: *Please phone*

Murupara

Farmhouse
Address: "Birchwood Cottage",
Troutbeck Road, Galatea, RD1, Murupara
Name: Desarei and Bob Covell
Telephone: (073) 64-827
Beds: 4 Single (2 bedrooms)
Tariff: Dinner, Bed and Breakfast Double $85, Single $50,
Children under 12 $25; Dinner $15; Campervans $20;
Nearest Town: City of Rotorua 50 miles, Large town of
Whakatane 50 miles, Murupara (pop. 2,000) 6 miles

My husband Bob and I live on a beef farm in the Galatea Valley on the border of the majestic Urewera National Park. We have exciting bush walks, river rafting, jet boating and hunting by helicopter or on foot for deer, wild pig and possum. Our fishing is second-to-none in our own lake Anewhenua, our rivers and tributaries. We have a beautifully-prepared golf course and squash club for alternative exercise. The giant Kaingaroa forest borders us on the west side and we look out on Mt Tarawera and Mt Edgecumbe which provide a good and interesting hike to the top on a fine day.

We have two guest rooms each with two single beds. We are always

continued over

81

delighted to have company for dinner and breakfast of your choice. Special diets can be catered for and a cut lunch can be supplied when necessary.

Guides can be found for special outings. We really enjoy meeting people and showing them around our beef farm, pig farm and new vineyard which will be produing wine this season. They are run on organic and bio-dynamic methods. We have three generations living on the estate as our son, our daughter-in-law and grandchildren are all keenly interested in the various facets of farming we follow.

We offer comfortable accommodation in a pleasant farm homestead in attractive surroundings.

Directions: *Please phone.*

Taupo

Farmstay + Self-Contained Accommodation
Address: 'Apple Tree Bridge Farm', Western Bays Road,
RD Mangakino (nr Taupo)
Name: James and Virginia Dysart
Telephone: (0814) 28-232
Beds: 4–6 in cottage, 1 twin in homestead (guest bathroom)
Tariff: B&B $55 per person, Bed + All Meals $150 per person;
Self-Contained Cottage (linen provided) 1–3 nights $130 per night,
1 week $400, meals arranged as extra if required; Campers,
Caravans and Campervans welcomed

We welcome visitors to our farm in the Taupo region. Ideally situated to explore this whole region of mountains, boiling mud, famous trout fishing lake and beautiful scenery and hospitality the self-contained cottage sleeps 4–6 comfortably. It is sunny, bright and very clean with all a family's needs met including a microwave oven and coal and wood burning range for winter that burns continuously.

The homestead offers a twin bedded room with private facilities with meals and living shared with the family. Dinner B&B, B&B, campers and campervans are welcomed.

The farm is 280 hectares, sheep and cattle as well as some cashmere goats and pine trees. Situated at the north west end of Lake Taupo it is ideally located for those wishing to explore the Taupo area with its lake, fishing, bush walks, skiing in winter, golf and hot pools. The Pureora Forest Park is close by for walking, bird watching and taking a picnic. The Waitomo Caves and Rotorua are an easy day's trip away. Mt Ruapehu is 1¼ hours drive.

Horse riding on the farm is available. Farm activities change with the seasons and such things as lambing, mustering with sheep dogs, haymaking, and various other farm activities can be observed or participated in by the visitor.
Simply phone us to book, or write, and you will receive a detailed map. We are very easily located, directions are not difficult.

Taupo

Homestay
Address: 51 Wakeman Road, Acacia Bay, Taupo
Name: Jim and Wilma Cousins
Telephone: (074) 88-901
Beds: 4 Single (2 bedrooms, guest bathroom)
Tariff: Bed and Breakfast, Dinner if requested, tariff on request, phone for reservations
Nearest Town: North west Taupo 6 km

We are a retired farming couple with one cat. Our house in quiet Acacia Bay has a magnificent view of Lake Taupo. Taupo and district have innumerable attractions from four golf courses to hot baths, walks, fishing, etc. Launch hire for fishing or cruising can be arranged.
Directions: *Follow Acacia Bay Road signs for 6 km. Wakeman Road on right.*

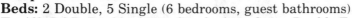

Taupo

Intimate Lodge
Address: 50 Koha Road
(cnr Gillies Ave,
Koha Rd), Taupo
Name: Koha Lodge
Telephone: (074) 87-647
Beds: 2 Double, 5 Single (6 bedrooms, guest bathrooms)
Tariff: B&B Double $100, Single $80, Suite Double/Twin + single sleep 3 $150; Dinner $35; Campervans $25+

Built 12 years ago as a large comfortable home Koha Lodge has glorious views overlooking the lake, mountains, town and country. We now enjoy pampering guests from New Zealand and around the world, in a warm, friendly and relaxed atmosphere.

A separate guest area has private bathrooms adjacent to bedrooms, each with tables and comfortable chairs, electric blankets and woollen underlays on the beds, and electric heaters and bathrobes provided. Guests have refrigerator and tea and coffee making facilities. A lower level has a dining room and two lounges — with thermal heating and fire. There is a thermal pool, a games room with full-sized billiard table, as well as outdoor balconies, decks and sheltered garden areas including B.B.Q.

We offer an extensive breakfast selection, and serve N.Z. gourmet foods with N.Z. wine for dinner following complimentary pre-dinner drinks. Local restaurant menus are available.

As Taupo is superb for deer hunting nearby, famous trout fishing, water sports as well as many other activities, wilderness areas and sightseeing, we recommend longer than an overnight stay. We are happy to arrange guides, and have a courtesy car.

Directions: *From State Highway 1 along lakefront at fire station, turn onto Rifle Range Road, about 1 km to Koha Road on right. Two blocks to Gillies Avenue corner.*

New Zealand is known as the friendliest
country in the world and our hosts
will live up to that reputation.

Taupo

Farmhouse
Address: "Dunfyne", RD1, Taupo
Name: Len and Beth Vickers
Telephone: (074) 84-494
Beds: 3 Single (2 bedrooms)
Tariff: B&B $25 per person; Dinner $20; Children half price

We are situated six miles (9½ km) from Taupo on a 430 acre farm with magnificent views of lake and town. On the farm we have sheep, cattle, horses and goats.
Taupo lake is noted worldwide for trout fishing which we can arrange with commercial guides.
You are welcome to have dinner with us or if preferred only bed and breakfast.
If transport is not available guests can be met and returned to public transport.
Directions: *Take the road to Acacia Bay from State Highway 1 on the northern side of Taupo. Continue till the turn to the right onto Mapara Road. Travel approximately 2 km and our cattle stop is on the right with name on railing.*

NZ phone numbers are being changed. Ring 018 for directory.

Turangi

Homestay
Address: 4 Huriana Grove, Turangi
Name: Eleanor MacRae
Telephone: (0746) 8977
Beds: 3 Single (2 bedrooms)
Tariff: B&B Double $55, Single $35; Dinner $15;
Children ½ price; Campervans $20 (4 persons)
Nearest Town: Taupo 53 km north

I live in a three bedroom house with private barbecue. I am close to the shopping area and local park with swimming pools and tennis courts. I enjoy other people's company and don't mind having children to stay. Turangi is an all seasons region and has a lot to offer such as tramping, hunting, canoeing, skiing, white water rafting, fishing and golf.
I am very close to the central mountains, Lake Taupo and Tongariro River. Close by at Waihi is a lovely Maori Pa and Catholic Church which has Maori artefacts. Hot mineral pools are close by at Tokaanu.
Directions: *Turn at Turangi Hotel, turn left, first right, first right again past the shopping area. Huriana Grove is the third street on the right.*

Gisborne and District

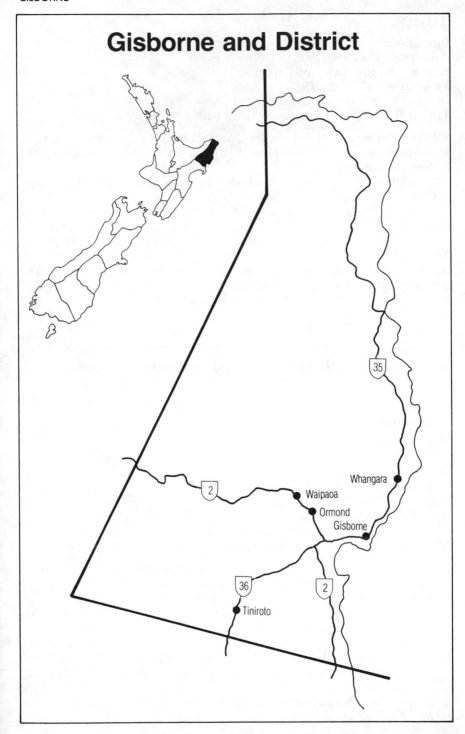

Whangara, Gisborne

Farmhouse
Address: 'Hikatu',
Whangara, RD3, Gisborne
Name: Ian and Sue Fraser
Telephone: (079) 22-850
Beds: 1 Double, 4 Single (3 bedrooms, guest bathroom)
Tariff: B&B Double $50, Single $30, Children half price;
Dinner $15; Campervans $15
Nearest Town: 30 km from Gisborne via East Coast Road

We live on a farm in the old family homestead which was built in the early 1900s. It is a comfortably sunny old place that we have renovated over the years and happily still retains the old world atmosphere we enjoy so much and would like to share. We have three spare bedrooms. One has a double bed, one has two single beds and the third is for children and is often occupied by our grandchildren in the holidays. The second bathroom does not open off any of these rooms and is for the exclusive use of our guests.

Our garden would be of particular interest to gardeners and garden lovers alike as we have spent many years creating a varied and interesting place which is now frequently visited by garden clubs from near and far. We feel it is at its best from early spring to summer.

There is a swimming pool and a tennis court too, the latter used for social tennis.

The farm runs sheep, a Hereford stud and thoroughbred horses. You are welcome to watch seasonal work in progress while you are here or go for walks over the farm or through a large adjoining bush reserve. There are also beautiful quiet beaches in easy driving distance.

You may dine with us or just have bed and breakfast, as you wish. Light lunch free.

To those who wish to enjoy the simple country way of life and a much loved garden a visit to Hikatu will be well worthwhile.

Whangara, Gisborne

Farmhouse
Address: Makorori Station, RD3, Whangara, Gisborne
Name: Richard and Robyn Busby
Telephone: (079) 78-027
Beds: 1 Double, 2 Single (2 bedrooms)
Tariff: B&B Double $60, Single $40; Dinner $15; Campervans $15
Nearest Town: 10 km north of Gisborne on State Highway 35

We are a young couple and live just ten minutes on the main coast road north of Gisborne at Makorori Beach. Our farm is 1430 acres and we

87

continued over

farm sheep and cattle. A farm tour can easily be arranged including spectacular views of Young Nicks Head and Poverty Bay.

Makorori Beach is excellent for swimming or you may like to try surf-casting or a horse ride along the beach.

Directions: *Please phone — the best time to contact us is in the evenings.*

Waipaoa, Gisborne

Farmhouse
Address: "The Willows", Waipaoa, RD1, Gisborne
Name: Rosemary and Graham Johnson
Telephone: (079) 25-605
Beds: 1 Double, 4 Single (3 bedrooms, guest bathroom)
Tariff: B&B Double $55, Single $40; Dinner $20 (including wine); Campervan facilities $15
Nearest Town: Gisborne 20 km

We live near the world's 'first city to see the sun' and enjoy some of the longest sunshine hours in New Zealand. We enjoy the amenities available in the city and also the country life on our 550-acre farm involving sheep, cattle, deer, grapes and cropping.

Gisborne's beaches are renowned for surfing, swimming and scenery. We also have beautiful natural beauty with our rivers and bush — a lovely way to unwind and relax.

Our home is probably best described in the American Colonial style with a panelled entry and dining room of our own oak timber milled from our own trees of which we have some lovely specimens planted by our forefathers. The guest rooms have two single beds in each and there are separate bathroom and toilet facilities available for guests. We welcome you to have dinner with us, or if you prefer only bed and breakfast.

We have a swimming pool and a grass tennis court which, as our three sons pursue their own interest, can only be described as available for a 'fun game'.

We would appreciate it if you could ring prior to your arrival.

We enjoy meeting people and look forward to your visit.

Directions *We are situated 20 km north of Gisborne on State Highway 2 through to Opotiki and the Bay of Plenty approximately 6 km from the Ormond Store or 9 km from Te Karaka. We have a sign "The Willows" at the end of our driveway. Our house is white with a black tiled roof situated on a hill overlooking the Waipaoa river.*

Ormond, Gisborne

Farmhouse
Address: "Meadowbank", Ormond, Gisborne
Name: Tim and Elizabeth Burke
Telephone: (079) 25-610
Beds: 1 Double, 2 Single (2 bedroom, guest bathroom)
Tariff: B&B Double $50, Single $30, Children half price; Dinner $15
Nearest Town: Gisborne 19 km

Our family of four children is grown up now so we have a large old homestead waiting to be filled. There is a tennis court and swimming pool for use during the summer and a spa pool for those that like the water warmer in winter.

Our farm is 490 hectares running sheep, cattle, horses and goats with a small amount of cropping, mostly for stock feed. We have the usual domestic animals associated with farming — ducks, chooks, pigs, dogs, cats, peacocks and lambs in season. We have a house cow too. It is a family affair we would love to share.

Fly fishing is available about one hour's drive from here and day trips to suitable rivers can be arranged. We are 20 minutes away from Gisborne's good swimming and surfing beaches. Horses are a large part of our lives and riding can be arranged for anyone interested — basic instruction too. Time needs to be allowed for riding.

Gisborne

Homestay
Address: 75 Stout Street, Gisborne
Name: Alec and Barbara Thomson
Telephone: (079) 89-675
Beds: 1 Double, 2 Single (2 bedrooms, guest bathroom)
Tariff: B&B Double $55, Single $35; Dinner $15; 10% discount for any bowlers who are in Gisborne for local tournaments

Our home is situated about 1 km from town, and a very pleasant walk over the river will take you to the botanical gardens, or another short walk will see you at the museum. Also within walking distance is the Ballance Street Village shopping centre, P.B. Bowling Club and bus stops.

The room with the double bed has a study, and also its own toilet and handbasin. The other room has two comfortable single beds.

We both enjoy meeting people and are active members of both indoor and outdoor bowling clubs. We also enjoy a game of bridge.

Tariffs are constant for this year. However, some
may have had to change slightly. Always check.

All telephone numbers in New Zealand are being changed during 1990 so the numbers listed may not be current. Ring 018 for directory assistance if you cannot contact your hosts.

Tiniroto, Gisborne

Self-Contained Accommodation
Address: Kai Kino Station, Private Bag, Tiniroto, Gisborne
Name: Pam and Darcy Hamilton
Telephone: (079) 37-192
Beds: 1 Double, 4 Single (self-contained cottage)
Tariff: B&B Double $55, Single $35; Dinner $15; Campervans $20
Nearest Town: Gisborne city 50 km, Wairoa 50 km — on State Highway 36

We live in a district which is well known for its excellent fly fishing in the area's lakes and rivers — a fisherman's dream! There are good walking tracks and the river offers many swimming holes.
Kai Kino Station breeds sheep and cattle — visitors are invited to join in farm activities.
There is a tennis and croquet court and barbecue area which guests may use.
It is three quarters of an hour's drive to Gisborne's beaches and one and a half hour's drive to Lake Waikaremoana.
The cottage is a modern, 3-bedroom house, carpet throughout, open fireplace, fully furnished with linen available. Meals are available on request.
Directions: *5 km in from Donneraille Park on Ruakaka Road, Tiniroto.*

Please let the hosts know if you have to cancel.
They will have spent time preparing for you.

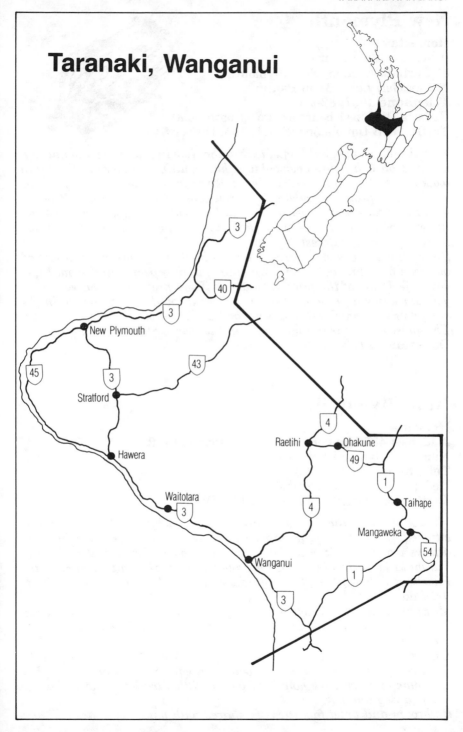

Taranaki, Wanganui

New Plymouth

Homestay
Address: "Puketotara",
31 Durham Avenue, New Plymouth
Name: Gerry and Beryl Paulin
Telephone: (067) 82-900
Beds: 1 Double (1 bedroom, guest bathroom)
Tariff: B&B Double $55, Single $35; Dinner $15

We have a two-storeyed home, within the New Plymouth city boundary, situated on a hillside overlooking the beautiful Te Henui River and walkway to the sea. The Te Henui River forms the boundary of our 4·5-hectare property where we grow cut flowers, mainly Proteas, Leucadendrons and Leucospermums for local and export markets. As flower growers we will be very happy to arrange garden visits and day trips to places of interest.
Since our three sons married and moved away we have travelled overseas on many occasions. We enjoy meeting people and would like you to feel part of the family. However if you prefer to be on your own you can enjoy a game of pool or browse through our bookcase in the rumpus room which adjoins your bedroom.
The guest room has a double bed and its own bathroom.
Directions: *Please phone.*

New Plymouth

Homestay
Address: 481 Mangorei Road, New Plymouth, RD1
Name: Evelyn and Laurie Cockerill
Telephone: (067) 86-090
Beds: 4 Single (2 bedrooms)
Tariff: B&B Double $45, Single $25, Dinner $10

We live close to the city but with a rural background. Our home is situated next to New Plymouth's well known Tupare gardens which are always worth a visit, especially in spring when they are at their best. Taranaki is world renowned for its beautiful parks and gardens — the Pukeiti Rhododendron Trust gardens being only a twenty-five minute drive away.
Mt Egmont can be viewed from our garden and can be reached within 20 minutes by car. We are only minutes from local beaches and the centre of the city.
Laurie is a blacksmith-farrier so we have a keen interest in horses. In fact two of our children were involved in equestrian sports until they left home to marry. We now have on our little farmlet a cow and a few sheep, a dog and cat.
Bathroom and toilet facilities are shared with us.

Bed and breakfast or family dinner available as you wish.
Off street parking available.
Directions: *Mangorei Road is a long one and can be approached from either north or south on entering New Plymouth boundaries. Our name is on the letterbox.*

Stratford

Homestay
Address: "Woodhill", Mountain Road South, RD23, Stratford
Name: John and Elaine Nicholls
Telephone: (0663) 5497
Beds: 1 Double, 4 Single (3 bedrooms, guest bathroom)
Tariff: B&B Double $60, Single $35, Children $15;
Dinner $17.50; Campervans $25 (up to 4 people)
Nearest Town: 46 km south of New Plymouth on State Highway 3

Come and enjoy the tranquility and beauty of the countryside in the heart of Taranaki. Our home is nestled in two acres of old English gardens and is over a hundred years old.
Each bedroom opens out onto the gardens and there is a separate guest bathroom.
We offer you warmth, hospitality and a haven from the stresses of everyday life. After a generous, leisurely breakfast enjoy a walk in the gardens or a swim in our large, outdoor pool. In the evenings you are welcome to join us for dinner, or if you prefer there are several restaurants in Stratford.
Our home is only 3 km from Stratford and 15 km from the Stratford Mountain House.
Stratford offers a wide range of activities including a pleasant golf course, lawn bowls and all types of mountain sports. For garden enthusiasts there is the Taranaki trail of gardens of which our home is a participant.
Directions: *We are situated 3 km south of Stratford on State Highway 3, adjacent to the Ngaere railway overbridge.*

Hawera

Farmhouse
Address: 11 Fraser Road, Hawera
Name: Ruth and John Hicks
Telephone: (062) 85-925 (day) 28-337 (evening)
Beds: 1 Double, 4 Single (3 bedrooms)
Tariff: B&B Double $50, Single $25; Children half price; Dinner $10
Nearest Town: 12 km north of Hawera, 9 km south of Eltham

We have a very attractive five-bedroom home built of native wood on 57 acres of farmland with native birds, bush and trees. Excellent cuisine, swimming pool set in private garden. Walks, mountain views, picturesque and peaceful.
We have our own supply of spring water — ample hot water for shower and bath. We grow our own meat and eggs. Breakfast — cooked bacon and eggs or Continental. Dinner, 3 course — roast meals.
Sheep shearing and mustering on request. We can arrange trips to Mt Egmont or to Lake Rotorangi for trout fishing. Also close to Tawhiti Museum.
All in all we can give you a warm welcome, excellent food and a truly rural experience you will never forget.
Directions: *Please ring.*

Waitotara

Farmhouse
Address: Bramham Park, Parekama Road, Waitotara.
Postal: 'Bramham Park',
Box 40, Private Bag, Waitotara, Wanganui
Name: Betty and Vic Falkner
Telephone: (064) 65-920
Beds: 1 Double, 2 Single (2 bedrooms, guest bathroom)
Tariff: B&B Double $25, Single $15, Children half price;
Dinner $10; Campervans $15 (2 people), $20 (4 people)
Nearest Town: Wanganui, 40 km south of Waitotara
on State Highway 3

'Bramham Park' is situated at the end of Parekama Road, set in a peaceful, quiet area with spacious lawns and gardens.
We farm an area of 1,600 acres — sheep, cattle (mainly angus beef cattle) and goats. Our family of five are all married and living away from home.
Guests are free to enjoy the relaxed atmosphere of a country home and enjoy home cooking and farm activities if desired.
For those who like walking and tramping it is an ideal spot. Guests, if they wish, can be taken on a guided tour of histori Maori sights. Wainui beach, where line fishing is popular, is only a few kilometres away.
Views of Mt Taranaki and Ruapehu can be seen from the farm which is 6 km from State Highway 3.

Waitotara

Farmhouse + Self-Contained
Accommodation
Address: Ashley Park,
State Highway 3,
Waitotara
Name: Barry Pearce
and Wendy Bowman
Telephone: (064) 65-917
Beds: 4 Single (2 bedrooms, guest bathroom)
Tariff: B&B Double $60, Single $30; Dinner $20; Power points
for caravans and campervans with full facilities; Cabins available;
Self-contained unit for 7 people

*We are 2 km from Waitotara village and 8 km to the beach. We have a
mixed farm, sheep cattle, deer and cropping. We have a large, comfortable home set in an attractive garden with a swimming pool and
avaries with exotic birds and pheasants. Also in the garden is an
antique and craft shop which also serves Devonshire teas and sand-
wiches from 9 am–5 pm daily.*
*Situated 100 metres from the house and garden is a 4-acre park of
native and English trees, surrounding a picturesque lake with
waterfowl.*
Guests have their own bathroom facilities.
*We like to serve New Zealand fare and hope you enjoy the tranquility of
the countryside. Guests are welcome to observe farm activities where
possible and there are scenic drives locally.*
Directions: *We are situated 32 km north of Wanganui and 12 km
south of Waverley on State Highway 3.*

Wanganui

Self-Contained Accommodation
Address: Bushy Park Lodge, Rangitatau East Road, 8 km from
Kai Iwi (16 km from Wanganui on State Highway 3)
Name: Alan Johnston
Telephone: (064) 29-879
Beds: 3 Double, 10 Single (6 bedrooms)
Tariff: Accommodation only Double $45, Single $40,
Additional adult $10, Children 7–15 $10
Nearest Town: Wanganui 24 km

*The Lodge is a large, wooden homestead built in 1906 for Frank Moore
who farmed a large estate. On his death in 1962 it was left to the Royal
Forest and Bird Protection Society who now run it as a lodge for all
members of the public.*
*Comfortable accommodation is provided in six bedrooms furnished in
the style of earlier years; five have their own vanity units. All have*

95

continued over

electric blankets and fan heater. Bedding and linen is provided though there is a charge of $3 per room if staying just one night. A discount of $5 per room is offered for Sunday to Thursday night excepting holiday periods.

Guests bring their own food and use a well-equipped kitchen. There are two large lounges and a smaller dining room/TV lounge with library books and table games. A recreation room in the basement provides a pool and table tennis tables.

Campervans are welcome. There are two caravan power points on the old stables. A bunkhouse can supply overflow accommodation.
Behind the homestead lie 97 hectares of fine native bush, well tracked and containing New Zealand's biggest Northern Rata tree.
Wanganui and its district offer many attractions and is only 20 minutes away by car.
Directions: *Travel west from Wanganui's main street onto State Highway 3 to Kai Iwi then turn north on a sealed road 8 km to Bushy Park Lodge.*

Wanganui

Farmhouse
Address: "Rusthall", No. 2 Line, RD2, Wanganui
Name: Tom and Derryn Johnson
Telephone: (064) 24-865
Beds: 2 Single (1 bedroom, guest bathroom)
Tariff: B&B Double $55, Single $35; Dinner $15; Campervans $20
Nearest Town: Wanganui 5 km

Our five-year-old home, which is situated on a 240-hectare sheep, cattle and cropping farm was designed to blend with the background of beautiful English trees. We enjoy the country life as well as having the advantage of the living in close proximity to the city of Wanganui.
Guests may enjoy our farm walks where there is natural beauty in the

native trees, birds and patches of native bush — added beauty with the excellent views of Mt Ruapehu and surrounding countryside.
Our guest room has two single beds — guests have their own bathroom and toilet facilities.
We enjoy meeting people and offer warm, friendly hospitality.
We do request guests phone in advance.
Directions: *After crossing the Wanganui town bridge turn left into Anzac Parade, then 2nd turn right to Fordell. Continue along No. 2 Line towards Fordell until reaching 152 No. 2 Line.*

Raetihi

Farmhouse
Address: State Highway 4, Raetihi
Name: Brian and Pixie Chambers
Telephone: (0658) 54-894 (bus) 54-310 (home)
Beds: 2 Single (1 bedroom, guest bathroom)
Tariff: B&B Double $50, Single $30; Dinner $15; Campervans $20
Nearest Town: Raetihi 1 km, Wanganui 85 km

We live 1 km north of Raetihi in a recently built splitstone home. We have an outdoor swimming pool in garden setting and a built-in spa pool for all seasons. We have a magnificent view of the Waimarino farming area and the central volcanic mountains.
We live on a 400 acre sheep and cattle farm with all the usual farming activities. For the more venturesome there is another 1000 acre farm with tramping and hunting available.
Being in the Waimarino we are just 30 minutes from Turoa Skifield, the beautiful Manganui-a-te-Ao river and Tongariro National Park. We are 45 minutes from the Wanganui river which caters for jetboating and tramping — there is also a good golf course within 3 miles.
Accommodation is twin bedroom with private shower and toilet.
Directions: *1 km north of Raetihi.*

Raetihi

Guest House + Self-Contained Accommodation
Address: Queen Street, Raetihi
Name: Bavarian Lodge
Telephone: (0658) 54-389
Beds: 5 Double, 20 Single, Self-contained 3-bedroom apartment sleeps 9
Tariff: B&B Double $85, Single $46, Children half price; Dinner $22
Nearest Town: Wanganui 1 hour

The Bavarian Lodge — home of operating, interesting farmers — can offer outdoor adventures and activities for all seasons, ages and abilities.
Farm Life, Tongariro National Park, trout fishing (experienced taxidermist available for home delivery), tramping, picnics, ornithology, painting, photography, magnificent native flora and fauna, a wealth of educational studies and historical pursuits, small game shooting, mountains, clean fresh air, rivers, lakes, peace, and nature 'in the raw', all offer a memorable holiday.
Evenings are always interesting — usually hilarious with local characters, lively banter, dancing and fun — making new friends for all.
Having hosted successfully for many years, we guarantee an unforgettable stay.
Transport to and from airports can be arranged if required — additional charge.

Raetihi

Farmhouse + Self-Contained Accommodation
Address: Pipiriki Road, RD4, Raetihi
Name: Ken and Sonia Robb
Telephone: (0658) 54-581
Beds: 1 Double (ensuite bathroom), 2 Single (2 bedrooms)
Tariff: B&B Double $50, Single $25, Children half price; Dinner $10
Nearest Town: Raetihi

From a family of nine children we now have only one son attending primary school and living at home so we enjoy being able to welcome visitors from New Zealand and overseas to a farm stay experience.
We live on a 400 hectare (1000 acres) hill country sheep and cattle farm and guests are welcome to partake in farm activities.
Sonia is a nurse and works part-time at the local hospital.
The double guest room is large and comfortable, has en-suite facilities, and (weather permitting) a lovely view looking up Mangaeturoa Valley to Mt Ruapehu. The twin bedroom has share facilities.
Shearers' quarters are available with linen and cooking utensils supplied on request.
Directions: *From Raetihi take the road to Pipiriki. We are 6 km along it on the right.*

Ohakune

Homestay/Farmhouse
Address: "Mitredale", Smiths Road, Ohakune
Name: Audrey and Diane Pritt
Telephone: (0658) 58-016
Beds: 1 Double, 2 Single (2 bedrooms)
Tariff: B&B Double $60, Single $30, Children −25%;
Dinner $10; Campervans $20
Nearest Town: Ohakune 6 km, Raetihi 9 km

*We are farmers who farm sheep and goats in a beautiful peaceful valley
with magnificent views of Mt Ruapehu. The Waimarino is an excellent
area for holidaying summer or winter. The Tongariro National Park
offers excellent walks, opportunities for photography and great skiing
at Turoa and Whakapapa. The rivers offer good sport for the fisherman
or canoeists and an excellent 18-hole golf course only 3 km from our
door. We are keen members of the Conservation body Ducks Unlimited.
Diane also manages the wine shop in Ohakune.*
*We have two guest rooms — one with two single beds, the other has a
double bed. All equipped with electric blankets. The home is heated
with a log fire and open fire — excellent for drying gear after a day's
skiing, a comfortable, cosy atmosphere to relax in.*
*We offer dinner with the traditional farmhouse fare or just breakfast —
gives you the opportunity to sample our excellent home-made jams.*
*We enjoy sharing our lifestyle with others so come and spend some time
on the farm.*
Directions: *Take the Raetihi Road (State Highway 49) at Ohakune
Hotel corner, travel 4 km to Smiths Road, second side road on the left.
An unsealed road. We are the last house 2 km at the end of the road. If
you prefer you may call at the wine shop in Ohakune for directions.*

Taihape

Homestay
Address: 12 Lark Street, Taihape
Name: Jack and Joyce Gilbert
Telephone: (0658) 80-915
Beds: 2 Single (1 bedroom)
Tariff: B&B Double $55, Single $35; Dinner $15; Children half price
Nearest Town: Taihape

*We are a retired farming couple. Our home is situated on the hill with a
comprehensive garden layout. We enjoy extensive views of farmlands
with the Ruahine Ranges in the background.*
*Taihape is the centre of good, high country farming. Pleasant bush
walks can be taken. Farm visits, all types of rafting and jet boating can
be arranged.*
*We are only one hour's drive from Ruapehu Skifields or Lake Taupo
(renowned for its trout fishing), also Titoki Point Gardens.*

continued over

Our family of three daughters and a son are all married with families. Our son runs the home farm of sheep, cattle and grain. Our hobbies are spinning, weaving and gardening.
Our guest room has twin beds with electric blankets. Dinner would be by arrangement.
Directions: *Please phone.*

Taihape

Homestay
Address: "Korirata", 25 Pukeko Street, Taihape
Name: Noel and Pat Gilbert
Telephone: (0658) 80-315
Beds: 2 Double, electric blankets (2 bedrooms, guest bathroom)
Tariff: B&B Double $55, Single $35, Children by
arrangement according to age; Dinner $15
Nearest Town: Taihape

We have recently renovated and added to a 62-year-old residence in an extremely quiet area of Taihape. Warmth and comfort is a feature.
The entire section — three quarters of an acre — has been landscaped with shrubs, a hydroponic house (supplying us with vegetables), an orchid house and a very large area planted in chrysanthamums and gladioli.
We are situated on top of the hill and have panoramic views of Mt Ruapehu, Ruahine Ranges and extensive farming country.
We are one hour to skiing on Ruapehu, 1 hour to Lake Taupo, 2½ hours to Rotorua or Wellington.
Farm visits, tramping, all types of rafting, river fishing and jet-boating are within 30 minutes plus Titoki Point Gardens.
Dinner and lunch are available on request. Almost all types of meals are available. Meals with hosts. Cooking is one of our hobbies.
Separate toilet, bathroom and shower is available for sole use of guests.
Directions: *Please phone.*

Mangaweka

Farmhouse
Address: "Cairnmuir Farmstays",
State Highway 1, Mangaweka
Name: David and Elizabeth Buchanan
Telephone: (0658) 25-878
If no reply (0658) 25-745
Beds: 4 Single (2 bedrooms, guest bathroom)
Tariff: B&B Double $80, Single $45, Children half price; Dinner $20
Nearest Town: 18 km south of Taihape

Our farmstay can offer you a comfortable, relaxed and fun-filled time with us. We have a grownup family of three so we are free to spend time with our guests.

Both of us enjoy outdoor life, have a keen love of gardening, enjoy tennis on our court, golf, and all the recreational activities this unique area offers.

We live on a 735 hectare sheep and cattle hill-country property which offers panoramic views from Mount Ruapehu to the South Island. Our spacious home has a welcoming atmosphere. The open fire and pleasant living room give people an opportunity to relax and enjoy the country lifestyle.

We like our guests to have dinner with us. We use home-grown produce which is presented with flair, imagination and creativity. We provide a breakfast of your choice.

Mangaweka abounds in opportunities for all to have a welcome break from city life.

Mangaweka

Farmhouse
Address: "Mairenui Holidays",
Ruahine Road, Mangaweka
Name: Sue and David Sweet
Telephone: (065825) 564
Beds: 1 Double, 2 Single (2 bedrooms, guest bathroom)
Tariff: B&B Double $75, Single $45; Dinner $20, Lunch negotiable;
Campervans $5 per person (all prices GST exclusive)
Nearest Town: Mangaweka

Farmhouse accommodation. We are members of and have been inspected by the New Zealand Association of Farm and Home Hosts. Our double bedroom has small sitting area, ensuite modern bathroom with sunken bath, and small private verandah, or share latter with twin bedroom.

We have a concrete tennis court (racquets available), horse riding, farm walks, river swimming. Trout fishing nearby and we can arrange whitewater rafting or canoeing and heliskiing in season.

We can offer sport or adventure (eg tramping in the Ruahine ranges) or you can enjoy a peaceful rest in the tranquil countryside.

There is excellent cuisine and we have the best New Zealand wines available. We enjoy meeting people and sharing our unique lifestyle. Both German and French are spoken.

We can collect guests from the train in Taihape or bus in Mangaweka. We will also collect from the airport in Palmerston North (additional cost).

Directions: *The farm is situated 12 km from Mangaweka and 84 km from Palmerston North on State Highway 54. There is a sign on the roadside "Mairenui Holidays".*

Hawkes Bay

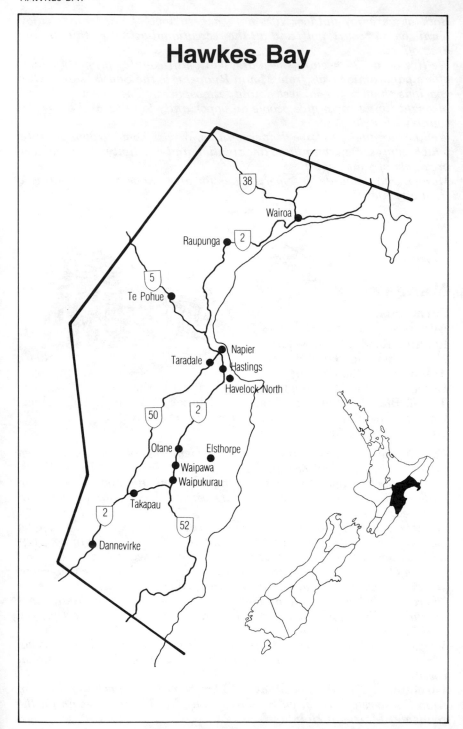

Raupunga

Tourist Lodge
Address: Waikohe Sportsmen's
Farmstay, RD4, Raupunga,
Northern Hawkes Bay
Name: Brian and Janice Batson
Telephone: (0724) 6969
Beds: 1 Double, 2 Single (2 bedrooms)
Tariff: On application
Nearest Town: Wairoa

We are situated in a very remote farming area adjacent to the Urewera National Park and a one-hour drive north-west of Wairoa. We farm an 815 acre sheep and cattle property. Recently we diversified into a Sportsmen's Lodge catering for game hunters and trout fishermen worldwide which has proved very popular and successful.

Our isolated lakes and rivers are well-stocked with quality rainbow and brown trout and guests like the fact that they can fish all day without seeing another angler. Top quality red deer, goat, wild ram and wild boar trophies are readily available.

Our ranch style home, at an elevation of 1500 ft has panoramic views of the countryside. This is complemented by well-manicured gardens, fish pond with waterfall, swimming pool, concrete tennis court and spa pool on our spacious patio which is lovely for outdoor meals.

Whether you require our hunting or fishing services, or just require a few days on the farm relaxing or enjoying bush walks, mustering, shearing, visiting the Urewera National Park, we can assure you a warm and friendly hospitable stay.

Due to our isolation, we recommend a minimum stay of two days and it would be easier to phone for directions when booking.

Te Pohue

Farmhouse
Address: Rock Station, Te Pohue, RD2, Napier
Name: Beryl and Peter King   **Telephone:** (070-291) 851 Te Pohue
Beds: 1 Double, 2 Single (2 bedrooms, guest bathroom)
Tariff: B&B $30 per room; Campervans $20 per van
Nearest Town: Napier ¾ hr, Taupo 1 hr on Napier/Taupo Rd

We are a country family. Our children have grown up and left lots of room and space; and time to care for holidaymakers!

Our home is 35 years old built from timber cut from our farm. We are 1500 feet above sea level so winter woollies are required in winter.

Great scenery, fresh air and water. There are country walks and animals to see if you like them, also native birds.

Our home is friendly, cosy, quiet and comfortable. We are interested in woollen crafts. Our hobbies include gardening, trees, animals, painting and floral art.

Taradale

Homestay
Address: 34 Otatara Road, Taradale
Name: Tonka Towers
Telephone: (070) 446-542
Beds: 1 Double, 2 Single (1 bedroom, guest bathroom)
Tariff: B&B Double $55, Single $35; Dinner $14
Nearest Town: Taradale

Our home has been designed by renowned local architect John Scott. It is situated within easy walking distance of the town's shopping area and only 15 minutes drive to Napier or Hastings. Two minutes away is the Napier Golf Club's course at Waiohiki.

The accommodation offered is detached from the house — a delightfully decorated sunny room with separate shower, toilet and washbasin.

As well as the Continental breakfast provided an evening meal can also be organised.

We are a friendly, happy family and look forward to extending our hospitality to you.

Taradale

Homestay
Address: 50 Puketapu Road, Taradale
Name: Don and Sheila Copas
Telephone: (070) 442-182 (h), 357-933 (w)
Beds: 1 Double, 3 Single (3 bedrooms)
Tariff: B&B Double $45, Single $22.50, Children half price; Dinner $15
Nearest Town: Napier 10 km

Our home is situated in an attractive and interesting one acre garden with sheep in the orchard, free-range bantams, a putting green and a swimming pool contributing to its unique rural atmosphere although it is only five minutes walk from the town of Taradale and ten minutes drive from the city of Napier.

The climate of Hawkes Bay justifies the title of "Sunny Napier" and the area in and around the city has much to offer of interest and activity, i.e. sailing, fishing, windsurfing, bush walks, etc.

Napier is also well endowed with tourist attractions — museums, aquarium, Marineland and can lay a claim to being the "Art Deco" centre of the world.

We love to entertain and you will be assured of a warm welcome at our comfortable family home.

Directions: *10 km west from Napier. Area maps are available from the Information Centre on Marine Parade or the A.A. Centre in Dickens Street, Napier or phone us for directions.*

Napier

Homestay
Address: 19 Alamein Crescent, Napier
Name: Pam and Bill McCulloch
Telephone: (070) 436-744
Beds: 1 King Size Double, 4 Single, 1 Cot (3 bedrooms)
Tariff: B&B Double $70, Single $35, Dinner $15
Nearest Town: Napier

We are retired and enjoy sharing our home with overseas guests. We have hosted many guests through our involvement with Rotary, Servas and the Friendship Force.
Three of our four children are married and our youngest daughter is currently overseas touring England and the Continent combining work and travel.
We have a swimming pool, spa pool, rumpus room and a well kept garden.
Our guest's rooms have single beds or a king-size bed and there is a cot and highchair available.
Family dinner available each evening if required.
Napier has many tourist attractions, suitable for a good family holiday destination for young and old. Napier has an excellent climate, plenty of sunshine, attractive shops and restaurants and is only 25 km from the twin city of Hastings.

Hastings

Homestay
Address: Please phone
Name: Maralyn and Ray
Telephone: (070) 85-959
Beds: 1 Double, 2 Single (2 bedrooms, guest bathroom)
Tariff: B&B $30 per person

We are a professional couple with a large, old, very comfortable family home.
Our three adult children no longer live at home. Our main leisure activities are scouting and tennis.
Guests can enjoy their own sitting room and bathroom. Off-street parking is available.
We are situated four blocks from the heart of Hastings city.

When you stay at B&Bs you are meeting "dinkum Kiwis".

Hastings

Farmhouse
Address: Wai-iti Farms, Maraekakaho Road, Hastings
Name: Jan Graham and Dick Black
Telephone: (070) 797-951
Beds: 1 Double, 2 Single (2 bedrooms, guest bathroom)
Tariff: B&B Double $40, Single $25; Dinner $15;
Children half price
Nearest Town: Hastings 12 km, Highway 50 3 km, Highway 2 9 km

*Last century our house began life as a ploughman's cottage but like
Topsy has grown to gracious and generous proportions.*
*We have spacious lawns and an attractive garden which hosts a variety
of pets from peacocks to puppies.*
*Hundreds of school children, parents and teachers visit us every year to
enjoy a variety of farm experiences which our guests would be most
welcome to enjoy also.*

Havelock North

Farmhouse
Address: Middle Road, 'Peak View' Farm
Name: Dianne and Keith Taylor
Telephone: (070) 777-408
Beds: 2 Single (1 bedroom)
Tariff: B&B Double $60, Single $35; Dinner $20
Nearest Town: Havelock North ¾ km, Hastings 6 km

*We own 25 acres of horticulture land and our house was built in 1900.
Our family are the 4th generation to live here. We have recently added
a second large living area.*
*Our home is surrounded by big lawns and trees with a lovely garden
which we are presently extending.*
*One son is married, another is away at university and as we only have a
daughter of 21 at home we are able to offer hospitality to visitors. We
enjoy meeting people — our aim is to provide a pleasant and memorable stay.*
*We are interested in caravanning, tramping and bushwalks. Keith
enjoys fishing, Dianne sewing, gardening and genealogy.*
*We offer comfortable accommodation with shared amenities. If you
have dinner with us be assured of wholesome and generous meals with
local wine (our compliments). Afterwards share an evening of relaxation and friendship or browse through our many New Zealand books.
We can advise on travel throughout New Zealand from our own family
experiences.*
*We are two minutes away from tennis and squash courts, indoor and
outdoor pools. It is only a short drive to Te Mata Peak with panoramic
views. Napier is a 20 minute drive away.*

No smoking inside please.
Be welcomed with tea or coffee. If travelling by public transport we are
happy to meet you for a minimal fee.
Directions: *Please phone.*

Elsthorpe, Otane

Homestay
Address: St Lawrence Road, Elsthorpe
Name: Margot and Bryan Tylee
Telephone: (0728-64) 898
Beds: 4–5 Single (3 bedrooms)
Tariff: Dinner, Bed and Breakfast Double $95,
Single $50, Children half price
Nearest Town: Waipawa 26 km, Otane 19 km

We live on a sheep and cattle farm, with horses for experienced riders.
It is lovely rolling country with beautiful views. Kairakau Beach is half
an hour away.
Our country home has five bedrooms and a billiard room. The two
guest rooms have single beds.
We will provide traditional farm-cooked meals, home-killed meat and
home-grown produce.
We look forward to meeting you.
Directions: *Turn off the main highway at Otane, follow the signs to*
Elsthorpe. At Patangata Hotel, come over the long, narrow bridge, over
the hill to the first road on left, St Lawrence Road. We are 2 miles down
St Lawrence Road on the right hand side, with our name on the
mailbox.

Waipawa

Homestay
Address: "La Maison de Bienvenue", 81 Great North Road, Waipawa
Name: Roma and Harold Leckie
Telephone: (0728) 78-438
Beds: 4 Single (3 bedrooms — 1 double room)
Tariff: B&B $27 per person, Children $15, Cot $1.50;
Dinner by arrangement $12; Fully serviced caravan
available at cheaper rates for backpackers.
Nearest Town: Waipukurau 10 km south, Hastings 42 km north

Our home is situated on the main highway from Hastings/Wellington.
We are at the northern fringe of Waipawa with farmland across the
road and behind us, therefore we offer very restful, rural surroundings.
Breakfast is served in the conservatory where one can enjoy the beauty
of lawns, gardens and gentle rolling hills. We have a large swimming
pool.
My husband and I live alone on the bottom floor and the three guest

107

continued over

rooms are upstairs where guests also have their own sundeck and balcony if they prefer to be alone.

Dinner is a family affair (by prior arrangement) or guests may prefer to eat at one of the two restaurants in the village.

Waipawa has a very interesting museum, new shopping complex, country walks, fishing. There is a lovely beach thirty minutes' drive from our home. Why not break your travels and rest awhile, taking time out to be refreshed by country walks, swimming and even taking a picnic lunch to the beach?

We serve a Continental breakfast of fruit and cereal with home-made wholemeal bread, home-made marmalade and jam.

We run a few sheep, have fowls, one cat, one canary and our interests lie in spinning, painting, Toastmasters and languages. French and German spoken.

Guests are served with a New Zealand bedtime snack compliments of the hosts.

Waipukurau

Farmhouse
Address: "Oakworth",
Station Road, RD1,
Waipukurau
Name: Marilyn and Trevor Jane
Telephone: (0728) 58-255
Beds: 2 Single (1 bedroom)
Tariff: Dinner, Bed and Breakfast — Double $85,
Single $50; Children ½ price; Campervans $20
Nearest Town: Waipukurau 16 km

We are 7 km from the small country township of Takapau, and have a mixed farm, with sheep and cropping, also a small flock of black sheep for spinning.

Our family consists of two working sons who live at home, plus two daughters who live away from home.

We have a large comfortable home, set in an attractive garden with swimming pool. The guest room has twin beds.

We are in the midst of an intensive farming area and the rivers nearby are well known for trout fishing. There are several bush walks in the locality.

Dinner with the family will be high quality New Zealand produce.

Directions *Turn off State Highway 2 at Fraser Road, by "Richmonds" sign, 15½ km south of Waipukurau Post Office. Travelling north, 4 km from Takapau crossroads, turn left at railway line into Station Road, 4th house.*

Takapau

Farmhouse
Address: "Tukipo Terraces", Highway 50, Takapau
Name: Bay and Shona de Lautour
Telephone: (0728) 56-827 or 56-808, Fax (0728) 56-808
Beds: 2 Double, 1 Single (2 bedrooms, guest bathrooms)
Tariff: Dinner, Bed and Breakfast — Double $110,
Single $65, Bed and Breakfast — Double $75, Single $50;
Children ½ single rate
Nearest Town: Waipukurau 20 km, Takapau P.O. and general
store 8 km

Highway 50 is the alternate route between Takapau and Napier, through attractive Central Hawkes Bay farming country. We are situated approximately 5 km from the southern end on the banks of the Tukipo trout stream, midway between Wellington and Taupo.
Ours is a new home with self-contained guest wing comprising bedroom (with double bed and a single), sitting room and limited cooking facilities.
Beautiful mountain views form a background for farming scenes of deer, goats, sheep, cattle and cropping.
We can show you farming operations on a large scale or small. Lovely native bush walks nearby. Trout fishing day trips by arrangement with professional fisherman.
Members NZ Farm & Home Hosts Inc.
Directions *If coming from the south drive 30 km north from Dannevirke, turn left onto Highway 50, travel 5 km. We are on the right, just at the end of a long plantation of mature pine trees, and about ½ km in from the road.*

Dannevirke

Address: 42 Victoria Avenue, Dannevirke
Name: "Glendane" (Norma and Ian Pedersen)
Telephone: (0653) 46-453
Beds: 1 Double, 3 Single (2 bedrooms, guest bathroom)
Tariff: B&B Double $55, Single $35;
Dinner $15; Children ½ price
Nearest Town: 1 km west of Dannevirke Post Office

We have a lovely home approximately ten years old. It is set in one acre of beautiful garden and being on the outskirts of town has a rural view

109

continued over

with our Ruahine Ranges in the background. It is very quiet and restful, a great place to break your journey.

We have two bedrooms available, one with two single beds and one with one double and one single and you have your own bathroom and toilet.

You may enjoy dinner with us or bed and breakfast only if you prefer. Apart from our interests in gardening and farming we make from pure natural wool our own handspun, handmade woollen goods — jerseys, vests, hats, scarves, etc and these original garments are for sale.

Motea, Dannevirke

Farmhouse
Address: Private Bag, Motea, Dannevirke
Name: Peg and Tim James
Telephone: (065-325) 828
Beds: 1 Double, 2 Single (2 bedrooms)
Tariff: B&B $25 per person, Children half price;
Dinner $10; Campervans $10
Nearest Town: Dannevirke 23 km

Tim and I have a farm of 1000 acres on which we run sheep and cattle. It is lovely rolling country. We both enjoy meeting people so anyone wishing to spend time with an average New Zealand couple will find that is what we are.

We have a four-wheel-drive van which is used on the farm so guests may take part in our activities or feel free to do what they wish.

Our house is modest but cosy. Our food is simple but plentiful. You may have dinner with us or if you prefer, bed and breakfast.

If you wish to see some country away from the main roads you can travel north or south from Motea. There are a number of beaches, also the Waihi falls in our vicinity.

Directions: *We live 23 km east of Dannevirke. For further information please ring Motea 828 evenings.*

Manawatu

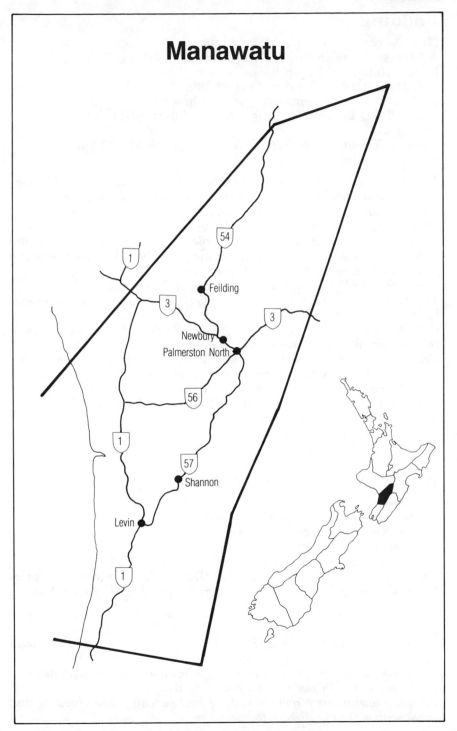

Feilding

Homestay
Address: "Denbigh Cottage", 172 Kimbolton Road, Feilding
Name: Helen and Bryan Roberts
Telephone: (063) 37-831 or (bus) 66-066
Beds: 2 Double (2 bedrooms, guest bathroom)
Tariff: B&B Double $50, Single $30, Children half price;
Dinner $15
Nearest Town: 20 km from Palmerston North and 13 km
from State Highway 1

Our home is a colonial cottage (1890s) restored and comfortable. Gas heating and open fire make it cosy in winter while oak trees in the adjacent park offer shade in summer.
We are ten minutes walk from Feilding shops.
We are an average New Zealand couple with room available to share with overseas visitors and New Zealanders alike. We enjoy meeting people and learning more about other places.
A separate bathroom and toilet is provided for guests.
Two cats have been left to us as children departed and a dog sometimes visits with a nearby daughter.
Our meals are home cooked, easy going affairs and we often barbecue in summer. We do not smoke but you may.
Feilding is central to the southern half of the north island so easy day trips to such places as Wanganui, Hastings, Mt Ruapehu, east or west coast beaches and Mt Bruce Wildlife Centre are possible.
Approximately 30 km away, near Kimbolton, there are fine rhododendron gardens to visit during spring.
We look forward to your visit.

Newbury, Palmerston North

Farmhouse
Address: No 5 RD, Palmerston North
Name: Keith and Margaret Morriss
Telephone: (063) 88-961
Beds: 4 Single (2 bedrooms)
Tariff: B&B Double $60, Single $35; Dinner $20; Children half price
Nearest Town: 8 km north of Palmerston North on State Highway 3

We enjoy country living, yet live only a short distance from Palmerston North.
A warm welcome awaits you at "Grinton", our 100-year-old home with family connections with its namesake in Yorkshire, England.
Our three daughters are all away, this allows us space to offer guests a comfortable stay in pleasant surroundings.
Farming operations consist mainly of beef fattening and cropping and large scale dairying also in the area.

We both enjoy travel and welcome the stimulation of overseas guests, ensuring them a sampling of some of New Zealand's fine food and wine.

Local scenic drives are within easy distance and may include Massey University, the Palmerston North Esplanade and Gardens open to the public.

Our interests include travel, tramping, trout fishing, golf, the Lions Club, music, floral art and dried flowers.

Directions: *8 km north of Palmerston North on State Highway 3 or 5 km south of Awahuri crossroads on State Highway 3.*

Palmerston North

Homestay
Address: 19 Phoenix Avenue, Hokowhitu, Palmerston North
Name: Vic and Judy Young
Telephone: (063) 61-156
Beds: 1 Double, 1 Single (2 bedrooms)
Tariff: B&B Double $50, Single $25, Children half price;
Dinner $12

We are a couple with a grown family living away from home and live in a pleasant suburb near to parks and fifteen minutes walk from the city centre. We have a cat and a Newfoundland dog.

The main guest room has a comfortable double bed with electric blanket and the bathroom adjoining has a spa bath.

Although a vegetarian household we will provide a meat meal if you wish, also breakfast of your choosing.

We would be happy to meet plane, bus or train.

Directions: *From south (Massey) side, turn off Fitzherbert Avenue, right into College Street then take third right (just before Victoria Avenue intersection) into Phoenix Avenue, which is a cul de sac. No. 19 is near the end on the left.*

Palmerston North

Homestay
Address: "Kilkenn Down", 143 Victoria Avenue, Palmerston North
Name: Keay and Ken McCormack
Telephone: (063) 73-491
Beds: 3 Single (2 bedrooms)
Tariff: B&B Double $55, Single $35; Dinner $10; Children half price

We are a typical New Zealand family although our children are now grown up and gone, interested in all sport (armchair variety except for bowls), music, live theatre and community projects and meeting people. We live close to the city in pleasant surroundings.
Palmerston North, "the rose city", is renowned for its lovely gardens, walkways and scenic drives. It is also a university centre with many cultural activities.

We offer friendly, warm hospitality with a family evening meal if you wish.
Ample off-street parking at rear of house — campervans welcome.
Directions: *From the city square travel south in Fitzherbert Avenue to College Street, turn left into College Street and travel approximately ½ km, then left into Victoria Avenue. Look for the palm tree in the front garden.*

The standard of accommodation in *The New Zealand Bed and Breakfast Book* ranges from homely to luxurious but you can always be sure of superior hospitality.

Palmerston North

Farmhouse
Address: Kelvin Grove Road, RD10, Palmerston North
Name: Terry and Barbara Fryer
Telephone: (063) 81-295
Beds: 1 Double, 2 Single (2 bedrooms)
Tariff: B&B Double $60, Single $35; Dinner $20; Campervans $15

If you are looking for good company, clean, attractive accommodation, a country setting only a few minutes from Palmerston North and superb food then look no further. Perhaps if the living conditions were not so attractive there would be two less working children at home and more rooms to let. Nevertheless, although our three children still live at home the house is large (and warm) and we have two bedrooms to offer our guests.

The house was built 15 years ago on 11½ acres of bare land and over that time we have established a garden of approximately one acre. In particular we have many rose bushes including old fashioned and modern roses but winter or summer there is always plenty of colour and interest. On the remaining acreage we run Hampshire sheep as a hobby. Ironically employment by the dairy industry supports our hobby and our love of roses and living in the country.

The district we live in is Whakarongo (that means 'listen'). Whaka-rongo borders Palmerston North and thus the attractions of a big city are only but a few minutes away. Transport to and from Palmerston North or the airport will be provided if required.

We look forward to meeting you.

Directions: *There are so many ways you may approach Palmerston North that it may be advisable to phone. In brief we are on Kelvin Grove Road in the fourth dip after Stoney Creek Road coming from Palmerston North along Tremaine Avenue. At our gateway there are three letterboxes (Jolly, Fryer, Matthews) and we are the first (repeat first) drive immediately after the three letterboxes.*

Shannon

Farmhouse
Address: Hennessy Road, Shannon
Name: Thaddeus's Place
Telephone: (069) 27-599, 27-623
Beds: 1 Double, 4 Single (3 bedrooms, guest bathroom)
Tariff: B&B Double $62, Single $38; Dinner $25;
Children less 10% on accommodation
Nearest Town: 2 km to Shannon, 10 miles to Levin,
20 miles to Palmerston North

My name is Thaddeus. I am a St Bernard dog.
We have a new Portalok home set in ten hectares of riverland situated

115

continued over

below the Tararua Ranges with the Mangahao river meandering through the property.

Colin is the local chemist. His interests are tennis, squash and music. Lynn runs the farmlet. Her interests are animals, gardening, cooking and music.

We have a large garden and there is a lawn tennis court. Colin loves having a game with the guests (actually he's not bad for his age!).

The farmlet raises vealer calves, mohair goats, sheep and has a palomino quarter horse. Lynn milks a house cow most of the year. I live outside!

In the Tararua Ranges within three minutes from here there are horse treks, bush walks, tours to Mangahao's three dams, the historical power station (still working) and a beautiful deer farm.

The Shannon Golf Club and Bowling Club welcome visitors. We have the National Bowling Museum in Shannon.

Within 30 minutes drive there are three beaches and Palmerston North (New Zealand's Rose City).

Lynn and Colin enjoy having guests and do their best to make their stay a happy one.

Directions: Take the road to Shannon from Levin, Foxton or Palmerston North. At the Albion Tavern turn towards the Tararua ranges and travel towards Mangaore along East Road until you have just left the built up area. Turn left by my sign and we are the second place on the left.

Love to see you

Thaddeus

Levin

Homestay
Address: 197 Bath Street, Levin
Name: Robin and Avis Barrie
Telephone: (069) 86-199 (during office hours),
87-266 (evenings, weekends and holidays)
Beds: 4 Single (2 bedrooms)
Tariff: B&B Double $50, Single $30, Children half price; Dinner $15
Nearest Town: We are adjacent to Main Highway situated
two minutes from town centre. Wellington 78 km to south
(1¼ hours), Palmerston North 46 km to north (35 minutes)

Levin has an attractive shopping centre, is the hub of a rural farming and horticulture area and is New Zealand's second largest textile centre having many light industries. The Horticultural Research Station is adjacent. The west coast beaches and the Tararua Forest Park are both five minutes travelling from Levin. Easy bush walks abound. The superb Moutere Golf Links are approximately 5 minutes by car.

We are a family of three, two of the family are now away for tertiary education. We are Rotarians and our business interests are Chartered Accountancy and Sharebroking.

Our home has a large and attractive garden — the guest room two single beds with own bathroom and toilet. A second room with two single beds is available (share facilities).

We welcome you to share family dinner with us. Bed and breakfast only if required.

Directions: *Turn off State Highway 1 in centre of town into Bath Street and ½ km towards hills.*

Levin

Homestay
Address: Roberts' Place, Arapaepae Road, Levin
Name: Alec and Noeline Dalton
Telephone: (069) 79-674
Beds: 2 Single (1 bedroom)
Tariff: B&B Double $55, Single $35, Dinner available if required
Nearest Town: Levin

We are a retired couple living in a modern home set in its own delight-
ful garden of one acre on State Highway 57 — the main route from
Palmerston North to Levin which itself is only 1½ hours drive from
Wellington.
Situated in horticultural country but only a few minutes' drive from the
shopping area of Levin, our property is well laid out with lawns, native
and exotic trees and we have ample off-street parking.
For those interested there is a games room with pool, table tennis and
darts.
Directions: *Two hundred metres north of the Queen Street inter-*
section and on the west side of Arapaepae Road.

All telephone numbers in New Zealand are being changed during
1990 so the numbers listed may not be current. Ring 018 for directory
assistance if you cannot contact your hosts.

Send us a comment form to tell us about your
B&B vacation. Forms are in this book and are
also obtainable from hosts.

Wairarapa

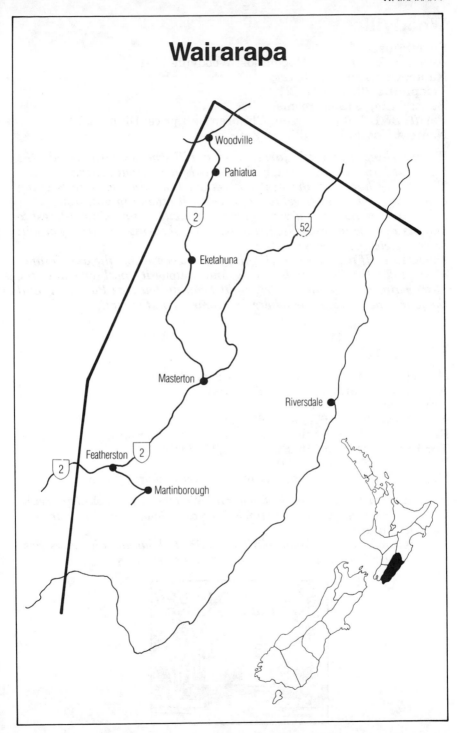

Woodville

Farmhouse
Address: River Road, Hopelands, Woodville RD1
Name: Chris and Jo Coats
Telephone: (06504) 47-521
Beds: 4 Single (2 bedrooms)
Tariff: B&B $30 per person, Children half price; Dinner $12
Nearest Town: Woodville 12 km

*We are sheep and cattle farmers on a hill country farm beside the
beautiful Manawatu River which is noted for its trout fishing.*
*The family have fled the nest but return from time to time, seeking
quiet from their busy lives, two of them still attending university.*
*Depending on the time of year, farming activities of possible interest to
tourists may be in progress, i.e. mustering, shearing, etc. and you will
be very welcome to participate.*
Directions: *If travelling on Highway 2 between Woodville and Dannevirke, take the Hopelands Road and follow it until crossing the
Manawatu River (6 km). Turn right heading towards Pahiatua, and
the fourth house (blue) is where 'Welcome' is on the mat.*

Pahiatua

Homestay + Self-Contained Accommodation
Address: 27 Tararua Street, Pahiatua
Name: Leonach House
Telephone: (0650) 67-054 or 67-056
Beds: 1 Double, 2 Single (1 bedroom, guest bathroom)
Tariff: B&B Double $50, Single $35, Children $5;
Weekly Tariff (7 days) $250
Nearest Town: Pahiatua, city of Palmerston North 33 km

*Welcome to a small, friendly township! We offer a free country break-
fast on arrival morning, and fresh fruit and flowers also, in our self-
contained unit.*
*Ours is an historical home built in 1896. It housed Pahiatua's first
mayor in 1897, and we are restoring it to former glory.*

Children are most welcome and a playground is available.
We are close to shops, restaurants, hotels, parks and river. Ideal for the trout fisherman, Pahiatua is one of the best trout fishing areas in New Zealand. A big trout fishing carnival is held annually.
Native bush reserves, glowworm caves, museum, craft shops, deer farms, native bird reserve and the spectacular Manawatu Gorge are all within a short driving distance.
If you need a relaxing break away, take it with us. We are 2½ hours from Wellington, 2½ hours to Napier.
Directions: *½ minute off State Highway 3. Please phone if possible.*

Eketahuna

Farmhouse
Address: 'Tidsfordriv' RD3, Eketahuna
Name: Ted and Glenys Hansen
Telephone: (06505) 8474
Beds: 2 Single (1 bedroom)
Tariff: B&B Double $55, Single $35; Children half price; Dinner $15
Nearest Town: Eketahuna 10 km, Masterton 50 km

We are a family of four with two teenage children. We are sheep-farming on a 900 acre hill country farm. We are the third generation to live on our farm. We are diversifying into Angora goats and also have a small flock of black and coloured sheep which provides the natural coloured wool for the spinning that is done in spare time.
Our home is 65 years old and has recently been modernised. The guest room has two single beds.

You may have family dinner with us or if you prefer only bed and breakfast — we can provide the breakfast of your choice. There is a diabetic in the family and we would be pleased to provide diabetic meals if required.
We have a waterfowl collection and are active members in waterfowl conservation group — Ducks Unlimited (N.Z.) Inc.
We recommend a visit to the National Wildlife Centre at Mt Bruce, just 23 km south on State Highway 2. Local rivers provide excellent brown trout fishing. There is an excellent 18-hole golf course open all year round at Eketahuna.
Directions: *Turn off State Highway 2 south end of Eketahuna and follow road to Alfredton for 10 km. Good sealed road. Farm name on gate.*

121

Lansdowne, Masterton

Homestay
Address: 65 Titoki Street, Lansdowne, Masterton
Name: Gordon and Doleen McNeilage
Telephone: (059) 83-817
Beds: 3 Single (2 bedrooms)
Tariff: B&B Double $50, Single $30; Dinner $15; Children half price

We are a family of four, with two girls at university, plus one sleepy cat. We are fortunate to live in the beautiful suburb of Lansdowne, about one mile north of the town of Masterton.
Our home is nearly fifty years old and we have altered and improved it to give us more living space. It is surrounded by gardens and has an outdoor court area.
You may have family dinner with us or, if you prefer, only bed and breakfast.
Masterton has a lovely park, attractive shops and restaurants. It is a very appealing town and we wish to extend warm, friendly hospitality.

Masterton

Homestay
Address: 2 Keir Crescent, Masterton
Name: David E. Barnes
Telephone: (059) 81-567 (home), 82-345 (bus.)
Beds: 2 Single (1 bedroom)
Tariff: B&B Double $50, Single $30, Children half price;
Dinner by arrangement $15
Nearest Town: 41 km south of Eketahuna, 100 km n.e. of Wellington on State Highway 2

I live in a semi-detached flat in a quiet street which looks out on to part of Masterton's scenic hill suburb of Lansdowne. I am situated within 10 minutes walk of our lovely Queen Elizabeth Park and 15–20 minutes walk from the Masterton town centre.
Day trips to Mount Holdsworth, Castlepoint beach, Cape Palliser and the Putangirua Pinnacles, National Wildlife Centre at Mt Bruce, glowworm caves near Martinborough and even Wellington by train can be easily made from Masterton.
I enjoy travel and have recently travelled extensively overseas and within New Zealand.
The guest room is best suited to one person but there are two beds. Bathroom/toilet facilities are on a shared basis.
Directions: *From the north, on State Highway 2 turn left into Third Street soon after entering the built-up area. Proceed to the end. Turn right into Totara Street then left. You are now in Keir Crescent. From the south, on State Highway 2 continue through the town centre past*

the Fire Station, over the Waipoua River bridge heading north to Woodville on Highway 2, but turn right when you reach First Street. You will pass through the suburban shopping centre of Lansdowne. Turn left at Totara Street, Keir Crescent is the third turn right.

Masterton

Farmhouse + Self-Contained Accommodation
Address: Harefield, 147 Upper Plain Road, Masterton
Name: Robert and Marion Ahearn
Telephone: (059) 84-070
Beds: 1 Double, 1 Single (1 bedroom, guest bathroom); 1 Double and 3 Single in detached, fully equipped, self-contained flat
Tariff: B&B Double $50, Single $30, Children half price, Flat $20 per adult self-catering; Dinner $15; Campervans $15
Nearest Town: Masterton PO 5 km

We are farmers whose family have all left home. Seven years ago we built our cedar house on 13 acres, 5 km from P.O. and 1½ km from Bypass Road.

Our guest room with its own bathroom is well away from ours and the kitchen. A cottage garden surrounds the house and flat, well back from the road. We look out on to the beautiful Tararua mountains and paddocks with sheep, cattle, deer and free range red hens which give us eggs for breakfast! We have a para pool, dartboard, pool table and croquet set.

We have been home hosting for some years and have ourselves been guests in Europe, Australia and New Zealand.

Our interests include travelling and travellers' talk, workshop inventions, Lions Int, wildlife (animals), reading, tramping, walking, gardening, Rose Society, aerobics, painting (oils and watercolour) and spinning.

We would be pleased to pick up from the bus depot, railway station or Wairarapa Airlines.

If you stay in the flat you can choose to be self-catering or have dinner and/or breakfast with us. Guests staying in the house can have dinner or just breakfast. Reductions for longer stays.

We are half an hour's drive to the National Wildlife Centre and two hour's drive from the Inter-Island Ferry.

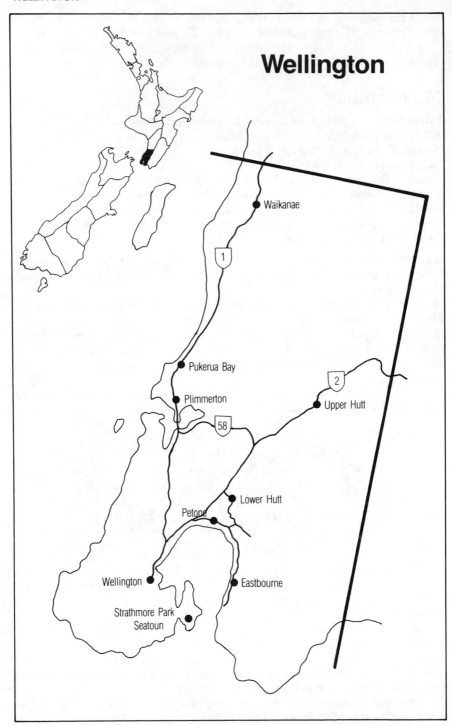

Wellington

Waikanae

①

Pukerua Bay

Plimmerton

②

Upper Hutt

58

Lower Hutt

Petone

Wellington

Eastbourne

Strathmore Park
Seatoun

Waikanae

Homestay
Address: Please phone
Name: Madeline Reid
Telephone: (058) 33-689
Beds: 1 Double, 2 Single (2 bedrooms)
Tariff: B&B Double $40, Single $20, Children half price; Dinner $15
Nearest Town: 60 km north of Wellington, 20 km south of Otaki on State Highway 1

My home is situated in quiet surroundings being in the garden area of Waikanae, halfway between Waikanae village and Waikanae beach. I am of English heritage (from North Cornwall) and have lived in New Zealand off and on since 1953. I am a widow with a family of two who are now pursuing their own careers in nursing and film-making respectively.

Waikanae and district has a variety of interesting attractions — fishing, boating, a beautiful beach, arts and crafts, bush walks, agricultural displays, and much more.

I do request that my guests be non-smokers.

Directions: *Please phone.*

The double bedroom opens onto a deck with sea views. Guests have their own toilet and shower.

Can't contact your host? Ring 018 for directory assistance.

Waikanae

Homestay
Address: "Waimoana", 63 Kakariki Grove, Waikanae
Name: Ian and Phyllis Stewart
Telephone: (058) 37-158
Beds: 2 Double, 2 Single (2 bedrooms, ensuite bathrooms)
Tariff: B&B Double $60, Single $40; Dinner $15;
Campervans $15 (shower and toilet for two people)
Nearest Town: 58 km north of Wellington on State Highway 1

We are a recently retired couple. We have two adult daughters who work and live in the city and come home when they can. Both of them speak German and French. We are non-smokers.

Waikanae is a delightful township, popular for holidays because of its climate.

Our centrally-heated home is newly completed and spacious, designed for comfort and warmth. We have only two guest rooms, allowing a friendly, personal atmosphere. Each room has both a double and a single bed and its own ensuite. Each has a spacious balcony for admiring the fantastic views. Relax around our heated internal

continued over

125

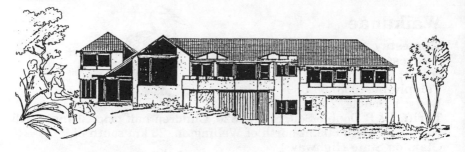

*swimming pool and sun-deck. (Pool not usually heated in winter,
unless by special arrangement.)*
*You are welcome to have family dinner with us or there are restaurants
nearby. We provide a choice of breakfasts.*
No pets please.
*Beach and river, bird sanctuary, bush walks, pottery and crafts all
within easy distance.*
Directions: *Please telephone.*

Phone numbers may have changed. Ring 018 for directory.

Plimmerton

Homestay
Address: 14 Roys Road
Name: Val and David Griffith Jones
Telephone: (04) 338-296
Beds: 1 Double, 2 Single (2 bedrooms, guest bathroom)
Tariff: B&B Double $50, Single $30, Children half price; Dinner $8
Nearest Town: Porirua

*Plimmerton is a seaside village half an hour's drive on the motorway
north of Wellington. Our house is 3 km from State Highway 1 and
enjoys magnificent views across Cook Strait, all-day sun and often
spectacular sunsets.*
*An interesting 15 minute walk takes you to Plimmerton village where
you will find a good variety of shops including a hairdresser, pharmacy,
delicious deli, quality craft shop, supermarket and bookshop, also a
church and a doctor's surgery. An alternative return trip can be made
along the sea front past sandy swimming beaches to Karehana Bay and
the boating club.*
*There are good restaurants within easy reach and a takeaway shop in
the village. A 30-minute train ride takes you to the centre of
Wellington.*
Three of our four sons live at home and Val works as a fibre artist.
*It is a comfortable and homely place and we make no apologies for the
busy family atmosphere. We enjoy children and young guests are
welcome.*

126

The double bedroom opens onto a deck with sea views. Guests have their own toilet and shower.
Dinner with the family can be arranged and breakfast is of your choosing.
Please telephone first.

Trentham, Upper Hutt

Private Hotel
Address: 42 Camp Street,
Trentham, Upper Hutt
Name: Ascot Lodge (Dorothy-Anne Bonner)
Telephone: (04) 278-835 or 277-511
Beds: 10 bedrooms
Tariff: B&B Double $75, Single $43; Dinner $15
Nearest Town: Upper Hutt 7 minutes, Lower Hutt 15 minutes

Although Ascot Lodge is a private hotel I run it as a large private house. Guests live here in an atmosphere that I hope is warm, congenial and relaxed amongst antiques and treasured possessions.
The lounge and dining room are wood-panelled which gives a lovely old-world charm and ambience.
Outside there is a pretty courtyard and small garden to sit in and enjoy under umbrellas. Coffee and tea are available 24 hours a day.
My interests include antiques, cats, theatre, gardening, travel, shopping, restaurants, cooking and interior decorating — not necessarily in that order.
Ascot Lodge is immediately opposite Trentham Race Course, one of the finest courses in the Southern Hemisphere, very close to Trentham Military Camp, Central Institute of Technology and Trentham Memorial Park and less than one hour away from the beautiful Wairarapa countryside. Picnic baskets packed on request.

127

Petone

Homestay
Address: 1 Bolton Street, Petone
Name: Anne and Reg Cotter
Telephone: (04) 686-960
Beds: 2 Single (1 bedroom)
Tariff: B&B $25 per person, Dinner $5 per person
Nearest Town: Lower Hutt 5 km, Wellington 8 km

We have an older type home by the beach which we have modernised. It has three bedrooms, a large lounge, diningroom, kitchen, bathroom with shower and bath.
We are two minutes from the museum on the beach, two minutes from the shops and the bus route into the city. The Fisherman's Table Restaurant is only 2 minutes away also.
We have three children, two girls and a son who have left home.
We offer two single beds with room for one extra or a child's cot which is available. Children would be very welcome as we have several children's play things in the back yard.
My husband is a keen amateur ornithologist and he goes to the Chatham Islands with an expedition trying to find the nesting place of the Taiko — a rare sea bird which is on the endangered list. We are keen to show any folk interested in birds the local places of interest.
He is also a member of the genealogy society. We have an old 1937 Austin 10 Car and belong to the Austin Vintage Club.
We are 10 minutes by road to the Picton ferry.

Mt Cook, Wellington City

Homestay
Address: Please phone
Name: Miss Jamie Bull
Telephone: (04) 846-505
Beds: 1 Double (1 bedroom)
Tariff: B&B Double $60, Single $40; Dinner by arrangement
Nearest Town: Wellington inner city

I am a self-employed choreographer, performer and tutor of dance. Consequently my work takes me around the country (which I love and know well) but when I'm at home I really enjoy sharing my home and my energy with others.
I live in an eighty-year-old inner-city cottage which I am gradually restoring. I think it has character as well as comfort.
It is a 15–20 minute walk to the heart of the city, there are buses nearby and the National Art Gallery and Museum is virtually on the doorstep.
Directions: *Please phone.*

Mt Victoria, Wellington City

Homestay
Address: 58 Pirie Street, Mt Victoria,
Wellington
Name: Robert and Elizabeth McGuigan
Telephone: (04) 858-512
Beds: 1 Queen, 3 Single (3 bedrooms, guest bathroom)
Tariff: Double $60, Single $40

We are a family of five, our three teenage children still living at home. Our 100-year-old Victorian 2-storey home is situated in Mount Victoria, an historic and quaint suburb, just a few minutes easy walk from the city.

We live upstairs and have our own facilities while downstairs is for guests. We have a TV lounge and a dining room with tea and coffee making facilities. There are three bedrooms and two bathrooms — one queensize ensuite, a twin room and a single room.
Wellington area has a lot to offer — good restaurants and shopping and a good public transport system. A beautiful coastline with wonderful views from Mt Victoria and up the cable car and through the botanic gardens. We also have parliament buildings, museums, art galleries and live theatre.
Directions: *Off motorway into Ghuznee Street, Taranaki Street, Vivian Street, across Kent Terrace and up Pirie Street to No. 58. From Airport take Airport bus to Kentucky Fried Chicken. From Railway Station take city bus no. 2 or 5 (2 sections), ask driver.*

Strathmore Park

Self-Contained Accommodation

Address: "Treetops", Strathmore Park, Wellington
Telephone: (04) 886-923
Beds: 1 Double, 1 Single (in en-suite cabin, electric
blankets, lambswool underlays, narrow foldaway bed on request)
Tariff: B&B Double $60, Single $40, Children under 5
no charge; Dinner by arrangement $20 (includes pre-dinner drinks
and wine with dinner); Special rates for children
Nearest Town: Wellington city 10 minutes (9 km)

*We are on the main bus route to the city and 1½ km from Wellington
Domestic and International Airport and could pick you up by prior
arrangement.*

*We are a home-loving couple whose children are now independent.
However our large, friendly dog keeps us in trim by demanding his
daily walk around Wellington's rugged coastline at the harbour
entrance or on the hills above the sea — you would be most welcome to
join us. We would also be happy to take you on a short, local sightseeing
drive. We love travelling ourselves and thoroughly enjoy talking to
everybody.*

*Although only one room, our comfortable cabin is spacious and has its
own bathroom, fridge, toaster, tea-making facilities, radio and television. Make your own Continental breakfast at your leisure or come
down to the house for a cooked breakfast.*

*If you don't feel like joining us for lively conversation over dinner, then
two minutes' walk to the local shops provides cold cuts and salad to
bring back to your cabin or perhaps the favourite New Zealand
takeaway, fish and chips (Chinese takeaway two minutes' drive).*

*The closest licensed restaurants are five minutes' drive away. Seatoun
beach and Miramar Golf Course are two minutes' drive or an easy
walk.*

*We look forward to your visit. "There are no strangers here — only
friends we haven't met."*

Directions: *Please phone.*

Seatoun

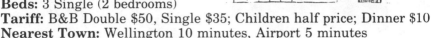

Homestay
Address: 87 Marine Parade,
Seatoun, Wellington 3
Name: Barbara Cleverley
Telephone: (04) 887-930
Beds: 3 Single (2 bedrooms)
Tariff: B&B Double $50, Single $35; Children half price; Dinner $10
Nearest Town: Wellington 10 minutes, Airport 5 minutes

My husband is a lecturer in graphic design and between us we have a wide range of interests — sport, theatre, handcrafts and we both enjoy meeting people.
Seatoun is a seaside suburb of Wellington. We have a lovely view of the sea and it is a pleasant area for walks and swimming in the summer. We are 10 minutes from the city by car, five minutes from the airport and close to public transport. We look forward to meeting you.
Directions: *By bus, catch a Seatoun bus, get off at the shops and walk down to the water and we are six houses past the wharf. Our home is five minutes away by car from the airport.*

One of the differences between staying at a
hotel and staying at a B&B is that you don't
hug the hotel staff when you leave.

All telephone numbers in New Zealand are being changed during 1990 so the numbers listed may not be current. Ring 018 for directory assistance if you cannot contact your hosts.

Nelson, Marlborough

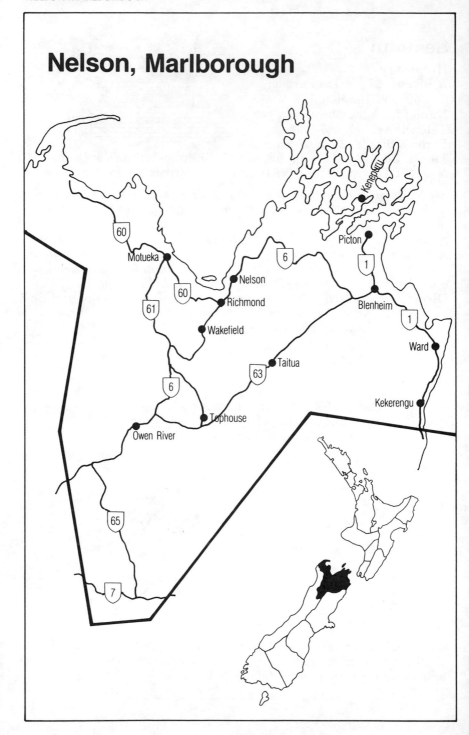

Motueka

Guest House
Address: Whites Guest
House, 430 High Street,
Motueka (just south
of junction
Highway 60 and 61)
Name:
Laddie and Rachael White
Telephone: (0524) 87-318
Beds: 3 Double Rooms, 2 Single Rooms, 1 Triple Room
Tariff: B&B Double $55, Single $33 (Winter Discounts, May–Aug, for
2 nights or more); Dinner by
arrangement $16.50
Nearest Town: Motueka 1·6 km

*Rachael and Laddie offer stylish hospitality and personal service in a
no smoking atmosphere, in their newly renovated home. Room to relax
in the spacious lounge and garden. Sleep in quality inner-sprung beds.
Enjoy a home-cooked evening meal served with fresh garden vegetables. Rachael's meals are cooked and presented with flair and pride.
(For optimum satisfaction meals should be ordered by 4 pm).*
*Books on New Zealand and up-to-date local information is displayed.
Laddie has the knowledge and is happy to advise and assist with your
ongoing travel plans.*

*Both Skyline and Newmans bus services will set you down near the
Guest House on request. This will save a walk back from Motueka
centre (which is only 1·6 km).*
Off-street parking is available for your car.
*Should you be walking the Abel Tasman Park we can store your car or
belongings. A limited amount of tramping gear is available for hire.*
*A laundry service is also available at a small charge. Tea and coffee
facilities are self-service at all times.*
*The sunny Motueka area offers beautiful beaches, wine and crafts trail,
horticulture tours and the unique and peaceful Abel Tasman Park.
Forward booking is advisable December through March in this area.*

Motueka

Homestay
Address: 96A Poole Street, Motueka
Name: Brian and Margaret Bird
Telephone: (0524) 88-436
Beds: 5 Single (2 bedrooms, guest bathroom)
Tariff: B&B Double $55, Single $35; Dinner $20
Nearest Town: Nelson 50 km

Motueka is a small town servicing an intensive horticultural area of hops, tobacco and fruit with one of the best climates in New Zealand. Motueka is the ideal stopping place for visitors to Abel Tasman National Park, Northwest Nelson Forest Park and Golden Bay. Kaiteriteri beach, 10 km away, is a popular holiday resort. Local attractions include alpine and coastal walks, trout and sea fishing, boating, goldpanning and an interesting variety of cottage crafts. We have compiled five interesting scenic day trips for you to select from.
Our modern two-storeyed home of old English style is set on a large section with swimming pool and garden.
Our family have grown up and left home allowing us space to offer a comfortable stopover in this area.
The guest rooms have single beds and there is a separate bathroom and an excellent view looking out to the mountains.
A friendly welcome is assured. Overseas visitors preferred.
We usually include a horticultural tour of nearby kiwifruit, hops, tobacco and tea.
Directions: *Please phone.*

Motueka

Self-Contained Accommodation
Address: Kairuru, State Highway 60, Takaka Hill, Motueka
Name: David and Wendy Henderson
Telephone: (0524) 88-091
Beds: 2 Double, 2 Single (2 bedrooms, guest bathroom)
Tariff: B&B Double $50, Single $25, Children half price;
Self-Contained Cottage $40 per night up to 4 people, including
linen and self-catering, $5 per person extra for breakfast, children
half price for breakfast; Dinner $15

Nearest Town: 17 km from Motueka on the Takaka Hill on State Highway 60

We are a farming family of four (two girls aged three and 10 years). We farm sheep, cattle and angora goats on our 4000 acre hill country property called Kairuru.

Our farm is handy to Kaiteriteri beach, Golden Bay and Abel Tasman National Park. There is a marble quarry in operation on our property. We are offering to travellers a modern, fully-equipped two-bedroom cottage with open plan kitchen, living and dining area and its own bathroom and laundry. The cottage is wooden inside and outside giving a rustic but warm feeling. A balcony along the front of the cottage provides an area to take in the sun and views of the bays and surrounding hills.

Your accommodation is handy to our home for dinner and socialising. A good selection for breakfast is supplied, but made by yourselves at your leisure in your own fully-equipped kitchen.

We enjoy visitors from all over the world and look forward to your stay with us.

Directions: *From Motueka take the road to Takaka (State Highway 60). Pass through the small town of Riwaka and travel up the Takaka Hill for 11 km. 'Kairuru' is on the right hand side and our name is on the gate. Takaka is 40 km further. The journey from Motueka takes about 25 minutes.*

Nelson

Homestay
Address: 20 Martin Street, Monaco, Nelson
Name: Jean and Jack Anderson
Telephone: (054) 76-739
Beds: 1 Double, 2 Single (2 bedrooms)
Tariff: B&B Double $48, Single $25, Children half price; Dinner $12.50
Nearest Town: Nelson

We are a couple who like meeting people. We are members of Friend-

135

continued over

ship Force International and have made lasting friendships with overseas visitors staying with us.

We live beside the sea where it is lovely to walk or put your boat in for a leisurely cruise. Waterskiing is prominent here in the summertime.

Shopping is close at Nelson, Stoke or Richmond. Also very near to historic houses, museum, gardens and craft habitat. In the winter time it is only about an hour's drive to the skifields.

We are near the airport and will meet planes or buses at depots. A phone call or a letter would be appreciated before arrival.

Directions: *Take the road from Nelson to Stoke. Turn right at the lights into Songer Street. Travel right to the bottom of Songer Street around the bay into Monaco turning in front of the Monaco Point Club into Martin Street.*

Nelson

Homestay
Address: 15 Riverside, Nelson
Name: Hunts Home Hosts
Telephone: (054) 80-123
Beds: 1 Double, 2 Single (2 bedrooms, guest bathroom)
Tariff: B&B Double $50, Single $30, Children $20; Dinner $15
Nearest Town: Nelson city

Take a break in sunny Nelson — the geographical centre of New Zealand — with your Home Hosts, David and Edith Hunt at their beautiful home by the crystal clear River Maitai in the centre of the city. Sightseeing, excursions, picnics, barbecues, fishing, gold panning, visits to local potteries and weavers, museums, theatres — all within easy reach.

Bed and cooked breakfast and meals as required including packed lunches.

Guest suite with one twin, one double bedroom. Guest lounge with colour TV, private facilities, kitchenette, lock-up garage.

Our service car is available to pick up guests from the Airport or Bus Depot or for sightseeing trips, etc. My wife speaks English, German and Czech.

Our upstairs quarters always have a warm welcome for those who want our company. Our brochure with city plan shows the way to our sunny home.

We want our guests to feel comfortable and at home — and a little spoilt.

When you stay at B&Bs you are meeting "dinkum Kiwis".

Nelson

Bed and Breakfast Inn
Address: 29 Collingwood Street, Nelson
Name: California House
Telephone: (054) 84-173
Beds: 3 Double, 2 Queen, 2 Twin (5 bedrooms, private or shared bathroom)
Tariff: B&B Double $95–$135, Single $67.50
Nearest Town: 3 blocks from town centre

A spacious, colonial home, built in 1893, with original English oak panelling, 24 stained glass windows, three fireplaces and a sunny verandah facing a large lawn and gardens. The house is set well back from the street in a quiet residential area, only five minutes' walk from the centre of town. Guest rooms are furnished with comfortable antiques, fluffy quilts and fresh flowers from our garden.

We serve only the finest home-baked California breakfast, which may include fresh orange juice, fresh berries and cream, ham and sour cream omelettes, apricot nut bread, apple and cheese blintzes, Finnish pancakes with pure Canadian maple syrup and freshly ground coffee.

We also provide a peaceful and relaxing atmosphere and gracious hospitality in the tradition of fine northern California inns.

The emphasis is on peace and quiet (no TV, no radios, no young children), gracious hospitality and the feeling of being a guest in an historic home.

Bicycles, beach towels and courtesy transport available.

NO SMOKING in the house at any time. The house is classified by the New Zealand Historic Places Trust on the basis of its historic and architectural significance.

Tariffs include the full specialty breakfast, wine or fruit juice on arrival, coffee, tea, sherry and biscuits (cookies) available at any time.

Nelson

Homestay
Address: 7 Titoki Street, Stoke, Nelson
Name: K. and L. Carr
Telephone: (054) 76-307
Beds: 1 Double, 2 Single (2 bedrooms)
Tariff: B&B Double $44, Single $22, Children half price; Dinner $15
Nearest Town: Nelson

We are a homely couple in a comfortable home, very fortunate to live within walking distance to Stoke centre, to beautiful parks and rose garden. Both have historic homes and museums.
There is a swimming baths complex nearby. By car, a short distance to airport, beautiful beaches, swimming, walkways, potteries, arts and crafts, farmlands, berryfruit farms, orchards and wineries.
Our home has two guest rooms, two single beds and one double. There is a separate shower room with handbasin.
You may have dinner with us or just bed and breakfast.
Directions: *Coming from the north (Picton), take State Highway 6 to Stoke, turn left at traffic lights (Turf Hotel) into Songer Street. Titoki Street is the last street on the right before the hill. From the south on State Highway 6 turn right at the traffic lights into Songer Street. If you do not have transport we can meet your plane or coach.*

Stoke, Nelson

Homestay
Address: 15 Aldinga Avenue, Stoke
Name: Russell and Mavis Thornton
Telephone: (054) 76-890
Beds: 2 Single (1 bedroom, guest bathroom)
Tariff: B&B Double $55, Single $30, Children half price; Dinner $12
Nearest Town: Nelson

We are a family of five with three schoolage boys. We live in a new home five minutes from Nelson airport and beach and our home opens onto a reserve.
We have recently achieved a long-standing dream to build our own home to cater for our lifestyle as we enjoy having guests, friends and family to stay.
Our guest room has two single beds with your own shower and toilet facilities nextdoor.
We would enjoy your company at dinner or if you wish only bed and breakfast.
Nelson has a host of things to do and see being a popular holiday resort. If you would like to come and stay with us, please phone and we can give you directions or meet you if necessary.

Nelson

Homestay
Address: 201A Annesbrook Drive, Nelson
Name: Jim and Audrey McMahon
Telephone: (054) 85-146
Beds: 2 Single (1 bedroom + ensuite)
Tariff: B&B Double $60, Single $40; Dinner $15
Nearest Town: 5 km west of Nelson city centre on Highway 6

*We live near the sea in our sunny, comfortable, three-year-old home.
You will find us very easy to locate, our driveway being directly off
Highway 6. It is a pleasant 8–10 minute drive around the waterfront by
car or bus from Nelson central city. En route to Abel Tasman Park.*
*Being on a slight rise we enjoy rural sea views. A babbling brook winds
by the pleasant secluded courtyard you may choose to relax in.*
*The guest accommodation is spacious and spotless. You have your own
bathroom, fridge and tea/coffee making facilities. Your bedroom has
two single beds, comfortable chairs, colour TV and an ample supply of
books and magazine. A glass door leads off into the garden.*
Breakfast is of your choice. Large or light from a varied selection.
*Tahuna Beach Reserve (safe swimming, tennis, jogging, fishing,
windsurfing) is within comfortable walking distance as are the village
shops and restaurants (three minutes by car).*
*We are also only a few minutes drive from Nelson Airport and will
happily collect you if required.*
*Your hosts — a middle aged couple are well travelled with wide
ranging interests. We have provided hospitality for visitors from many
countries. Our objective is to supply good quality accommodation and
food in a welcoming and friendly atmosphere.*

Pass the message on to campervanners. The
New Zealand Bed and Breakfast Book has some
great stopovers.

Central Nelson

Guest House
Address: Collingwood House, 174 Collingwood Street, Nelson
Name: Alan and Cecile Strang
Telephone: (054) 84-481
Beds: 1 Double, 4 Single (3 bedrooms, guest bathroom)
Tariff: B&B Double $50, Single $30, Children half price; Dinner $15
Nearest Town: A block away from Nelson

After travelling extensively overseas and enjoying meeting so many people, my husband and I decided to return home, retire early and find a lovely old New Zealand home from which to offer bed and breakfast in the best British tradition. After some time we found 'Collingwood House' with its lovely big guest rooms and bathroom with shower and bath, separate upstairs, each room having lovely views of the city — central but quiet.

We are close enough for our guests to walk to town and to the many excellent restaurants. As we love living in Nelson we are eager to share its delights with our guests.

Should you require dinner we will be happy to supply it.

We have lots of ideas for day's outings apart from our fabulous beaches.

Collingwood House, Nelson

All telephone numbers in New Zealand are being changed during 1990 so the numbers listed may not be current. Ring 018 for directory assistance if you cannot contact your hosts.

As distances in New Zealand are not great check out the maps of the neighbouring provinces for other B&Bs nearby.

140

Nelson

Homestay
Address: Please phone
Name: Dorothy and Bob Brown
Telephone: (054) 84-751
Beds: 2 Single (1 bedroom, guest bathroom)
Tariff: B&B Double $60, Single $40
Nearest Town: Nelson (5 minute walk)

My husband and I are a retired couple and we would like to welcome you to our comfortable, modern home which is in a garden setting on the banks of the Maitai River and close to the Queens Gardens, just five minutes' walk to the city centre, shops and restaurants, art gallery, covered heated swimming pool and spa. Central yet quiet. Off-street parking.
The guest room has two single beds and you have your own bathroom, also your own sitting room with colour TV and tea and coffee making facilities or you may prefer to join us in our lounge and just sit and talk, maybe share a common interest, travel. Why not spend a few days exploring the wonderful Nelson area?
We just love meeting people and making new friends. We are non-smokers.
Directions: *Please phone.*

Richmond

Homestay
Address: Edens Road, Hope, RD1 Richmond, Nelson
Name: Laurie and Pat Rainbow
Telephone: (054) 45-766
Beds: 3 Single (2 bedrooms)
Tariff: B&B $25 per person, Children half price; Dinner $12;
Campervans (with power) $15 (also Caravan available)

With three of our family having left the nest there are now just three of us at home, our youngest son just having started work.
Our home is rurally situated on a 10 acre block being part of the horticulture-rich Waimea plains. We dabble in market gardening, goats and sheep.
There are numerous picnic spots by the nearby rivers and we're just 25

141

continued over

minutes from Nelson city. If you want to relax we can recommend Rabbit Island about 12 km away with its beautiful safe beach and large sheltered park-like areas surrounded by exotic forest.
Our house is fifteen years old and it attracts the sun for as long as it shines. The two guest rooms have three single beds in total. The bathroom is shared.
If you wish an evening meal is available and we'll provide either cooked or Continental breakfast.
P.S. We'd enjoy seeing your family photos.
Directions: *If travelling south through Richmond carry on 4 km from traffic lights to Edens road and turn right (Aniseed Valley goes left, can be confusing). If travelling north from Brightwater, pass over Wairoa river and at 2nd crossroad turn left. You're in Eden's Road.*

NZ phone numbers are being changed. Ring 018 for directory.

Wakefield, Nelson

Farmhouse
Address: Absarokee Appaloosa Stud, 144 Whitby Road, Wakefield, Nelson
Name: Denis and Jessie Blanche
Telephone: (054) 28-198
Beds: 2 Single (1 bedroom)
Tariff: B&B Double $55, Single $35, Children half price; Dinner $15; Light Meal $7; Campervans (barbecue facilities and light refreshments in evening with hosts) $20
Nearest Town: Richmond 16 km, Nelson 32 km

We are a family of three with one adult son still living at home.
We have a comfortable family home. It is on the main road to the west coast, 1½ km north of Wakefield Village. We enjoy meeting people having had visitors over the years through Young Farmers Clubs, 4H Club and International Friendship Force. We like our visitors to feel welcome and to feel that our home is theirs while they are here.
Meals are wholesome country fare of three courses with plenty of fresh fruit and vegetables, having our own vege garden. We also like to use local produce.
We run an Appaloosa horse stud, having imported a stallion from the USA. We also have a hobby — making handcrafted soap — and we have a collection of geraniums.
Campervans are welcome.
Wakefield is one hours drive to skiing. Only quarter of an hour to the beach and rivers.
Directions: *We are on the main highway 32 km south of Nelson city, 16 km from Richmond. The property has a large sign "Appaloosa Stud" on stable.*

Wakefield, Nelson

Homestay
Address: 6 Anslow Place, Wakefield, Nelson
Name: Ngaire and Norman Lochhead
Telephone: (054) 28-321
Beds: 4 Single (2 bedrooms, guest bathroom)
Tariff: B&B Double $55, Single $35, Children half price;
Dinner $15; Campervans welcome
Nearest Town: Nelson 32 km, Richmond 16 km

Our house is situated about two minutes off the main road in a cul-de-sac, quiet area.

Recently we have retired to Wakefield after enjoying a farming life. We both enjoy meeting people and like to think we make them very welcome.

The village of Wakefield is surrounded by mixed farming, also logging activities.

We have a steam museum, very good golf course, tramping available, snow skiing one hour away.

In our village we are very lucky to have a Post Office, large supermarket, chemist and two takeaway/dairies. We are a very caring and sharing village.

Some hosts are away from home during the
day. It will help if you phone them the evening
before you want to stay.

Wakefield, Nelson

Homestay
Address: "Claydon's Ridge", 88 Valley, RD1, Wakefield, Nelson
Name: Pam and Colin Ladley
Telephone: (054) 28-265
Beds: 2 Single (1 bedroom)
Tariff: Dinner, Bed and Breakfast Double $85; Campervans
Nearest Town: Richmond 15 km, Nelson city 30 km,
Wakefield village 4 km

We are a family of five — three children Scott, Nicola and Katie. We are very lucky to live in sunny Nelson on a beautiful sheep, cattle and deer farm in 88 Valley which is just south of Wakefield village.

Not far from us we have the Nelson lakes approximately one hour's

continued over

143

drive through an attractive forest. In the other direction Abel Tasman National Park and lots of lovely, sandy beaches.

On our farm we have a stream running through with two areas of native bush. We can offer a tour around the farm on a 4-wheel-drive vehicle seeing sheep shearing, sheep dog demonstration, deer and cattle and whatever is happening on the day including a children's pony and farmyard animals.

Our interests include gardening of which we have a large rockery landscaped area of alpine plants, sheep dog trialling, travel, barbecues and numerous handcrafts.

Secluded campervan sites available on farm.

Meals available.

Directions: *Please ring.*

Taitua

Farmhouse
Address: RD1 Taitua, State Highway 63, Blenheim
Name: Cathie and Robin Young
Telephone: (057) 22-816
Beds: 1 Double, 2 Single (2 bedrooms, guest bathroom)
Tariff: B&B Double $55, Single $38.50; Dinner $18;
Campervans $15 (private facilities available, spa bath),
Children half price

We have a new ranch-style house on a 440-acre sheep farm midway between Blenheim and Nelson Lakes National Park (50 km from each).

Robin is a kiwi (Crocodile-Dundee-type), Cathie an American (California, Pennsylvania, Massachusetts). We have one daughter of 17, 2 cats — 1 black, 1 colourpoint Himalayan and 2 angora rabbits.

We are keen card players — bridge, piquet, cribbage, pinochle, and more. Cathie collects antiques and books. Robin will provide a free farm tour by Landrover and a sheep-shearing demonstration (he does all his own). There is trout-fishing nearby, a heated swimming pool (open Sept.–May) and many walks.

Breakfast features waffles, pancakes, omelettes, muffins, fresh (or home-bottled) fruit. Dinner by arrangement, cut lunches available (on home-made bread).

Directions: *On the main highway between Blenheim and St Arnaud (Lake Rotoiti), 16 km past Wairau Valley village.*

Let the phone ring for a long time when telephoning.

Tariffs are constant for this year. However, some may have had to change slightly. Always check.

Our B&Bs are mostly private homes. Most do not accept credit cards.

Tophouse

Farmhouse
Address: Tophouse, Tophouse Road, RD2, Nelson
Name: Melody and Mike Nicholls
Telephone: (054) 36-848
Beds: 2 Double, 8 Single (5 bedrooms, guest bathrooms)
Tariff: Dinner, Bed and Breakfast — Double $84, Single $42, Children negotiable
Nearest Town: Blenheim 98 km, Murchison 57 km, Nelson 72 km, St Arnaud 8 km

We, Melody and Mike Nicholls, with our two young sons, invite you to share our unique home with its huge open fires, lovely setting and homely atmosphere.
Tophouse, a cob (mud) building, dating from the 1880's when it was a hotel, and reopened in 1989 as a Farm Guest House, has that 'good old days' feel about it.
Situated on 300 ha (730 acres) of picturesque high country farm running goats and cattle, with much native bush and an abundance of bird life, Tophouse is only 8 km from St Arnaud.
St Arnaud, gateway to Nelson Lakes National Park, is nestled on the shore of Lake Rotoiti, a popular holiday spot for its peace and beauty, bush walks, fishing etc and in the winter becomes a ski village serving the two local fields, Rainbow and Mt Robert.
A typical farmhouse dinner is included in the tariff and if the fire's going, which it usually is, 'real' toast for breakfast.
Directions: *Just off State Highway 63 between Blenheim and Murchison and 8 km from St Arnaud is Tophouse, that's us! The area took its name from the building. Look for the signpost. If travelling from Nelson, leave State Highway 6 at Belgrove and travel via Waiti Valley, Golden Downs Forest, Kikiwa, we're signposted from the main road and looking forward to your visit.*

Owen River, Nelson

Farmhouse
Address: 'Strathowen',
Owen River, Nelson
Name: Peter and Rankeilor Arnott
Telephone: (054) 39-075
Beds: 4 Single (2 bedrooms)
Tariff: B&B Double $60, Single $40, Children under 14 half price;
Dinner $15
Nearest Town: 18 km east of Murchison, 1½ hours from Nelson,
2 hours from Picton

We are a farming family of five with three teenage children attending boarding schools in Nelson.
Strathowen Farm is situated in a beautiful area in the Owen River valley, 1 km drive from the only highway to the west coast from Nelson and Blenheim.
Being surrounded by native reserves, rivers and lakes, we are ideally situated for those interested in the many activities and scenery that this beautiful area provides or, for the travel-weary, guests may like to relax in our attractive garden overlooking the Owen River.
We provide two comfortable bedrooms, good bathroom facilities and a separate sitting room.
We welcome visitors to join us in our daily activities on our hill country sheep farm. Fishermen are welcome to visit us and enjoy the excellent fishing in the many rivers of this area.
Directions: *1 km drive off main highway at Owen River. Signposted.*

Kenepuru Sound, Picton

Guest House
Address: St Omer House, Kenepuru Sound, RD2, Picton,
Marlborough
Name: Flora and George Robb
Telephone: (057) 34-086
Beds: 5 Double, 5 Single (16 bedrooms) (others with 3 or 4 bunks)
Tariff: $60.65 per person per day, all meals included;
Cottages $18–$22, $3 extra if linen and blankets supplied;
Campervans, tent sites $7–$12, $5 facility charge per person per day; Dinner $22, Lunch $12, Breakfast $8 (Continental $5.50);
Children under 2 no charge, Children under 12 half price
Nearest Town: Picton or Havelock, 2½ hours by road

A peaceful bay, a fifty-year-old, family-run guest house with plenty of historic interest is where my husband and I and two adult daughters welcome you. Our family are the fifth generation in the area.

146

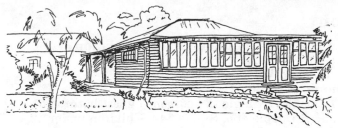

The Marlborough Sounds are a maze of waterways — you can cruise, yacht, canoe, row, dive, swim, fish, water ski or explore beaches and wrecks, climb bush-clad hills, tramp walkways, see farmland (sheep, cattle, deer, goats, rabbits), hunt deer and wild pigs, hire horses to ride. Nearby are mussel and salmon farms, bird sanctuaries, shag colonies and glowworm walks.

Our dining room has a BYO licence, we cater for all meals and tastes — venison, wild pork, shellfish, fish, fresh eggs, vegetables and fruit locally grown are on our menu.

The games room is large enough for dancing — has piano, table tennis, TV, etc. mini golf on lawn and tennis court.

Travel: *By car — part-metalled road, 2½ hours from Havelock. Fly float plane from Picton or Porirua or small plane from Wellington, 20 minutes. Watertaxi from Picton or Havelock.*

Picton

Self-Contained Accommodation
Address: Please phone
(preferably evenings)
Name: Geoff and Val Brannan
Telephone: (057) 37-177
Beds: 1 Double, 2 Single
(1 bedroom, 2 singles in living room, guest bathroom)
Tariff: B&B Double $35, Single $25, Children $10; Dinner $15 (3 course); Discounts for 3 nights or longer

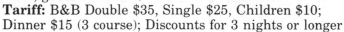

Welcome to our modern home with beautiful views over Picton's magnificent harbour and hills. We will provide breakfast, picnic lunches and dinner with prior notice or, if you prefer, our fully self-contained flat with own T.V. allows you to "do your own thing".

Our two daughters aged 12 and 15 and ourselves enjoy sailing, restoring and motoring vintage cars, travelling when time and finances allow, walking the lovely bush tracks available in this area and meeting other people.

We are about 15 minutes walk from the ferry terminal, railway station and town centre but can provide transport if requested.

147

Picton

Homestay + Self-Contained Accommodation
Address: PO Box 256, Picton
Name: Ron and Wendy Gabites
Telephone: (057) 36-491
Beds: 1 Double, 2 Single (2 bedrooms, guest bathroom)
Tariff: B&B Double $65, Single $40, Children under 12
half price; dinner $20

Picton is the main centre for the beautiful Marlborough Sounds, with its lovely bays and scenic views of water and bush-clad hills.
Our new home is situated by the sea in Waikawa Bay (three minutes from Picton). The property has an expansive view over the Bay and Queen Charlotte Sound where we can watch the inter-island ferries, pleasure yachts and launches.
A safe swimming beach, children's playground, boat launching ramp and general store are close by.
We have a fully self-contained and separate apartment downstairs which sleeps four with all facilities. It is very suitable for longer holidays.
Our family of four sons are all away from home and we now have time to pursue our own interests which include sailing, fishing, golfing, leathercraft, gardening and meeting people.
Relax for a few days with us in the beautiful Marlborough Sounds, enjoy sailing, sightseeing, bushwalking, fishing, picnics or a game of golf.
We are happy to meet and provide transport from buses, train or inter-island ferries.

Blenheim

Homestay
Address: Please phone
Telephone: (057) 89-562
Beds: 1 Double, 4 Single (3 bedrooms, guest bathroom)
Tariff: B&B Double $55, Single $35 (less 10% if prebooked
by night before); Dinner $15; Children half price
Nearest Town: Blenheim 3 km from town centre

Your hosts are a married couple with a grown up family offering a spacious, modern home in a quiet, southern suburb of Blenheim. We have one double and two twin bedrooms available — all beds with electric blankets. Guests have sole use of toilet/bathroom.
This landscaped property includes sundeck, pool, barbecue and off-road parking.
The host is an airline pilot with interests in all aspects of aviation from models to homebuilts and gliding — also builds miniature steam locomotives. The hostess loves cooking and will serve wine with meals. She

is also a spinner and woolcraft hobbyist. Both enjoy sharing travel experiences. We have a 1929 Model A Ford vintage car — soft top tourer — and offer guests the chance to ride and be photographed in it. Can also arrange sightseeing flights around Marlborough.

We can assure you of personal attention and a warm, friendly atmosphere, but should you require privacy that too will be respected. We are non-smokers but don't mind if you do. There are no household pets.

Nearby attractions include 2½ hour Wither Hills walk, Brayshaw Historical Park and Vintage Farm Museum, vineyards and winery trail, salt works, skifields, Nelson Lakes National Park, Marlborough Sounds Maritime Park, fishing, boating, etc.

Town centre 3 km. Suburban shopping 1 km.

Blenheim

Homestay
Address: 191 Redwood Street, Blenheim
Name: Alan and Mary Stevenson
Telephone: (057) 89-091
Beds: 1 Double, 5 Single, Cot available (3 bedrooms,
guest bathroom, room with double bed also has a single bed,
all beds have electric blankets)
Tariff: B&B Double $65, Single $40, Children $5; Dinner $17;
Campervans $5 per person

We have a lovely warm brick home on the rise at the southern end of Redwood Street (opp. Safe Street). We were farming at Seddon until our son's marriage (early 1984) and we are still very interested in everything pertaining to farming and community work.

As the house is built back from the street, ours is a very quiet, restful home.

We really enjoy meeting people from overseas. We have travelled a little and are members of the Marlborough Travel Club.

Guests may have dinner with us, or, if you prefer only bed and breakfast. We can provide the breakfast of your choice.

Guest area has its own bathroom with bath, separate shower and separate toilet. There is a small swimming pool and a pool table available. Ample off-street parking.

Directions: *Travel to railway crossing on Main Street (State Highway 1), turn between siding and main line into Redwood Street and travel approximately 2·7 km.*

B&B hosts do it because they enjoy meeting
people. It is a friendship business.

Blenheim

Homestay
Address: 722 Severne Street, Blenheim
Name: Charles and Pam Hamilton
Telephone: (057) 88-220
Beds: 2 Single (1 bedroom, guest bathroom)
Tariff: B&B $25 per person; Dinner $12; Campervans $15;
Children under 12 half price

Our home is situated on the town boundary of Blenheim and is built on an 8-acre block of land. We are fortunate to be able to combine the freedom of country living with the benefits of only a 20-minute walk to the Blenheim town centre.

We are a family of seven but during the working week and school term time our numbers drop to five. We range in age from an early teenager to our elderly grandmother so ours is a three-generation home. Consequently the house is large and fairly new.

The guest room has two single beds and you would have your own bathroom and a quiet upstairs lounge if you wished. TV viewing would be available with the family.

We can offer you dinner with our family if you wish or just Bed and Breakfast.

We provide a convenient stopping place either before or after you use the Cook Strait ferry.

Directions: *Take State Highway 6 from Blenheim to Nelson. Our street is the last on your left as you leave Blenheim.*

Blenheim

Farmhouse
Address: Maxwell Pass, Blenheim
Name: Jean and John Leslie
Telephone: (057) 81-941
Beds: 4 Single (3 bedrooms, guest bathroom)
Tariff: B&B Double $55, Single $30, Children half price; Dinner $15
Nearest Town: Blenheim 8 km

We live 8 km from Blenheim on a 1500 acre hill country property running sheep and cattle.
Our home is a modern two-storeyed house set in spacious grounds with a swimming pool and grass tennis court.
Guests have their own bathroom.
Now that our family have left home we enjoy spending time with guests. Marlborough is a major grape growing area with several wineries plus horticulture, agriculture and livestock farming from high country to the coast. Marlborough Sounds is nearby either by sea or road. Trout fishing is also close at hand and there is a golf course and hard tennis court in Blenheim.
Directions: *Please phone.*

Blenheim

Homestay
Address: Old Renwick Road, RD2, Blenheim
Name: Barbara Lancaster
Telephone: (057) 85-446
Beds: 1 Double, 2 Single (2 bedrooms)
Tariff: B&B Double $60, Single $35; Dinner $20; Campervans $20
Nearest Town: 8 km west Blenheim

Ashley and Barbara have recently sold their catering business and have semi-retired on the outskirts of Blenheim.
We have two acres of land for hobby farming and landscaping, gardening being one of our loves.
Our home is 11 years old with all modern facilities. We enjoy country style cooking and look forward to providing the meals of your choice.
An inground pool is just completed for summer swimming and outdoor barbecues.
We are five minutes from Blenheim Airport and right in the heart of the vineyards and orchards.
Directions: *Please phone.*

Ask your hosts for local information. They are
your own personal travel agent and guide.

Blenheim

Farmhouse
Address: Ugbrooke, Blenheim
Name: Hugh and Belinda Vavasour
Telephone: (057) 27-259
Beds: 1 Double, 4 Single (4 bedrooms, guest bathroom)
Tariff: Dinner, Bed and Breakfast — Double $135, Single $70,
Children under 10 no charge
Nearest Town: 26 km south of Blenheim

*Ugbrooke is a large, old family home, listed with the Historic Places
Trust. It is situated in the Awatere Valley, 26 km from Blenheim. The
farm is 850 acres mainly running sheep and some very friendly angora
goats.*
*We have two comfortable sitting rooms, billiard room and TV room.
The bedrooms have comfortable beds with electric blankets, bedside
lamps and electric heaters. Our guests have their own bathroom.*
*We have a tennis court, swimming pool and croquet lawn. Or you may
just want to relax on our long verandah and admire the view across
Cook Strait. The gardens are extensive and well-maintained.*
*Meals feature farm-killed lamb and the freshest fruit and vegetables
available according to the season. Freshly ground coffee is a specialty,
at Ugbrooke.*
*Ugbrooke is just 5 km from the main south road and so we are ideally
situated for those travelling on the ferries. We enjoy having guests and
sharing our lovely old family home with you. We are happy to show you
over our farm and take pride in telling you about the district.*
Directions: *Please phone.*

Ward

Farmhouse
Address: "Weld Cone",
Ward, Marlborough
Name: Charlie and Audrey Chambers
Telephone: (057) 20-816
Beds: 4 Single (2 bedrooms, top quality woolrest sleepers,
guest bathroom)

Tariff: B&B Double $60, Single $38; Dinner $16;
Campervans $15; Children half price; Morning and
afternoon teas free
Nearest Town: 45 km south from Blenheim on State Highway 1

*We are a family of four with two teenage children. We have a sheep and
cattle farm 1,550 acres near Ward beach which is a great place for "rock
hounds".*
*Our home is about 75 years old with lovely leadlight windows and
doors. It is a large gracious house with ample space for you to relax and
have a restful time if you so desire.*
*Our farm is part of the early "Flaxbourne Settlement". The Historic
Places Trust have an information noticeboard by our woolshed.*
*Our garden is very large, about 1 acre, with over 200 rhododendrons,
camellias and azaleas plus roses and lots of lovely trees and birds.*
Directions: *Our farm is 2.5 km from State Highway 1. Turn opposite
"Fuel Plus Tearooms" along Seddon Street over railway line and
bridge, "Weld Cone" on your right. We will pick up visitors who travel
by bus.*
Happy Holidays.

NZ phone numbers are being changed. Ring 018 for directory.

Kekerengu

Farmhouse
Address: Valley Road, Kekerengu
Telephone: (057) 20-606
Beds: 1 Double, 2 Single (2 bedroom, guest bathroom)
Tariff: B&B Double $55, Single $35
Nearest Town: Blenheim 67 km, Kaikoura 62 km

*We are a semi-retired couple originally from Scotland who enjoy
meeting people.*
*Our home is 1 km up the Kekerengu Valley Road behind the little
Church of St George.*
*We have a modern house with a double and twin bedroom available.
Guests have their own toilet/bathroom.*
*With our daughter we have a small farm of 100 acres — sheep and
cattle plus some goats, pigs, horses, dogs and hens. The animals are all
very friendly and would appreciate your company.*
*We have a swimming pool and the Kekerengu River flows through our
property — a good spot to find some interesting rocks or for the children
to enjoy a splash.*
*The property has an interesting history and some lovely, well-
preserved buildings remain (built in the 1860's) with mature trees
enhancing the peaceful surroundings.*
*Organically-grown vegetables, eggs and goat's milk are available if
required.*

Westland

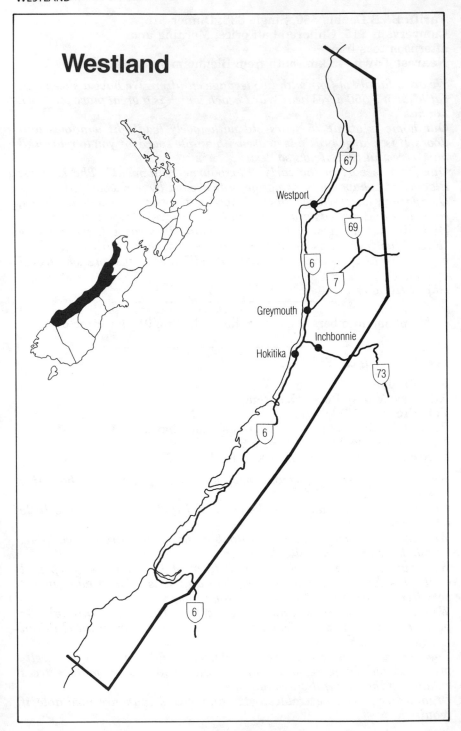

Westport

67

69

6

7

Greymouth

Inchbonnie

Hokitika

73

6

6

Greymouth

Guest House
Address: Golden Coast Guest House, 10 Smith Street, Greymouth
Name: Gladys Roche
Telephone: (027) 7839
Beds: 12 beds (5 bedrooms)
Tariff: B&B Double $55, Single $38; Children half price

Golden Coast Guest House is two minutes from town Railway Station and buses. It is built on a slight rise with lovely gardens and barbecue area. There is a TV lounge and tea and coffee making facilities. Laundry always available. There is also off-street parking. Electric blankets and heaters in all rooms.
Your comfort is our business.
Directions: *Main highway to South Road above Railway Station.*

Greymouth

Homestay
Address: "Aldwyn House", 48 Chapel Street, Greymouth
Name: Alun and Mary Owen
Telephone: (027) 6107
Beds: 4 Single (2 bedrooms)
Tariff: B&B Double $55, Single $33, Children half price

Aldwyn House is three minutes walk from the town centre in a quiet garden setting of two acres offering sea, river and town views.
The house was built in the 1920s and is a fine example of an imposing residence with fine woodwork and leadlight windows, whilst being a comfortable and friendly home.
We are ideally situated for travellers touring the west coast as Greymouth is central and a popular stopover.
We offer a courtesy car service to and from local travel centres and also provide off-street parking.

All telephone numbers in New Zealand are being changed during 1990 so the numbers listed may not be current. Ring 018 for directory assistance if you cannot contact your hosts.

New Zealand is known as the friendliest country in the world and our hosts will live up to that reputation.

Hokitika

Guest House
Address: 20 Hamilton Street, Hokitika
Name: Central Guest House — Joanna and Brent Williamson
Telephone: (0288) 58-232
Beds: 4 Double Rooms, 1 Single Room, 1 Triple Room, 1 Quad Room (ample bathroom and shower facilities)
Tariff: B&B Double $54, Single $34; Dinner $16; Full cooked breakfast available $5 extra per person

Our 1920s character home is centrally located in Hokitika. Hokitika is a pleasant, small town, once "the capital of the goldfields" and in recent years it has seen a resurgence in gold-mining activity.

The goldroom, greenstone factory, craft co-operative, museum, Tweed factory, three superb restaurants and banks are all within two minutes walk. Those who have a little more time may like to take a scenic drive around Lake Kaniere to the Hokitika Gorge, shanty-town — the authentic recreation of an 1880s goldrush town or the local glow-worm dell. For the more energetic Hokitika is surrounded by many walkways, gold panning, hunting, fishing, whitebaiting (in season) and rafting areas.

Both of us have travelled extensively and enjoy meeting others from around New Zealand and overseas.

We look forward to sharing the many wonderful features that made us choose Hokitika as our home.

We are only too happy to meet anyone arriving by bus or plane.

Hokitika is ½ hour from Shantytown, 1 hour from Punakaiki Blowholes, ½ hour from Greymouth, 5 hours from Picton, 4 hours from Christchurch, 6 hours from Wanaka, 7½ hours from Queenstown, 2 hours from the glaciers.

Directions: *Turn left at town clock and take first street to right.*

Phone numbers may have changed. Ring 018 for directory.

Inchbonnie

Self-Contained Accommodation
Address: Inchbonnie, Kumara RD1, Westland
Name: Russell and Jean Adams
Telephone: (027) 80-153
Beds: 1 Double, 4 Single (2 bedrooms in cottage)
Tariff: B&B Double $55, Single $35; Dinner by arrangement;
Campervans $20
Nearest Town: Inchbonnie is 80 km from Greymouth and Hokitika
and is easily accessible from Canterbury, especially via Arthurs Pass

*We offer a fully furnished cottage in a scenic rural retreat. Linen is
available. The cottage is on our property and we farm sheep, beef and
deer.*

*We are situated in the midst of some of the best trout fishing in the
South Island — Lake Brunner and Lake Poerua and rivers within 10
minutes travel.*

*Our homestead is set in a large established garden and guests are
welcome to join us. Jean has a special interest in woolcraft. Russell is
the farmer. Our two teenage children live in Greymouth during the
week. Craig is a very keen fisherman.*

Directions: *We are 10 km from Jacksons turnoff on
Inchbonnie–Mitchells Road. Please phone for details.*

The standard of accommodation in *The New
Zealand Bed and Breakfast Book* ranges from
homely to luxurious but you can always be sure
of superior hospitality.

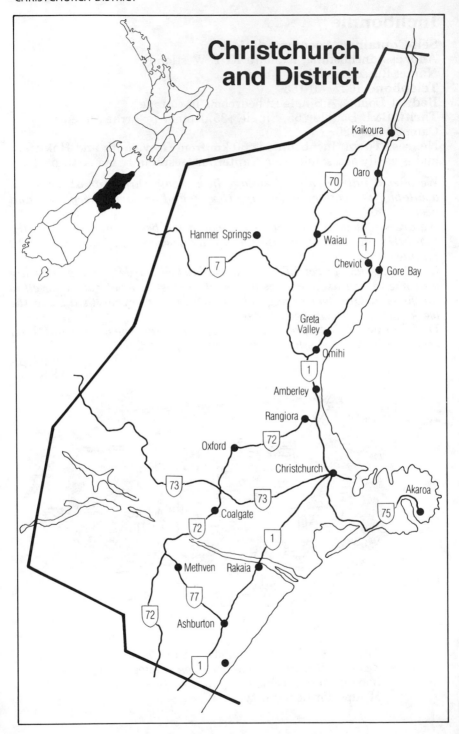

Christchurch and District

Kaikoura

Self-Contained Accommodation
Address: "Bayview",
296 Scarborough Street, Kaikoura
Name: Bob and Margaret Woodhill
Telephone: (0513) 5480. If no reply 5379
Beds: 2 Double, 2 Single (3 bedrooms)
Tariff: Double $40, Single $25; Dinner $15
Nearest Town: 130 km south of Blenheim, 183 km north
of Christchurch

We are a retired couple with four grown children and five grand-
children. Between us we have many interests including golf, lawn
bowls, woodwork, cake icing and stretch sewing. We are keen gar-
deners and grow tomatoes and cucumbers under glass. We also make
our own bread.
Our home on an acre of land is high on the Kaikoura Peninsula, about
3 km from the township, and we have a splendid view of the mountains
and sea. The accommodation attached to our home is a completely
self-contained unit with a large double, a small double and a twin
bedroom. We have a guest lounge, bathroom, laundry and kitchen
facilities for tea/coffee making. We offer both bed and breakfast and
evening meal with us.
We have our own swimming pool and other recreational activities in
the district include golfing, seaside and bush walks, beach swimming,
native bird watching, museum, Maori fortifications, aquarium, fishing,
wharves, seal colony, nature watch sea trips to view whales, dolphins,
seals and numerous sea birds, natural limestone caves and many more.
We offer transport for visitors travelling by train or bus.
Directions: *Scarborough Street, the access to the Peninsula, is off the*
main highway on the south side of the town.

Oaro, Kaikoura

Farmhouse
Address: Oaro, RD2, Kaikoura
Name: Kathleen and Peter King
Telephone: (0513) 5494
Beds: 2 Single (1 bedroom)
Tariff: B&B Double $55, Single $28, Children half price; Dinner $12
Nearest Town: 22 km south of Kaikoura

We are semi-retired living on 48 acres having sold our hill-country
property. Our three daughters all live away from home now. One is
married with three children.
This is a mild climate and we are experimenting in a small way with
citrus and subtropical fruits.

continued over

159

Oaro is close to the sea and we have a fine view north along the Kaikoura coast. A walk south along the coast is always popular.
We are happy for you to join us for dinner but if you prefer there is a restaurant 2 km north where they have takeaways as well as meals.
Directions: *We are 22 km south of Kaikoura on a side road just a short distance off the main north-south highway.*

Tell other travellers about your favourite homes.

Waiau

Farmhouse
Address: "Hillview", Waiau RD, North Canterbury
Name: Arthur and Margaret Pawsey
Telephone: (0515) 6044
Beds: 3 Single (2 bedrooms)
Tariff: B&B Double $55, Single $35, Children half price; Dinner $15
Nearest Town: 130 km north of Christchurch, 40 km from Hanmer Springs, 80 km south of Kaikoura.

We have four children working away from home. We live on a 690 hectare sheep and cattle hill country farm with spectacular views of the Waiau River which lends itself to fishing and recreation. The farm is situated very handy to the inland Kaikoura road, so we feel it is an ideal stopping place for people travelling north, south or west. An added attraction is the Hanmer resort which is approximately 40 km away.
We would be very happy to involve our guests in farm activities if they so desire. Guests may have dinner with us or if you prefer only bed and breakfast.
Our house is approximately 30 years old with a large living area overlooking a terrace and swimming pool in a well-planted garden setting of silver birches and gums.
Directions: *Please phone.*

Gore Bay, Cheviot

Homestay
Address: 'Saltburn', Gore Bay, Cheviot RD3, Canterbury
Name: Dorothy and Les Jefferson
Telephone: (05138) 686
Beds: 1 Double, 2 Single (2 bedrooms, electric blankets)
Tariff: B&B Double $35, Single $20, Children half price;
Dinner by arrangement $12
Nearest Town: Cheviot 9 km

Originally from England, my husband and I have retired to the house we have built overlooking the bay in this attractive area.
We have travelled extensively, both in New Zealand and overseas, and thoroughly enjoy meeting people from other countries.
At home we are keen gardeners and appreciate the mild climate we experience here.
We also enjoy tramping and there are many walking tracks, delightful views and a safe surfing and swimming beach.
Native birds abound and a seal colony lies a short walk along the coast to the north, while a walkway follows the coastline southward through natural bush to the Hurunui River mouth, an excellent fishing spot.
Cheviot, the nearest shopping area is 1½ hours drive north of Christchurch on State Highway One and 1¼ hours drive south from Kaikoura.

Blythe Valley, Cheviot

Homestay
Address: RD3, Cheviot
Name: Pamela and Paul Lagan
Telephone: (05138) 315
Beds: 1 Single, 1 Set Bunks (1 bedroom)
Tariff: B&B Double $30, Single $20, Children half price
(home-baked morning, afternoon tea and supper included);
Dinner $15; Campervans $20
Nearest Town: Cheviot 25 km, Christchurch 100 km

I would like to welcome you to our comfortable home set on 1⅓ acres in the picturesque Blythe Valley and share the peace, tranquility and beautiful scenery with you.
The guest room is spacious with a single bed, two bunks, electric blankets, heater and wonderful views of the valley, sea, trees and garden. A door opens on to a small terrace. The guest lounge has a Kent log fire and television. French doors open on to a large terrace where you can dine or relax while the bellbirds and fantails entertain you.

continued over

161

We are keen gardeners, breed Cavalier King Charles spaniels and have a backyard menagerie of fur, feather and fin.
There are many interesting walks, surfcasting at Nape Nape, fishing in the Hurunui River, a walkway at Port Robinson and swimming at Gore Bay. Packed lunches available (at an additional charge) with tea or coffee in your flask.
Booking is essential. We serve tasty vegetarian whole food cuisine. Homebaked morning and afternoon tea included in the tariff.
Directions: *We are near the Nape Nape scenic reserve, Hurunui river mouth and Gore Bay. Please phone for directions.*

Greta Valley

Farmhouse
Address: "Gorrie Downs", Greta Valley, RD, North Canterbury
Name: Janette and Rod McKenzie
Telephone: (050 443) 475
Beds: 1 Double, 3 Single (2 bedrooms, guest bathroom)
Tariff: B&B Double $55, Single $35, Children half price;
Dinner by arrangement
Nearest Town: Cheviot ½ hr north, Amberley ½ hr south,
Christchurch 1 hr south, Picton 3½ hrs

Our home is a very comfortable 40-year-old house, with established garden and trees, situated in a peaceful valley with magnificent views of the countryside.
The guest wing has a separate entrance, one double bed and one single bed, with own bathroom. The furnishings are designed with your comfort in mind and good heating is available in the winter. We can assure you of a most comfortable stay. A second twin room is available if needed, in our house.
We have both travelled extensively and enjoy meeting people from other countries.
We are involved in numerous business activities which we run from our 1000 acre farm. These include the farming of Friesian bulls, raising black and coloured sheep for handcraft wool and export, and international consultancy services. Between us we are involved in golf, spinning, gardening and tennis.
We offer delicious home-cooked meals and a cooked breakfast if required.
We are ideally situated for those travelling the Picton–Christchurch route, and we are only five minutes off the highway. Likewise we are five minutes from a quiet, safe swimming beach.
We look forward to you breaking the journey with us.
Directions: *Please phone or write for directions and reservations.*

If you find something missing that you are
accustomed to, simply ask you hosts for it.

162

Greta Valley, Waikari

Farmhouse
Address: Foxdown Greta Valley.
Postal: Amberley, RD3
Name: Alison and Peter Fox
Telephone: (0504 43) 704
Beds: 2 Double (1 queen), 3 Single (3 bedrooms, guest bathroom)
Tariff: B&B Double $60, Single $35; Dinner $18
Nearest Town: Farm is situated 1¼ hours drive north of Christchurch (90 km) on a valley road between Highways 1 and 7, 16 km from Greta Valley and 19 km from Waikari. 4 hours drive from Picton.

Foxdown is a farm of 1400 hectares (3500 acres) carrying 5500 sheep and 250 cattle in the rolling to steep North Canterbury hills. It has been in the Fox family for over 110 years.
Our home is a large, modern, two-storeyed homestead with own facilities for guests. If you wish you will be able to join in farm activities, be taken for a tour of the farm or relax, whichever you wish. Foxdown has a swimming pool, trampoline, tennis court, pool table for guests' use. Many walks are within easy distance of homestead.
In the area are fishing, golf, bowls, squash, walkway, beach (33·5 km), Hamner Springs Hot Pools (84 km) and Skiing (2 hours).
Our farm is run by Peter and son Andrew with some casual help. Our interests are contract bridge, local history, travel and meeting overseas people and fellow New Zealanders, farm forestry and wool.
Directions: *End of Foxdown Road which is off Waikari–Greta Valley Road.*

Omihi Valley

Homestay
Address: 'Cannobie-Lee', RD3, Amberley, North Canterbury
Name: Mark and Rosey Savill
Telephone: (0504) 45-868
Beds: 2 Double, 1 Single
Tariff: B&B Double $90, Single $70, Children under 10
no charge; Dinner $20

Cannobie-Lee is a picturesque old family home which was built in 1912 and is situated in the Omihi valley. It has extensive lawns and an old English garden full of 'old garden roses', shrubs and perennials, a swimming pool and a croquet lawn.
We are a family of five with two school-age children and our oldest daughter is at University. We all enjoy meeting people and our home is comfortable and a great place to relax at your leisure.
Our farm is 350 acres and is primarily, sheep, cash cropping and bull beef.

continued over

We are in close proximity to Hanmer Springs (1 hour), a beautiful Alpine village with hot springs, horse trekking, golf and skiing facilities.

At Cannobie-Lee we aim to please and a warm welcome awaits your arrival.

Directions: *We are conveniently situated on State Highway 1, 12 km south of Greta Valley township or 22 km north of Amberley (70 km to Christchurch).*

Amberley

Guest House
Address: RD1, Amberley
Name: Harleston Guest House
Telephone: (050229) 806
Beds: 5 Double, 1 Single (6 bedrooms, own bathrooms)
Tariff: B&B Double $74, Single $37; Dinner $22; Children half price, under 5 free; Campervans $20 per vehicle

We are very proud of the history associated with our 127-year-old farmhouse which is a North Canterbury landmark protected by the NZ Historic Places Trust.

Harleston is ideally situated for travellers wishing to use the inter-island ferries. Going north you can enjoy a half-hour start on city dwellers and for southbound travellers, instead of wearily trying to find accommodation in a strange city late in the day, you can stay with us and after a hearty breakfast drive to Christchurch with the advantages a new day brings.

Our home is welcoming, comfortably unpretentious and has a great deal of character.

Guests can enjoy acclaimed cuisine, the nearby (usually deserted) beach or perhaps visit a local vineyard, catch a fish, explore the varying countryside or simply relax in our garden.

Your hosts are Liz and Les and as Liz has worked in international tourism until recently she completely understands the needs of her guests and enjoys caring for them. Les will happily discuss horses and the races they never won, farming in general and after lengthy encouragement may even sing a song!

Directions: *State Highway 1, 40 km north of Christchurch, 10 km south of Amberley, sign at gate.*

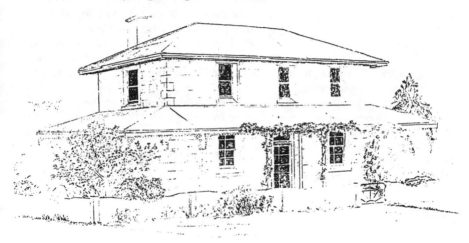

Ashley, Rangiora

Farmhouse
Address: "Woolly Meadows Farmyard", Cones Road, Ashley, Rangiora RD2
Name: John and Lynda van Beek
Telephone: (0502) 35-387
Beds: 1 Double, 3 Single (3 bedrooms)
Tariff: Double $55, Single $35; Dinner $15; Campervans (parking, own toilets) $20

Our home is new on our 40-acre farm 5 km from Rangiora, 25 minutes from Christchurch, 20 minutes to Christchurch International Airport, 5 km from Highway 72 and 12 km from Highway 1.

John was born in Holland and travelled to New Zealand with his family in the 1950s.

continued over

165

Woolly Meadows
Farmyard

Farm life takes up most of our time and recently we have developed part of our farm to cater for visitors such as senior citizens, school groups, etc. We have built a complex where we cater for afternoon teas, shearing and cow milking demonstrations, and most other farm activities. We always have pet sheep here which love to be fed, as well as most farm animals. We milk our cow each day, separate the milk with an antique separator and make our own butter and ice cream.

Near our farm we have a cheese factory, meadery, steam museum, specialist handmade chocolate shop, orchards, golf courses, beaches, fishing, horse trekking, winery, forest walks or you may wish to relax in our private garden setting.

Dinner is always available, leave a call back number on our answer-phone if necessary. We can meet you in Rangiora if you travel by bus from Christchurch and we look forward to meeting you — strangers are only friends you have not met.

Directions: *Take the road to Loburn from Rangiora and look for our "Woolly Meadows Farmyard" sign, 2 km over the Ashley River Bridge.*

Oxford

Homestay + Self-Contained Accommodation
Address: 37 High Street, Oxford
Name: Norton and Helen Dunn
Telephone: (0502) 24-167
Beds: 4 Single (2 bedrooms); Self-contained unit 2 single beds,
(1 bedroom, guest shower, toilet, sitting room, tea-making facilities,
verandah entrance)
Tariff: B&B Double $44, Single $22
Nearest Town: Walking distance to the shops, 55 km
from Christchurch

Our house is 60 years old and has a spacious garden — warm and sunny.
We are a contented married couple with a family of three grown-up sons. We retired from Dunedin to live in Oxford — a charming, restful town and a friendly community. Oxford offers scenic walks, horse treks, homecrafts, pottery, herbs, basket making and home spun hand-knitted garments, bowls, tennis, squash, restaurant, golf and bridge club handy.
Directions: *High Street is off the Main Road — left — sign outside the gate.*

Christchurch

Bed and Breakfast Inn
Address: Rockvilla Mansion, 24 Marriner Street, Christchurch 8
Name: Robin and Jenny Digby
Telephone: (03) 265-634
Beds: Various (5 bedrooms)
Tariff: B&B (cooked breakfast) Double $70, Single $58,
Suites $45 per person

*We are a family of four (two teenagers) living in Christchurch's super
suburb (Sumner — by the sea), which has all the water sports available.
Our home is quite unique constructed of volcanic rock. It is eighty-one
years old and has a very interesting history. The mansion has been
recently restored throughout so while retaining the atmosphere of
yesteryear, it is most comfortable for today's traveller.*

*Our suites have direct access to outdoor balconies, radio, television and
also sitting facilities, and are rather larger than the standard rooms.
Also they are located on the north wing of the house which favours
evening sun.*

*Our breakfasts are superb and are served in a dining room that is
unforgettable.*

*So bring along your sense of fun (also sense of humour), this is one
place you'll come back to again and again.*

Directions: *Marriner Street is the main street in Sumner. If you have
difficulty finding us, ask a local villager, they all know us.*

Please let the hosts know if you have to cancel.
They will have spent time preparing for you.

Bryndwr, Christchurch

Homestay
Address: "Allisford", 1/61 Aorangi Road, Bryndwr, Christchurch
Telephone: (03) 517-742
Beds: 2 Single (1 bedroom)
Tariff: B&B Double $55, Single $35; Dinner $12
Nearest Town: 5 km from Christchurch central post office

We have an attractive single-storey flat with a large twin bedroom available for guests, also a comfortable lounge opening onto a private garden. There is also off-street parking.
The nearest No. 17B Wairakei Rd bus stop is only three minutes walk away and this bus passes the Arts Centre, the Museum, the Botanical Gardens and the McDougall Art Gallery on the way into the city centre. Allisford is situated about halfway between the Airport and the city centre and is also easily reached from north, south and west main highways.
You may have the breakfast of your choice and are welcome to have dinner by arrangement.
Directions: *Please phone.*

NZ phone numbers are being changed.

Ring 018 for directory.

Christchurch City

Private Hotel
Address: 52 Armagh Street, Christchurch
Name: "Windsor" Private Hotel
Telephone: (03) 662-707, 661-503
Beds: 40 bedrooms
Tariff: B&B Double $67.50, Single $46, Children under 12 $15; (Quote this book for 10% discount)

Our charming colonial style home overlooks Cranmer Square and is centrally located to the city centre, Botanical Gardens, Art Centre and theatres.
We provide nicely furnished rooms all individually heated, also 24-hour tea and coffee making facilities, laundry, carpark.
Each evening at 9 pm we serve tea and biscuits in our spacious TV lounge.
All rates include a delicious full menu breakfast.

Christchurch

Homestay
Address: 12 Dublin Street, Christchurch
Name: Jan and Mike Cann
Telephone: (03) 661-861
Beds: 4 Single (2 bedrooms)
Tariff: B&B Double $50, Single $25

We have a large old comfortable family home built at the turn of the century. It is situated in the city, 100 m from the Avon River and Hagley Park, and only minutes walk from the city centre, Arts centre, city mall, Botanical Gardens, major hotels, restaurants, night clubs and top class vegetarian restaurant.
We are on all main bus routes including to Airport and beach. Car hire is available around the corner, and a few minutes walk takes you to an up-market shopping centre – Merivale.
In fact we have everything at our doorstep.

Christchurch City

Homestay
Address: 68 Fisher Avenue, Christchurch 2
Name: Peter Brine and Lynne Haye
Telephone: (03) 329-584
Beds: 1 Double, 3 Single (2 bedrooms, guest bathroom)
Tariff: B&B Double $50, Single $25

We are a professional couple with an interest in meeting overseas visitors. We have a lovely old home in a quiet tree-lined street handy to downtown.
Bedrooms are spacious and guests have use of their own toilet and shower. Cooking facilities can be provided by arrangement if required. We share our home with a German Shepherd dog.
We ask guests not to smoke inside the house and to phone for reservations.

Always telephone ahead to enquire about a
B&B. It is a nuisance for you if you simply
arrive to find someone is already staying there.
And besides, hosts need a little time to
prepare.

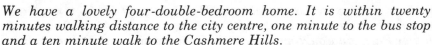

Christchurch City

Homestay
Address: 7 Selwyn Street, Christchurch 2
Name: Jaap and Riet van Hamelsveld
Telephone: (03) 328-141
Beds: 1 Single room, 1 Twin room
Tariff: B&B $18 per person

We have a lovely four-double-bedroom home. It is within twenty minutes walking distance to the city centre, one minute to the bus stop and a ten minute walk to the Cashmere Hills.
Christchurch has much to offer visitors and public transport is handy. We have Saturday (8.30 am–9 pm) shopping nearby in New Brighton, with lovely beaches a stone's throw away. There are many lovely walkways on our hills.
Daily departures by air and road to the southern lakes and alps.
Our five children have grown up so there is just my husband and me to warmly welcome you.
Off-street parking available.
Directions: *Please phone.*

Christchurch

Homestay
Address: 214 Main Road,
Moncks Bay, Christchurch 8
Name: Joan and Barrie Shakes
Telephone: (03) 843-147
Beds: 1 Double, 2 Single (2 bedrooms)
Tariff: B&B Double $55, Single $35;
Dinner $12; Children under 13 half price

We have a fifty-year-old two-storey house on the flat with lovely unimpeded sea views from our upstairs guest room. We enjoy welcoming guests to our home and sharing our interests of travel and music.
Some 2 km west of our home is located Ferrymead Historic Park — home of vintage trams, locomotives, historic houses, etc. Barrie helps to restore the trams there and is one of the drivers at the Park.
The attractive village of Sumner is about one kilometre away and over the hills at the back of our house is situated the picturesque port of Lyttelton, gateway to beautiful scenic drives.

Sumner can boast three of the best restaurants in Christchurch, but if you wish you may have dinner with us. Breakfast is of your choice.
Directions: *If travelling by coach, board a number 3K in the Square and alight first stop after Redcliffs Village. If travelling by car take the route of Sumner and our home is on the main road directly after Redcliffs village.*

New Brighton, Christchurch

Homestay
Address: 22 Pine Avenue,
South New Brighton,
Christchurch 7
Name: Isobel Mitchell
Telephone: (03) 883-439 or 884-811 (please phone anytime)
Beds: 1 Double, 2 Single (2 bedrooms, guest bathroom)
Tariff: Accommodation only $22 per person, Children up
to 12 $15; Dinner with wine $22, Breakfast from $2 to $10
(menu supplied in your room); Campervans $8 per person, Children $4

Come to Brighton by the sea. We have a lovely sandy beach, also estuary walks, local shops, bus stops only 200 metres away.
My home is situated in a quiet street with lots of private, off-street parking. I am four minutes drive from New Brighton shops, restaurants, 10 km to Cathedral Square, 20 km to Christchurch International Airport.
You are assured of comfortable and smoke-free surroundings. Choice of double or twin rooms. Separate bathroom for guests. You are welcome to use full laundry and drying facilities. Afternoon tea and light supper provided at no extra cost, baking is my speciality. Dinner by arrangement.
Campervans are very welcome. There are two power points, with toilet, hot and cold water, washing can be done in the laundry and the bathroom is for your use.
Directions: *Travel in an easterly direction from Cathedral Square to New Brighton shopping centre. Turn south 1½ km to Jervois Street and then turn into north end of Pine Avenue to number 22.*

Many homes have facilities for campervans.
The ideal camping spot with electricity,
bathroom, laundry and friendly hospitality. Tell
campervanners about this when you see them.

171

Akaroa

Homestay
Address: Please phone
Name: Gwen and Murray Manhire
Telephone: (0514) 7127
Beds: 2 Single (1 bedroom, guest bathroom)
Tariff: B&B Double $55, Single $35; Dinner $15
Nearest Town: Akaroa

Our home stands in the sunshine in an acre of bush and well-established garden, just about two minutes walk from the beach on the shore of the incomparable Akaroa harbour. The view is magnificent. The sea and shoreline are everchanging in colour, always lovely. Birdlife and birdsong are ever-present — wood pigeons, fantails and bellbirds as well as many seabirds nearby. We offer tranquility and peace.

We are recently retired with an adult family. Truly rural, we enjoy sharing the country life. We love our garden and have home-grown vegetables all the year round as well as our own honey and fresh eggs from our free range chooks.

I love cooking and if you choose I will prepare dinner for you, as well as the breakfast of your choice.

Our home is modern colonial and our guest accommodation consists of a twin-bedded room and adjacent private bathroom. We hope guests will feel at home and make tea or coffee when they choose.

Akaroa township is less than five minutes away — an excellent variety of craftshops, activities and our well-known herb farm and boat and fishing trips offer a wonderful holiday.

We will help with transport where necessary.

Can't contact your host? Ring 018 for directory assistance.

Akaroa

Farm Cottage
Address: Tree Crop Farm, Grehan Valley, Akaroa
Postal: PO Box 9, Akaroa
Name: Lynne Alexander
Telephone: (0514) 7158 (early morning or evenings)
Beds: 1 Double (1 bedroom)
Tariff: B&B $30 per person, Children half price; Dinner $15;
Campervans $15 (2 persons, one site only)
Nearest Town: Akaroa 2 km, Christchurch 80 km

Tree Crop Farm is a 20 hectare hillside property with a 100-year-old sod cottage tucked beneath giant walnut trees and beside a stream in a bird-filled valley above the small fishing village of Akaroa.

172

The accommodation is a rustic but newly added sunny, semi-detached double room with French doors onto a brick courtyard and guest carpark. Shared shower, bath and toilet facilities are also separate from the house.

The property is being developed from a small dairy farm into organic fruit and vegetable gardens with 'pick your own' dried flowers, tree crops such as hazelnuts, chestnuts, walnuts and also grazing for horses and sheep.

A trekking venture also operates from Tree Crop Farm taking experienced riders on day or overnight horseback trips over stock routes and farm tracks to outlying sheep stations on the coast which also offer dinner, bed and breakfast.

Specialities of the house include home brewed beer, porridge, ice cream, vast green salads, local fresh fish and mussels.

An easy 15 minute walk down the valley to Akaroa where there is a range of restaurants, cafes and three hotels.

Coalgate

Homestay
Address: 'Gowan Lea', Whitecliffs Road, Coalgate RD, Canterbury
Name: Diana and David Bates
Telephone: (051667) 823
Beds: 4 Single (2 bedrooms, guest bathroom)
Tariff: B&B Double $55, Single $30, Children half price; Dinner $15
Nearest Town: Darfield 20 km, Christchurch 65 km

Gowan Lea is a hill country farm with a spacious homestead set in a large garden with a backdrop of a native beech reserve.

Our family is now independent and away from home. We welcome you to stay and share what we enjoy.

There are two guest rooms with two single beds each with sole use of bathroom facilities.

You are welcome to join us for dinner by prior arrangement.

Directions: *An hour's drive from Christchurch and 10 km from Glentunnel off Highway 72 at the end of Whitecliffs road you will find us.*

Methven

Homestay
Address: Northfield, Dolma Street, Methven
Name: Roger and Jane Goldsbrough
Telephone: (053) 28-622
Beds: 2 Double, 2 Single, Cot (2 bedrooms)
Tariff: B&B Double $75, Single $40, Children under 12 half price;
Dinner on request $20 (all plus GST)
Nearest Town: Methven

*We are a family of six with four school-age children and a variety of
pets. We have a large family home built in 1914 which we have recently
renovated to retain its full character. It is surrounded by spacious
lawns and trees and is adjacent to a nursery garden.*
*We have two guest rooms both of which can be family rooms and we can
offer a taste of country living. We also have a swimming pool, grass
tennis court and trampoline.*
*We are within very easy reach of skiing at Mt Hutt, fishing, hunting,
golfing, jetboat safaris, river rafting and bush walks or you can just
enjoy the country air and spend a few relaxing days away from it all.*
*We are interested in wholefoods and herbs and Roger enjoys making
handcrafted furniture and restoring antiques. Jane comes from
England and we have travelled overseas as a family and enjoy meeting
fellow travellers.*
Directions: *Take the main south road from Christchurch. Once over
the Rakaia bridge take the sixth turning on the right (approximately
1 km after bridge), follow the road to Methven and Mount Somers for
approximately 32 km, turn left into Dolma Street, we are the third
house on the left.*

Ashburton

Farmhouse
Address: "Wescott",
Racecourse Road, Ashburton
Name: Maralyn Smith
Telephone: (053) 88-085
Beds: 4 Single (2 bedrooms, guest bathroom)
Tariff: B&B $25 per person, Children half price;
Dinner by arrangement $12; Campervans $15
Nearest Town: Ashburton 3 km, Christchurch 80 km

*I have an attractive home, swimming pool and large garden on 7 acres
of land in N.W. area of Ashburton, very handy to shops and facilities. It
is less than 1 hour's journey from Christchurch airport and 20 minutes
journey to Methven township which is near the Mt Hutt skifield. Also*

the ski-bus from Ashburton passes our gate and arrangements can be made for it to stop.

The area offers good fishing, jet-boat rides, hunting, railway museum, golf courses, etc.

I have a large guest room which contains two single beds plus a divan, but could also offer another room with two single beds if necessary arrangements are made. There is plenty of room for campervans which would be very welcome.

There would always be a warm, friendly welcome to guests and dinner can be supplied as an extra if required.

I also own a labrador dog and a cat and have several horses on my land which is situated approximately one mile past Hotel Ashburton on Racecourse Road.

Ashburton

Farmhouse
Address: 'Willowbank', RD1, Ashburton
Name: Shona Thomas
Telephone: (053) 84-195
Beds: 4 Single (2 bedrooms, guest bathroom)
Tariff: B&B $25 per person, Children half price; Dinner $12
Nearest Town: Ashburton approx. 2 km

We are a family of five — three boys, one married and living at the top of the farm, two other sons at home.

We live on a 535 acre farm and have sheep, cattle and cropping.

Because we live so close to Ashburton all the usual amenities are available. Lovely indoor swimming pool, tennis courts and golf course only 5–10 minutes away. On the farm we have our own swimming pool in summer and canoeing on our pond.

My garden is my chief interest and the pond with its golffish and white swans provide interest. The farm is on the bank of the Ashburton River and fishing is available. Some good walks are available, an historic village is five minutes away.

Directions: *Please phone for directions.*

As distances in New Zealand are not great
check out the maps of the neighbouring
provinces for other B&Bs nearby.

175

Ashburton

Homestay
Address: Eiffelton, RD3, Ashburton
Name: Anne and Colin Fleming
Telephone: (053) 37-017
Beds: 2 Single (1 bedroom, 3 extra beds suitable
for children available in another bedroom)
Tariff: B&B Double $50, Single $30, Children $7; Dinner $15
Nearest Town: 20 km south of Ashburton

*The Fleming family farm a large intensive cropping unit plus some
stock along the banks of the manmade Hinds River which is pleasant
and popular for picnics, swimming and trout fishing. We are keen to
welcome and entertain visitors.*
*Our modernised brick home is attractively set in a large garden with
swimming pool and grass tennis court.*
Guests are welcome to join in farming activities.
*Mt Hutt skifield is within easy distance, 12 km to salmon fishing on the
Rangitata.*
Ashburton, a well-appointed rural town (pop. 15,000) is 20 km north.
Directions: *Turn off State Highway 1 at Hinds (12 km south of Ash-
burton), travel east 8 km, turn left on to Poplar Road, 2 km along this
road (all sealed), beside the river bridge is our home and farm.*

Ashburton

Farmhouse
Address: 'Noumai', No 3 RD, Ashburton
Name: Norman and Anne McConnell
Telephone: (053) 37-296
Beds: 4 Single (2 bedrooms)
Tariff: B&B Double $50, Single $25, Children half price;
Dinner $12
Nearest Town: 30 km south of Ashburton, 8 km south of Hinds

*We live on an irrigated sheep farm. We have an adult family of three —
a daughter married and two sons working and travelling overseas at
present.*
*Our home is an older house surrounded by a large garden with
spacious bedrooms and generous living areas. There are two guest
rooms with twin beds and nearby shower and bathroom.*
*We are 12 km north of the turnoff to Mt Cook and Southern Lakes via
Geraldine. There is a salmon and trout river nearby and we are a
half-hour drive from Peel Forest native bush.*
Family activities include golf and squash and other outdoor activities.
Directions: *Mailbox on Highway 1. Turn over railway line and into
driveway.*

Send us a comment form to tell us about your
B&B vacation. Forms are in this book and are
also obtainable from hosts.

All telephone numbers in New Zealand are being changed during
1990 so the numbers listed may not be current. Ring 018 for directory
assistance if you cannot contact your hosts.

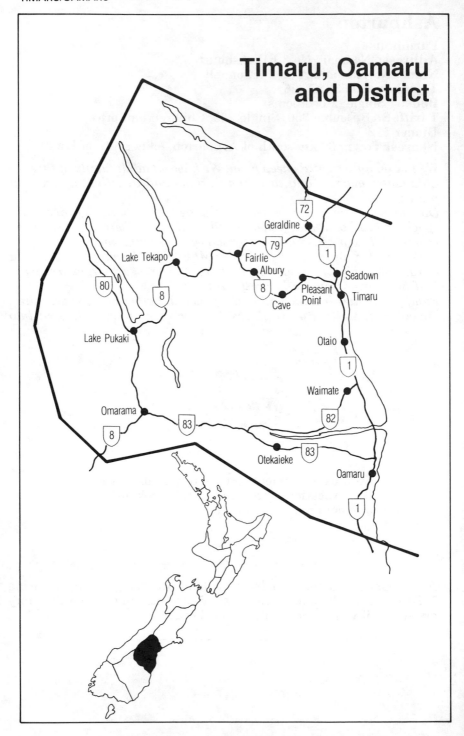

Timaru, Oamaru and District

Geraldine, South Canterbury

Homestay
Address: "Wharepuke Bed and Breakfast", Pye Road,
The Downs, RD21, Geraldine
Name: Joan and Peter Larsen
Telephone: (056) 38-982
Beds: 4 Single (2 bedrooms)
Tariff: B&B Double $55, Single $30; Dinner $15
Geraldine ½ km

The name "Wharepuke" means house on the hill in Maori, and our home is situated in an attractive 1¼ acre garden setting with magnificent views of mountain and countryside, and adjacent to Talbot Forest Reserve with its numerous bush walks.

We are a middle-aged couple, semi-retired who enjoy the opportunity of meeting visitors to New Zealand and promise you relaxing, comfortable hospitality.

Our spacious old home built about the turn of the century has been renovated to modern standards, with all the atmosphere of the past being retained.
A breakfast of your choice is served at your requested time and an evening meal is available by arrangement if required.
The Geraldine area is very picturesque and day trips to the Gorges and Peel Forest Scenic Reserve 15 km away make a day to remember.
Directions: *At roundabout in main street by Mobil garage turn into Pine Street, left into Jollie Street, right up hill (Totara Street) which runs onto Pye Road. "Wharepuke" is second on left.*

Fairlie

Homestay + Self-Contained Accommodation
Address: "Shinness Lodge", Kimbell, Fairlie
Name: Noreen Gallagher
Telephone: (05656) 8470
Beds: 1 Double, 1 Single (1 bedroom); 4 self-contained units
Tariff: B&B Double $55, Single $35, Children half price;
Campervans $15; Self-contained units for four people ($10 each)
Nearest Town: Fairlie 8 km, Timaru 75 km *continued over*

179

I love meeting people and having them stay in my home. I also enjoy cooking meals and presenting and serving them attractively.
Gardening, art and crafts and music keep me busy.
For skiing holidays Fox Peak is 17 miles from here and Mt Dobson access road just 3 km past my home (the Mt Dobson skifield bus passes at 9.15 and returns at 4.30 pm daily).
I have a 10 acre property with sheep and cows, two goats, a corgi and fowls, stream and river to fish. Our estate farm, managed by my two sons is 1 km away and they enjoy showing people all farm activities and can organise night hare shoots.
Fairlie has a country and western carnival for ten days over Christmas and New Year and Fairlie Easter Show is renowned.
I would be happy to meet guests in my car at Fairlie or at Timaru airport.
Directions: *Please ring.*

Lake Tekapo

Homestay + Self-Contained Accommodation
Address: The Chalet, Pioneer Drive, Lake Tekapo
Name: Zita and Walter Speck
Telephone: (05056) 774
Beds: 3 Double, 3 Single, 4 Bunkbeds, 2 Self-Contained Flats
(4 bedroom flat sleeps max 10, flatette sleeps max 3)
Tariff: B&B Double $68, Single $37; Accommodation only Double $56, Single $30, Additional Person $14
Nearest Town: 100 km northwest of Timaru, 230 km southwest of Christchurch; 250 km northeast of Queenstown

Lake Tekapo is a delightful lakeside resort nestled amongst some of New Zealand's most beautiful mountain scenery. It is well-known for the colour of the lake and the Church of the Good Shepherd. It is an ideal stopover place between Christchurch and Queenstown. This region is a great place for people who like the outdoors — walking, tramping, riding, golf, watersports, fishing and hunting are the main summer activities. During the winter months alpine and crosscountry skiing, skitouring and iceskating attract many holidaymakers. Tekapo is also a base for scenic flights over the magnificent Southern Alps. The scenic splendour in the MacKenzie and the sunsets provide plenty of impressions for painters and keen photographers.
We are a family with two little boys; wir sprechen deutsch, nous parlons français.
Our home is a two-storey building along the lakeshore and close to the famous church. Our guests can stay in a self-contained flatette (sleeps 3) or the bigger self-contained flat (sleeps 10). There is a barbecue area for our guests.

Fishing gear can be hired. It is possible to take our guests for fishing or hunting trips by previous arrangement.
Our aim is to make your stay in Tekapo a memorable and enjoyable part of your holiday.
Directions: *From the bus stop in Lake Tekapo (at the petrol station near the Post Office), you follow the main road direction Timaru, pass the bridge and turn left into Pioneer Drive, down to the church and the sheepdog monument. You will find our house 100 metres from the monument away on the right hand side. Distance from the Post Office to the house is approximately 700 metres.*

Lake Pukaki

Farmhouse
Address: 'Rhoborough Downs', Lake Pukaki, P.B. Fairlie
Name: Roberta and Logan Preston
Telephone: (05620) 509
Beds: 1 Double, 2 Single (2 bedrooms)
Tariff: Dinner, Bed and Breakfast Double $100, Single $50
Nearest Town: Twizel 10 minute drive

Our property of 18,000 acres which carries merino sheep in the MacKenzie country has been in the family since 1919.
We have a family of three grown children occasionally at home.
We are approximately halfway between Christchurch and Queenstown. It is a one hour drive to Mount Cook National Park and Ohau State Forest. Skifields, ice-skating, water sports, fishing and tramping are all handy. Glorious mountain views from the homestead.
I serve delicious New Zealand cuisine, mostly home grown, in quiet and relaxing surroundings.
Twizel township has a bank, doctor, hairdresser, shops, etc. plus golf, tennis and squash facilities.
Directions: *Please phone a day before or preferably earlier as bookings are necessary.*

Albury

Farmhouse
Address: "Golden Hill", Chamberlain Road, Albury, RD16,
Highway 8, Main Road to Mt Cook
Name: Jennifer and Roger McKeown
Telephone: (05055) 707
Beds: 1 Double, 2 Single (2 bedrooms)
Tariff: B&B Double $50, Single $25; Dinner by arrangement

Roger and I live in a warm, family farmhouse amongst attractive gardens and tennis court on our sheep and cattle farm. Two of our family are married and the youngest is working in London.

181

continued over

Our home is situated on a ridge overlooking farmland, hills and mountains. There are beautiful views from every room.
Several skifields — Mt Dobson, Round Hill, Fox Peak, Mt Hutt and Ohau — are within one to three hours drive from our home.
Farm activities can be enjoyed — walking up the meandering stream into the hills or exploring our beautiful MacKenzie country within one half an hours drive from our door. You are welcome to stay more than one night.
Directions: *Chamberlain Road runs west of Albury. We are eight miles up this road, the last farmhouse on left. Please ring before 8 am or the evening before arrival.*

Cave, Timaru

Self-Contained Accommodation
Address: Mount Nimrod, 14 RD, Cave
Name: Marion R. Patterson
Telephone: (03) 23-747
Beds: 2 Single (1 bedroom, guest bathroom)
Tariff: B&B Double $40, Single $20, Dinner by arrangement
Nearest Town: Timaru 52 km inland

We are a family of three — all adult. We have a modern, brick home situated close to Mount Nimrod Scenic Reserve which has broadleaf forest, native birds, wallabies and walking tracks maintained by the Department of Lands and Survey. Golf links about 8 km.
Interests include gardening, handcraft and farming activities.
Directions: *Please phone.*

Phone numbers may have changed. Ring 018 for directory.

Pleasant Point, Timaru

Farmhouse
Address: "Mt Gay", Pleasant Point, RD12, Timaru
Name: Florence and Roger Carter
Telephone: (056) 27-153
Beds: 4 Single (2 bedrooms, guest bathroom)
Tariff: B&B Double $60, Single $40, Children half price; Dinner $20
Nearest Town: Timaru

"Mt Gay" (1000') the family property for over a hundred years, is a sheep, goat and agro forestry farm thirty-five minutes drive from Timaru, two hours from Christchurch and Mt Cook. Bus, train and plane arrivals met at Timaru. There are limestone outcrops with sheltered valleys for walking, Maori drawings, and extensive beautiful views of snow-capped mountains, plains and sea.
In our modern, architecturally-designed home with its pleasant garden surrounds will be found a relaxed atmosphere and good country cuisine which has grown from many years of hosting experience.
One horse for experienced rider or lead-rides for children (no charge). Guns available for rabbit shooting. Five minutes drive to trout fishing river, 30 minutes drive to salmon fishing (tackle available), sixty to ninety minutes to three skifields, thirty minutes to the beach, fifteen minutes to golf, squash, tennis and Olympic pool.
Directions: *Please ring.*

Seadown, Timaru

Farmhouse
Address: Seadown, RD3, Timaru
Name: Margaret and Ross Paterson
Telephone: (056) 82-468
Beds: 2 Single (1 bedroom)
Tariff: B&B Double $55, Single 35, Children half price; Dinner $15
Nearest Town: Approximately halfway between Timaru
and Temuka

We are a mixed cropping farm situated in South Canterbury between Timaru and Temuka, east of State Highway 1 with a lovely view of the Southern Alps and a 20-minute walk from the sea coast.
We have a family of four with two married and two still living at home. One son works on the farm and is interested in competitive ploughing. We grow grass-seed, clover, grain crops and peas and also have 600 sheep.
Our home is an older type home which has been modernised. The guest room has two single beds with electric blankets and bathroom and toilet close by. Guests can use the laundry facilities. A very warm spacious living area, a swimming pool can be enjoyed in the warmer

continued over

183

*weather, also large lawns and garden. You are welcome to have your
meals with us.*

*Your hostess is interested in spinning, woolcraft and gardening. She
also makes her own bread which guests can enjoy.*

*Day trips can be comfortably taken to Tekapo, Mount Cook, Hydro
Lakes and skifields. A five-minute drive to the mouth of the Opihi River
for salmon fishing and whitebaiting in the season, a few minutes drive
to where Phar-Lap was born, the Timaru golf course a short driving
distance away.*

Directions: *From north approximately 5 km from Temuka to
Dominion Road on left. Turn right if travelling from Timaru approx
11 km. To the end of Dominion Road — turn right then left onto Beach
Road, till you come to Hides Road on left — first house on left on Hides
Road.*

Timaru

Homestay
Address: 16 Selwyn Street, Timaru
Name: Margaret and Nevis Jones
Telephone: (056) 81-400
Beds: 3 Single (2 bedrooms)
Tariff: B&B Double $55, Single $35, Children half price; Dinner $15

*We are a family of six but with only one child left at home. Our home is
a spacious, comfortable, two-storeyed brick house with a grass tennis
court in use from October until March.*

*Situated in central Timaru — 5 minutes walk from the beach and 15
minutes from town, our home is set back from the road in a private
garden surrounded by trees.*

*We have travelled and worked overseas with our four children three
and a half years of our married life, and share an enjoyment of meeting
people from other countries and feel we have an appreciation of what it
is like to be a visitor in a foreign country.*

184

Our main interests centre around music and the theatre in which we are both actively involved. We also play tennis and golf. We enjoy making use of the many walks and opportunities to get into the mountains which are so accessible from Timaru.

Timaru is centrally situated in the South Island — 2 hours from Christchurch, 2½ hours from Dunedin and Mt Cook and 2–2½ hours from five skifields.

Directions: *Please phone.*

Otaio, Timaru

Farmhouse
Address: "Cedar Downs",
Otaio, RD1 (Horseshoe
Bend Road), Timaru
Name: Mary and Graeme Bell
Telephone: (056) 26-647
Beds: 4 Single (2 bedrooms, guest bathroom)
Tariff: B&B Double $55, Single $35, Children half price; Dinner $15;
Campervans $6 per person (2 campervan points)
Nearest Town: 28 km south from Timaru, 28 km north
from Waimate

"Cedar Downs" is a farm of 600 acres only 1 km from main State Highway 1. Located in a pleasant valley we farm sheep, deer, cattle, goats and cropping. At times a demonstration of shearing can be arranged.

A comfortable brick home and warm hospitality await you. The two guest rooms have two single beds in each, all with electric blankets and you have your own bathroom. There are two campervan power points with shower and toilet facilities.

Meals can be provided for live-in or campervan guests if required.

A swimming pool and barbecue area is set in an attractive garden where you are welcome to relax. If you prefer you are welcome to join in farm activities.

Day trips can be comfortably taken to Mt Cook, the lakes and ski fields. At Makikihi 4 km away there is a good craft shop.

Directions: *28 km south of Timaru or 28 km north of Waimate on Horseshoe Bend Road (signposted on main road), first farm on left.*

Always telephone ahead to enquire about a
B&B. It is a nuisance for you if you simply
arrive to find someone is already staying there.
And besides, hosts need a little time to
prepare.

185

Waimate

Farmhouse
Address: "Te Moana Nui", Willowbridge, RD10, Waimate
Name: Don and Lorna Hayman
Telephone: (0519) 28-837
Beds: 4 Single (2 bedrooms, guest bathroom)
Tariff: B&B Double $50, Single $25, Children half price; Dinner $15;
Campervans $20 up to 4 people
Nearest Town: 44 km south from Timaru, 41 km north from
Oamaru, 12 km east from Waimate

We are midway between Christchurch and Dunedin and have a mixed cropping and livestock farm situated on the banks of the Waihao river and bounded on the east by the sea. Fishing, boating and waterskiing within walking distance.
Our attractive home is in a tranquil setting of trees and garden (sheltered and sunny) with a lovely view of the hills and mountains.
Two guest rooms are available, each with twin beds and serviced by a bathroom and shower room. Ample parking for campervans, power, toilet and shower room handy.
You are assured of warm, friendly hospitality and are most welcome to have family dinner with us or bed and breakfast if preferred.
Waimate has lovely gardens, bush walks, scenic drives, golf, etc. A pleasant day trip to Mt Cook is possible, or you may prefer to just relax and enjoy our surroundings. You are very welcome to stay more than one night.
Directions: *On State Highway 1 44 km south of Timaru, or 41 km north of Oamaru, turn into Lucks Road opposite a bright yellow barn, first turn left, second left, first right into Low's Road, second house on left (5 km from State Highway).*

Waimate

Homestay
Address: Wainono Homestead, RD10 Waimate
Name: Ken and Cynthia Henderson
Telephone: (0519) 28-883
Beds: 1 Double, 2 Single (2 bedrooms, guest bathroom)
Tariff: B&B $35 per person, Children under 13 years half price;
Dinner $15
Nearest Town: Waimate

Our olde worlde homestead set in a peaceful 5 acre garden setting is situated on State Highway 1, 800 metres south of the Waimate/Kurow turnoff, midway between Timaru and Oamaru and only 2½ hours drive from Christchurch.
It was built in 1910 as a gentleman's residence for Paul Studholme, a son of Michael Studholme, the first white settler in Waimate.

The homestead is handy to salmon and trout fishing in the Waitaki River and is an easy drive to the hydro lakes and Mount Cook.

A craft and art gallery featuring an extensive range of high quality crafts and paintings has been established in the former ballroom of the homestead.

There is a choice of guest room, with either a double or single beds and your own bathroom.

Your hosts' interests include spinning and weaving, porcelain dolls and railway preservation and modelling.

Waimate

Farmhouse
Address: Trebell Farm,
8RD Waimate,
South Canterbury
Name: Diane and Brian Foley
Telephone: (0519) 25-722
Beds: 2 Single (1 bedroom)
Tariff: B&B $25 per person, Children half price;
Dinner $12; Campervans $15
Nearest Town: 3 km from State Highway 1, 11 km Waimate

We are a family of four, the two children attend the local high school. We live in an 80-year-old home that has both character and charm. The views in all directions are pleasing to the eye and extend from the ocean to the Hunter Hills.

On our farm we breed the uniquely New Zealand sheep — Drysdales. We also have many pets that like people and plenty of attention.

We are fortunate to own a 'wetlands' area which is the home of many New Zealand birds.

The Waimate area offers the opportunity for many sporting activities such as hang gliding, tramping, fishing, shooting and boating.

Our guest room is reached by a spiral staircase and has two single beds. The bathroom is shared with the family.

Meals may be taken with the family or separately as preferred.

We love meeting people from new walks of life with whom we can share conversation in our relaxed environment.

Directions: *We may be found by turning off State Highway 1, 4 km south of Makikihi onto O'Neils Road. Our home is at the junction of O'Neils Road, Nolans Road and Rathgens Road.*

187

Omarama

Farmhouse
Address: Dunstan Downs, Omarama
Name: Tim and Geva Innes
Telephone: (02984) 862
Beds: 1 Double, 2 Single
Tariff: B&B $25 per person; Dinner $20
Nearest Town: Omarama — 17 km west on State Highway 8

*Dunstan Downs is a sheep and cattle station in the heart of the South
Island highcountry.*
We have two school-age children, one at boarding school.
*Our home is full of country warmth and you are welcome to join us for
dinner or bed and breakfast.*
*We have a beautiful river for fishing nearby and also for pleasant
walks. Ohau skifield is only an hour away.*

Waitaki Valley, Oamaru

Farmhouse
Address: 'Sunny Downs', Otekaieke, 9k R.D., Oamaru
Name: Kaye and Keith Dennison
Telephone: (0297) 22-741
Beds: 2 Double, 1 Single (2 bedrooms), Sleepout with 2
good single beds
Tariff: B&B Double $50, Single $25, Sleepout $10, Children under
13 half price; Dinner $15; Campervans $20 (up to 4 people,
includes light breakfast)
Nearest Town: 60 km west of Oamaru on State Highway 83,
60 km east of Omarama,
15 km east of Kurow

*We invite you to share our home with us and experience the peace and
tranquility of the country. We are a family of four with two teenage
children. We live on a farm just 2 km from State Highway 83 and 3 km
from the Waitaki river which is well-known for its fishing and jet-
boating. Fishing trips and jetboat rides can usually be arranged. We
are en route to and from Mt Cook. Skifields are very accessible.*
*On our farm we have sheep, cattle and the usual farm animals. We
enjoy showing people around and having them join in farm activities.
We have a swimming pool and a pony for children to ride.*
*The farmhouse is large and modernised. The beds have woolrest
sleepers and electric blankets. Full accommodation or just bed and
breakfast available. Longer stays are very welcome. We have a power
point for a campervan.*
*Quiet surroundings. Families welcome. Friendship and warm hospi-
tality assured.*

We are members of N.Z. Association of Farm and Home Hosts.
Kaye is a schoolteacher so please phone after 4 pm or before 8 pm on schooldays — other days phone at any time, or just arrive. There is usually someone around.
Directions: *From Oamaru or Christchurch turn onto State Highway 83 and continue through Duntroon, take second road on left which is Eastern Road. We are second place on right with 'Sunny Downs' on the gate. From Mt Cook/Omarama pass through Kurow, take 6th road on right — Eastern Road.*

Can't contact your host? Ring 018 for directory assistance.

Oamaru

Homestay
Address: 107 Reservoir Road, Oamaru
Name: June and Ken McAuley
Telephone: (0297) 71-360
Beds: 3 Single (2 bedrooms)
Tariff: B&B Double $50, Single $30, Dinner $15;
Campervans welcome $15 (facilities available)
Nearest Town: Oamaru 3 kms

We welcome you to join us on our small farm where we have cattle, goats and a friendly dog. Our modern home is centrally heated and is very comfortable. The guest rooms are twin and single. Beds all have electric blankets and a large bathroom next to guest rooms. We have a great rural, mountain and ocean view.
You may join us for an evening meal if ordered before 2 pm or if you prefer just bed and breakfast.
Visit beaches, penguin colony, museum, historic buildings. Day trips to Waitaki basin, hydro lakes, fishing rivers or Mount Cook.
Directions: *On State Highway 1 at Waitaki Girls High School turn up Dusle Street and follow white line up the hill into Reservoir Road (1·5 km). Name and number on letterbox.*

189

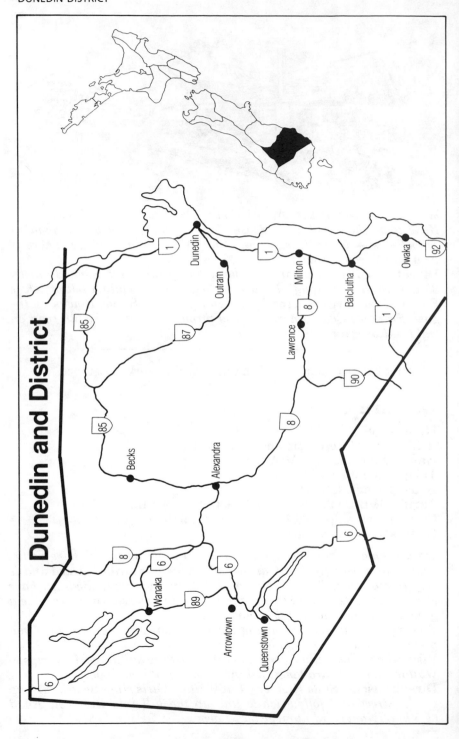

Dunedin and District

Wanaka

Homestay
Address: 15 Norman Terrace, Wanaka
Name: Sue and Dick Williman
Telephone: (029) 437-135
Beds: 1 Double, 2 Single (2 bedrooms)
Tariff: B&B Double $50, Single $25, School Children $10
Nearest Town: Town centre 2 km

Our modern, family home includes a warm visitors flat with twin and double rooms, dinette (tea-making facilities) and bathroom.
Our home is less than 100 m from Lake Wanaka. There is easy access to it through a beautiful lakeside park. From here too there are pleasant lakeside walks.
Wanaka is one of New Zealand's faster-growing holiday centres. Its opportunity for watersports, its picturesque golf course and proximity to Aspiring National Park have made it a popular summer resort.
Recently two large commercial skifields have been developed in the area.
The town offers a variety of good restaurants and activities for visitors. Dick and I have travelled overseas extensively and have now made our base in Wanaka.
As we are both high school teachers and run a small bus company as well we would request that visitors ring in the evening for bookings or be brave and use the answerphone. We welcome the opportunity to meet and greet overseas visitors as do our two boys Jonathan and Malcolm. We do request visitors not to smoke in our home.
Directions: *From the town centre follow the road west around the lake towards Glendu Bay. Second road on the right (Sargood Drive) leads into Ripponlea subdivision. Norman Terrace is the first road on the right off Sargood Drive. Ours is a back section.*

Can't contact your host? Ring 018 for directory assistance.

Arrowtown

Homestay
Address: 20 Wiltshire Street, Arrowtown, Central Otago
Name: Mrs Cynthia Balfour
Telephone: (0294) 21-326
Beds: 1 Double, 2 Single (2 bedrooms)
Tariff: B&B Double $70, Single $45; Dinner $25
Nearest Town: Arrowtown, 19 km from Queenstown

I am a semi-retired businesswoman, well travelled with a variety of interests including gardening, cooking, arts and crafts and skiing. I welcome the opportunity of offering hospitality to visitors to New Zealand.

My attractive colonial-style home is located in the historic centre of Arrowtown, an old gold mining town in Central Otago.
The area offers both summer and winter activities such as hiking, bungie jumping, trout fishing and skiing in the winter.
Queenstown, an international tourist resort, is about 20 minutes away. It offers quality shopping, jetboating, rafting, helicopter sightseeing and excellent restaurants, as well as other popular attractions.
My warm and comfortable home has two guest rooms — one double and one twin. I prefer non smokers.
Interesting home cooking is a speciality.
Skiers are welcome from approximately mid-June to mid-October depending on the season. Four internationally-recognised ski areas are within easy reach.
Reservations ahead by phone or letter please.

One of the differences between staying at a
hotel and staying at a B&B is that you don't
hug the hotel staff when you leave.

Lake Hayes, Queenstown

Homestay
Address: Speargrass Lodge, Speargrass Flat Road,
Lake Hayes RD1 Queenstown
Name: Denis and Jenny Jenkins
Telephone: (0294) 21-411
Beds: 1 Double, 7 Single (4 bedrooms, guest bathroom)
Tariff: B&B Double $70, Single $35, Children under 13
half price; Dinner $20
Nearest Town: Queenstown 15 minutes, Arrowtown 5 minutes

Our home is known as Speargrass Lodge, set in 11 acres of landscaped garden and meadow amidst the beautiful mountain scenery that this area is so famous for.

We are a busy household with two schoolage children, an assortment of friendly farmyard animals and we enjoy opening our home to visitors from all over the world.

Guests are invited to relax in the peaceful, rural environment yet be within short driving distance of the many tourist and recreational activities that Queenstown has to offer.

Accommodation for up to 10 guests is spacious and comfortable and includes ensuite facilities, large living area with huge open fireplace, games room, barbecue area and children's trampoline.

As qualified chefs we take pleasure in cooking memorable meals for our guests from light summer dishes to hearty après ski dinners.

Our home is in a central location to four major snowfields so skiing plays an important part of our southern winters. We also own and operate the 'Flower Barn' on our property which is a year-round tourist attraction well-known for its displays of dried flowers and country cottage crafts.

Directions: *Speargrass Lodge is easy to find. Heading north on the main Cromwell highway from Queenstown turn left to Arrowtown after passing Lake Hayes. Then it is first left along Speargrass Flat Road. AA signage at the intersection. Heading south to Queenstown from Cromwell turn right to Arrowtown on first sight of Lake Hayes then again first left along Speargrass Flat Road.*

193

Queenstown

Homestay
Address: 6 Oregon Drive,
Kelvin Heights, RD2,
Queenstown
Name: Audrey & Kathie Galbraith
Telephone: (03) 44-29665
Beds: 1 Double, 2 Single (2 bedrooms, guest bathroom)
Tariff: B&B Double $60, Single $35; Dinner by arrangement $20

We are two sisters who have "been there, done that" overseas — now relaxing in beautiful Queenstown.
Our home is a new two-storeyed colonial style with panoramic views of lake and mountains. The two guest rooms are on the ground floor serviced with own bathroom/toilet facilities.
Our home overlooks lake Wakatipu and across to Queenstown centre. Driving times are Queenstown 20 minutes, airport 10 minutes, Frankton village 10 minutes, golf course 2 minutes.
As Queenstown is an international tourist resort it offers excellent 7-day-week shopping, sightseeing fishing, skiing (in season) and many top class restaurants.
We do request guests not to smoke in our home.
Directions: *Please phone before 9 am or after 4.30 pm.*

Queenstown

Homestay
Address: 396 Peninsula Road, Kelvin Heights, RD2, Queenstown
Name: Janet and Don Anderson
Telephone: (0294) 29-467
Beds: 5 Single (3 bedrooms, guest bathroom)
Tariff: B&B Double $50, Single $25
Nearest Town: Queenstown 11 km by road

We have been retired for several years and our family of two boys and two girls are all away from the nest.
We are living in an area we have always loved. From our home the view is an artist's dream encompassing lake and mountain scenery of great beauty.
A fine 18-hole golf course and the deer park are close by. Below the house a lakeside walkway offers trout fishing or strolling in tranquil surroundings. There are several skifields within easy reach.
We would be glad to advise you on any of the exciting adventures available.
Directions: *At Frankton take Invercargill road, cross Kawarau Bridge and take first turn to right to Kelvin Heights. Pass Deer Park entrance and continue approximately 0·8 km and our house is on left above Peninsula Road.*

Queenstown

Homestay
Address: No 2 Boyce Crescent, Frankton, Queenstown
Name: Lois and Ivan Lindsay
Telephone: (0294) 23-162
Beds: 4 Single (2 bedrooms, guest bathroom)
Tariff: B&B Double $50, Single $30; Dinner $15
Nearest Town: Frankton 1 km, Queenstown 6 km

We are retired sheep and grain farmers from Southland. We have a family of six, all married. Our interests are gardening, sport, knitting and meeting people.

We have two twin guest rooms overlooking the lake with electric blankets, bedside lamps and heaters. Guests have a separate bathroom. Also a sunny conservatory to relax in.

Our home is in a sunny situation on the Frankton arm of Lake Wakatipu by the Kawarau River, six kilometres from Queenstown with pleasant walking tracks in the area. We are at the base of the Remarkable mountains where excellent skiing is available. Coronet Peak and Cardrona fields are also in the area.

There is a shopping centre in Frankton with airport, coach-stop, medical facilities, golf, tennis, water sports, jetboating, fishing, helicopter flights and coach and plane tours to Milford Sound all within 1 km of our home.

For those arriving by coach transport can be arranged to and from Queenstown where many more tourist attractions are available.

Directions: *1 km from Frankton on Invercargill State Highway 6. Name on letterbox on right.*

Phone numbers may have changed. Ring 018 for directory.

Becks

Farmhouse
Address: Becks, RD2, Omakau, Central Otago
Name: Earl and Pam Harrex
Telephone: (029 443) 609
Beds: 1 Double, 1 Single (2 bedrooms)
Tariff: B&B $28 per person, Children half price;
Dinner $14; Campervans $15
Nearest Town: Alexandra 45 km

We farm sheep and deer at Becks in Central Otago. Guests are always welcome to take part in the everyday running of the farm. We are a family of five — three schoolage children.

We have recently renovated our older-style homestead, set in picturesque grounds with a swimming pool and barbecue area. A large open fire, plus central heating provides a cosy home during the winter months.

The guest rooms have one double bed and one single bed, sharing the bathroom and laundry facilities with hosts.

Our family interests include gardening, swimming, fishing, patchwork, music, summer and winter sports including curling — a traditional winter sport unique to Central Otago. We are two hours drive from four major ski-fields.

We offer guests motorbike rides, horseriding, short trips to nearby historical St Bathans and other nearby goldmining ghost towns.

We really enjoy showing visitors our quiet, peaceful rural setting with magnificent views of the vast openness of Central Otago.

Directions:*From Alexandra take State Highway 85 to Becks Hotel. First left turn to St Bathans. Our farm is 2 km from turnoff — named motor gate. From Palmerston take State Highway 85 for 120 km to Becks School. Right turn to St Bathans.*

NZ phone numbers are being changed. Ring 018 for directory.

Alexandra

Homestay
Address: 13 Schaumann Street, Alexandra
Name: Mrs Kay Adam
Telephone: (0294) 86-322
Beds: 2 Single (1 bedroom, guest bathroom)
Tariff: B&B Double $50, Single $30

The guest area has a room with 2 single beds, a small sitting room and a bathroom with a shower.

I live alone except for my golden labrador and three variegated cats, all of whom are excluded from the visitors' area. I do relief teaching at the local high school and interview for the Department of Statistics.

Alexandra lies at the junction of the Clutha and Manuherikia rivers and is the centre of farming and fruit growing. It is well-known for its climate — cold and dry in winter, hot and dry in summer. It has some pleasant shops, many restaurants, a museum, swimming pool and parks.

On many weekends, particularly when it is hot, I go to my holiday house at St Bathans — 60 km from Alexandra. This is an old gold mining town with small pub, ten houses and a lake. I have a guest room with two single beds but the furnishings are simple and there is only one bathroom which contains bath, basin and toilet. The charge is the same as Alexandra but includes simple lunch and dinner. The telephone number is Omakau 689.

Directions: *From Post Office (and bus stop) go up Centennial Avenue (road to Clyde and Cromwell and Queenstown), take the fourth road on the left (Matau Street) and then second right which is Schaumann Street.*

Dunedin

Homestay
Address: 6 Kiwi Street, St Leonards, Dunedin
Name: Shirley and Don Parsons
Telephone: (024) 710-690
Beds: 1 Double, 2 Single (2 bedrooms)
Tariff: B&B Double $50, Single $30, Children half price;
Dinner $12–$15
Nearest Town: 5 km from Dunedin

We live in a quiet suburb 10 minutes from the city centre. Our home overlooks the lovely Otago Harbour and is within easy reach of many of the local attractions — Larnach Castle, Olveston, the Albatross colony and Disappearing Gun, Portobello Aquarium and harbour cruises.

Dunedin is a lovely city situated at the head of the Otago harbour with many interesting and historic stone buildings to view.

There are also many lovely bush walks within easy reach of the city.

We have a family of five who have all left home so we have two rooms available, one double and one twin, with a cot also available as children are very welcome. The bathroom facilities are shared.

We have a generous amount of living space and you may have an evening meal with us or if you prefer only bed and breakfast.

Directions: *From the Dunedin Railway Station follow Anzac Avenue onto Ravensbourne Road. Continue down the harbourside approximately 5 km until you reach St Leonards. Turn left into Moa Street then left into Kaka Road then straight ahead to Kiwi Street and turn left.*

Dunedin

Homestay
Address: 1 Eagle Street, Burkes, Dunedin
Name: Allan and Judith Hutton
Telephone: (024) 710-753
Beds: 1 Double, 2 Single (2 bedrooms, guest bathroom)
Tariff: B&B Double $55, Single $35; Dinner $15

We have a comfortable home and promise you relaxing, comfortable hospitality. We enjoy having guests and catering for them. You have your own bathroom and toilet facilities.
We enjoy yachting and have a love of good music. From our home we have a view of our beautiful Otago harbour which we never tire of.
Directions: *Take Highway 88 from Dunedin to Port Chalmers. Burkes is the second suburb from Dunedin, a distance of 7 km from Dunedin Railway Station, it is situated on the second harbour inlet.*

Dunedin

Homestay
Address: 84 London Street, Dunedin
Name: Bruce and Val Duder
Telephone: (024) 778-638
Beds: 1 Double, 4 Single (3 bedrooms, guest bathroom)
Tariff: B&B Double $75, Single $40, Children half price; Dinner $18

We offer the unique experience of staying in one of Dunedin's historic mansions, seven minutes walk to the Octagon, and near the special attractions in central Dunedin.
The house is full of French polished mahogany, beautiful stained glass windows, and original brass fittings. Despite its grandeur, it is a very comfortable home.
Our guest rooms are upstairs, with superb views of the city. The main guest room has a queen-size bed and a single, and a vanity unit. There is a twin bedded room and a single room. There are two bathrooms, one solely for guests, the other shared with us. Also upstairs is a "galley" where guests can make a cup of tea or coffee anytime, plus a small reading room.
We share our living room, which has a beamed ceiling and an inglenook with an open fire, with our guests. We do provide dinner, with a little notice, using good New Zealand produce. Special diets can be catered for given 24 hours notice. Breakfast can be as substantial as you choose.
Allergy sufferers should note we have three cats.
Send for free map and brochure.

Dunedin

Homestay
Address: Magnolia House, 18 Grendon Street, Maori Hill, Dunedin
Name: Joan and George Sutherland
Telephone: (024) 671-999
Beds: 1 Double, 3 Single (3 bedrooms, guest bathroom)
Tariff: B&B $30 per person; Dinner $20
Nearest Town: Dunedin city centre 2 km

We live in a superior suburb on half an acre of land, one third of which is native bush with wood pigeons, tuis, bellbirds and fantails. The rest is in lawn and attractive gardens.

Our 1906 house is spacious with a large dining room and drawing room, and a more intimate sitting room.

The double room has its own large balcony looking out on lawns and bush. The guest rooms are airy and have antiques. Guests share their own bathroom with shower and tub. There are fireplaces in most of the rooms and central heating in all. Two nights in Dunedin is a must.

We are very close to Otago Golf Club and can supply clubs, bag and trolley free. Also nearby is Olveston stately home and Moana Olympic-size swimming pool. The Otago peninsula is a wonderful day's sightseeing.

We can provide a fine New Zealand meal with wine, liqueurs, candles and conversation if given sufficient notice (4 hours).

We have two cats, a courtesy car, bus nearby and no smoking.
Directions: *Please phone.*

Outram

Farmhouse
Address: "Lee Ridges", Hindon, RD2, Outram
Name: Bruce and Nola Dick
Telephone: (024) 891-477
Beds: 4 Single (2 bedrooms, guest bathroom)
Tariff: B&B Double $60, Single $45, Reduced rates
for more than 2 persons; Dinner $15
Nearest Town: 40 km west from Dunedin, Mosgiel 25 km

Our 560-acre sheep farm offers you the opportunity to experience

199

continued over

"everyday" rural New Zealand. At 1300 ft above sea level we have a panoramic view of surrounding countryside.
Our near-new home has a guest bedroom and games room upstairs, extra beds available. Electric blankets and heaters in all rooms. A warm welcome awaits you.
Bruce's hobbies are wood turning and hunting trips. He is always willing to take interested people around the farm. Nola is accustomed to cooking for guests — "Lee Ridges roast lamb" a speciality. Wine or non-alcoholic drinks served with dinner. We have two children at boarding school, a son and daughter at home. We also have a variety of pets, including one indoor cat.
We are adjacent to the Taieri River Gorge which offers jet-boating and white-water rafting, horse riding and train excursions.
Directions: *Travelling south from Dunedin turn off State Highway 1 into Mosgiel and continue through Mosgiel's main street towards Outram on State Highway 87. Cross the bridge over the Taieri river (1 km before Outram) and at the end of the bridge turn right into George King Memorial Drive. Continue on this tar-sealed road 15 km. We are the second house on the left after the Lee Stream Gorge.*

Can't contact your host? Ring 018 for directory assistance.

Milton

Farmhouse
Address: "Marylea", Clarksville, Milton
Name: Ian and Eleanore Clark
Telephone: (02997) 8621
Beds: 2 Single (1 bedroom)
Tariff: B&B Double $50, Single $30, Children half price; Dinner $15
Nearest Town: Milton on State Highway 1 at junction
of State Highways 1 and 8

Ian and myself plus our two teenage daughters live on a mixed farm in an older-style farmhouse. We have sheep, cattle, hens and two pet goats plus the usual pets. The girls and myself are very interested in the Girl Guide Movement.
We are close to forest walks and lovely beaches.
Milton is a small country town, supplying a larger farming area.
We are 30–35 minutes travel to Dunedin airport, also at the turnoff for Central Otago.
Directions: *Please phone.*

Tariffs are constant for this year. However,
some may have had to change slightly. Always
check.

Owaka

Farmhouse
Address: Glenomaru, RD1, Balclutha
Name: Bruce and Kathryn Wilson
Telephone: (0299) 58-282
Beds: 2 Single (1 bedroom)
Tariff: B&B Double $25 per person, Children half price;
Dinner $12; Campervan off-street parking
Nearest Town: Balclutha 22 km, Owaka 11 km

We are a family of six — three daughters and a son. Our son lives at home and is leasing an adjoining property.
We live on a 900 acre mixed farm running beef, sheep and deer. Guests may be taken on a farm tour.
We are very near Kaka Point, renowned for beach, lighthouse and yellow-eyed penguins.
The guest room has two single beds and shares our bathroom.
You may have family dinner with us or if you prefer only bed and breakfast.
Guests can be collected off public transport from Balclutha free of charge.
Directions: *Take Highway 92 from Balclutha towards Owaka, first turn right past sawmill. From Owaka turn left beside sawmill up gravel road.*

Owaka

Farmhouse
Address: Glenomaru, RD1, Balclutha
Name: Roger and Isla Jones
Telephone: (0299) 58-469
Beds: 2 Single (1 bedroom)
Tariff: B&B Double $50, Single $30, Children half price; Dinner $12
Nearest Town: Owaka 12 km, Balclutha 23 km

We are a family of four with two teenage children who usually have plenty of pets around.
On our 850 acre farm we run sheep and cattle and enjoy showing people around and have them join in any farm activities if they wish.
There are many walks and things of interest to do around the Catlins area — one being the Nugget Lighthouse where a reasonably fit person can get right down amongst the seals, etc.
We have a modern, centrally heated farmhouse offering full accommodation or just bed and breakfast. We can also accommodate two children who would share with our son and daughter.

Owaka

Farmhouse
Address: "Tarara Downs", RD2 Owaka, South Otago
Name: Ida and John Burgess
Telephone: (0299) 58-293
Beds: 1 Double, 2 Single (2 bedrooms); Sleepout for 3
Tariff: B&B Double $55, Single $35, Children half price;
Dinner $15 (3-course), $10 (2-course); Sleepout $10 per person
Nearest Town: Owaka 16 km

Our 1325-acre farm is situated in an area renowned for its bush and coastal scenery. Also the beautiful Purakaunui Falls are within walking distance. The farm runs sheep, cattle and deer and we also have horses to ride and riding instruction available.
Many farm activities may be seen and participated in, eg sheep shearing and dogs working. Fishing trips and bush walks may be arranged. Our pets love people and attention!
We live in a comfortable New Zealand farmhouse and enjoy eating our own produce and local delicacies.
Children very welcome.
Directions: *Follow State Highway 92. Approximately 1¾ hours drive from Invercargill or Dunedin on a scenic, coastal road, follow signposts to Purakaunui Falls — we are the closest house to them.*

Phone numbers may have changed. Ring 018 for directory.

Owaka

Farmhouse
Address: "Greenwood", Tarara, RD2 Owaka, South Otago
Name: Alan and Helen-May Burgess
Telephone: (0299) 58-259 (if no reply, phone after 6 pm)
Beds: 4 Single (2 bedrooms)
Tariff: B&B Double $55, Single $35; Dinner $15, Lunch if required;
Campervans $20; Self contained house at Papatowai beach (sleeps 8)
$50 per night (4 persons), $10 each extra person
Nearest Town: Owaka 14 km

We farm in the Catlins district with our homestead situated within walking distance from the beautiful Purakaunui Falls (features on the front cover of Wild New Zealand *book).*
Our home which is set in a large garden offers warm, comfortable accommodation for up to four persons. The main guest bedroom opens through to a day-room furnished with vanity unit (hand basin), divan, table and chairs, giving you private living facilities. The sunny room opens out to the outdoor barbecue area. The bathroom, toilets and shower room would be shared with our family.
A three-course dinner may be provided.

Our 1500 acre farm is hilly to rolling country, farming sheep, cattle and some deer. Alan is always willing to take interested people around the farm or have them partake in farm-related activities. Horse riding can be arranged.

Our district features many beautiful scenic drives and walks through native forest and beaches. Trout, salmon or rock fishing may be enjoyed.

Directions: *Take the road (Highway 92) to Owaka from Balclutha or Invercargill. From Owaka follow the signposts to Purakaunui Falls for 14 km. Our name and farm name is on the gate entrance (just before you reach the falls).*

Ask your hosts for local information. They are your own personal travel agent and guide.

New Zealand is known as the friendliest country in the world and our hosts will live up to that reputation.

All telephone numbers in New Zealand are being changed during 1990 so the numbers listed may not be current. Ring 018 for directory assistance if you cannot contact your hosts.

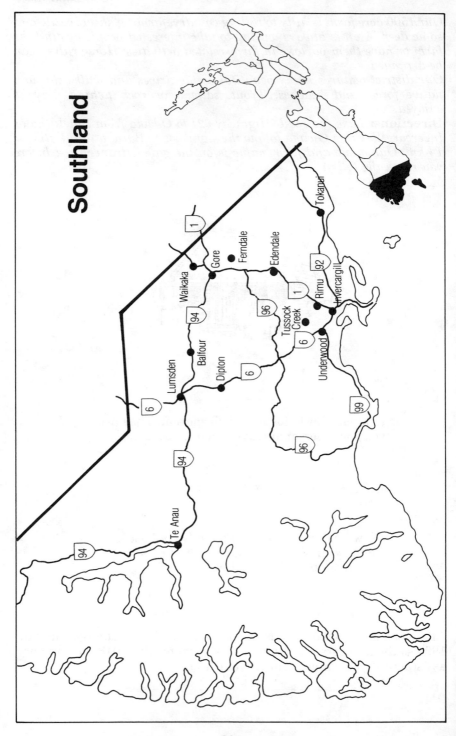

Te Anau

Farmhouse
Address: Sinclair Road, RD1, Te Anau
Name: Teresa Hughes
Telephone: (0229 7581)
Beds: 2 Single (1 bedroom, guest bathroom)
Tariff: B&B Double $55, Single $35
Nearest Town: Te Anau 5 km

My husband, Dave, and I, and our three children aged between ten and fourteen years old) live on a deer farm overlooking Lake Te Anau.
The guest room, which has your own private bathroom, has a beautiful view of the Lake and mountains.
Te Anau is the centre of all tourist attractions in Fiordland. We would suggest a stay of more than one night to allow more time to enjoy them, e.g. a day trip to Milford Sound (116 km) or a visit to Doubtful Sound — a very relaxing day. There are also many interesting bush walks and the lakes and rivers have excellent fishing — only 5–10 minutes drive away.
We can assure you of a very warm and friendly stay. (It is usually better to ring before 8 a.m. or after 6 p.m.).
Directions: *Continue through Te Anau on road to Milford Sound for about 5 km, turn right at Sinclair Road and continue for 1 km. We are the second house on the left, our name is on the letterbox.*

Some hosts are away from home during the
day. It will help if you phone them the evening
before you want to stay.

Te Anau

Farmhouse + Self-Contained Accommodation
Address: Please phone
Name: Ross and Joan Cockburn
Telephone: (0229) 7082
Beds: 4 Single (2 bedrooms, guest bathroom)
Tariff: B&B Double $70, Single $35; Self-Contained Farm Cottage
$50 (up to 4 persons); Self-Contained Farm Quarters $40 (up to
4 persons); Dinner $15
Nearest Town: Te Anau 18 km

*We live on a rolling, hill country sheep, cattle and goat station, situated
18 km from Te Anau and offer walks/tramping, native bush and horse
riding. Also swimming and trout fishing in the white stone river.*
*You are welcome to join in with the daily working of the property or use
us as a base for day trips to all Fiordland.*
*We have three teenagers who are usually away at school. As a family
we enjoy meeting and entertaining people.*

Te Anau

Farmhouse
Address: Kakapo Road, Te Anau, PO Box 69
Name: Naomi and David Hughes
Telephone: (0229) 7081
Beds: 3 Single (2 bedrooms)
Tariff: B&B Double $70, Single $35; Dinner $15
Nearest Town: Te Anau 8 km

*Our farm, running deer, sheep and angora goats, overlooks Te Anau
and offers superb views of the lake and mountains.*
*Fiordland, one of the world's largest national parks, is renowned for its
rugged beauty and pristine mountain and valley environment.*
*We enjoy sharing our broad experience of tramping in this region and
can assist with ideas, planning and reservations for your Fiordland
experience — sightseeing, fishing, tramping, etc. Picnic lunch and
transport to and from Te Anau can be arranged, also safe storage for
your vehicle and belongings whilst you 'walk the tracks'.*
Directions: *Turn off State Highway 94 onto Kakapo Road 4 km on
Mossburn side of Te Anau. Our place (name on letterbox) is on top of
the hill 4 km from turnoff on the left.Tar sealed road.*

Let the phone ring for a long time when
telephoning.

Lumsden

Farmhouse
Address: Josephville, No. 4 R.D., Lumsden
Name: Annette and Bob Menlove
Telephone: (0228) 7114
Beds: 2 Single (1 bedroom, guest bathroom)
Tariff: B&B Double $55; Dinner $15 per person
Nearest Town: 9 km south of Lumsden, Invercargill 80 km

We live on a 520-hectare farm on State Highway 6 to the lakes. We enjoy meeting people and would like to have you to stay with us.
We live beside a river well-known for its trout fishing. Our farm has got sheep, cattle, deer and goats.
You would be welcome to have the family meal with us or if you prefer bed and breakfast.
Please phone before 8.30 am or after 5 pm.

Balfour

Farmhouse
Address: Longridge North, No. 6 R.D., Gore
Name: Ivor and Margaret Black
Telephone: (020) 46-090
Beds: 4 Single (2 bedrooms)
Tariff: B&B Double $40, Single $20, Children half price;
Campervans welcome
Nearest Town: Lumsden 15 minutes, Gore 35 minutes north-east

We live in a beautiful farmland valley surrounded by majestic mountains. We are on the main tourist route to Milford Sound, Lakes Te Anau and Manapouri and Queenstown. Our home is comfortable and warm. The beds have electric blankets and feather duvets.
Our family are grown up and away from home. We have travelled and we enjoy meeting and having people to stay.
We farm sheep, deer and cattle and are very fortunate to be only ten minutes from one of the most famous trout fishing rivers in the world, the Mataura River, with two others not much further away (the Oreti and Waikaia). So, if it is fishing, farming or just relaxing in our tranquil garden and surroundings, we will enjoy sharing it with you.
Invercargill is 1¼ hours away, Lake Manapouri (New Zealand's loveliest lake) and Doubtful Sound 1 hour, Lake Te Anau (gateway to Fiordland and the famous Milford Track) 1 hour, Queenstown and Lake Wakatipu 1¼ hours.
Directions: *From Gore (½ hour) you turn right at Balfour crossroads then second turn left (signpost) follow tarseal, we are fifth house on left hand side (5 min). From Lumsden you take the road to Gore, just out of Lumsden at signpost you keep left and follow tarseal over hill. We are fifth house on right hand side (10 min).*

Balfour

Farmhouse
Address: "Hillcrest", No. 1 R.D., Balfour
Name: Ritchie and Liz Clark
Telephone: (020) 46-165
Beds: 1 Double, 2 Single (2 bedrooms)
Tariff: B&B Double $46, Single $23, Children under 12 half price;
Dinner $12; Campervans $15
Nearest Town: Lumsden 16 km, Gore 40 km

*We welcome you to join us on our farm. We are a family of four with two
young boys and as a family enjoy working together, meeting people and
enjoy playing social tennis and squash.*
*On our 650-acre farm we run 2,500 ewes, a few cattle and some
cropping.*
*Our semi-detached guest room has two single beds and if required we
have a double room in our home. We are happy to put up an extra bed if
required. I am fond of cooking and welcome you to share our family
dinner or if you prefer only bed and breakfast.*
*Our farm is situated 3 km from Balfour which is a popular stopover,
being on the main tourist route from the lakes to Dunedin via Gore. We
are only minutes from some of the top trout fishing rivers.*
Directions: *Balfour is on the main highway 16 km from Lumsden and
40 km from Gore. When arriving at Balfour crossroads, take the road to
Waikaia, then the first turn to the left before transport depot and travel
2½ km, we are on the right. Please phone.*

Dipton

Farmhouse
Address: "Bilberry Oak",
Dipton R.D.
Name: John and Judy Buchanan
Telephone: (0228) 5228 (booking essential please)
Beds: 1 Double, 2 Single (2 bedrooms)
Tariff: B&B Double $60, Single $30, Children under 13 half price;
Dinner $10
Nearest Town: Lumsden 24 km, Invercargill 70 km

*Our farm is situated on one of the main roads from Invercargill
through to the attractions of Te Anau, Milford Sound and Queenstown
so it is a convenient stopover point during your travels.*
*Our comfortable farmhouse is set in a large garden which includes a
covered swimming pool and a barbecue area which we use a lot during
the summer months.*

We welcome you to have dinner with us or just bed and breakfast, the choice is yours. We also offer the use of our laundry facilities if you so desire.

John is always very willing to take folk about the property, explain about the New Zealand way of farming and if at all possible, let you see at close hand such activities as shearing. Our is mainly a sheep farm with a little cropping and a few cattle. We also have a Hampshire Sheep Stud.

We are interested in most sports and if you feel like a day's break from sightseeing, a game of squash or golf or a few hours fishing on the Oreti River could be easily arranged. I am a keen knitter and often have a selection of sweaters and other knitted articles for sale — no ridiculous mark-ups added here! Please ask if you are interested.

Our three sons are at boarding school so as yet we have not had the opportunity to travel overseas so we really enjoy the chance to hear first hand about other countries and cultures.

Directions: *Take the Dipton–Castlerock road (west side of Oreti river), turn on to Boundary Road, second house on right.*

Dipton

Farmhouse
Address: "Glenrannoch", Brices Road, Dipton
(Postal address: PO Box 11, Dipton)
Name: Garth and Adrianne Stewart
Telephone: (0228) 5088 (booking is essential please)
Beds: 2 Single, 1 Double (2 bedrooms)
Tarrif: B&B Double $50, Single $25; Dinner $15
Nearest Town: Invercargill 70 km, Te Anau 92 km,
Queenstown 130 km

Our farm is situated on the sunny north-west corner of the Hokonui hills. We live at 1,000 ft above sea level allowing magnificent views of mountains and farms.

We offer friendly rural hospitality on one of Southland's larger farms, also the opportunity to experience day to day activities of New Zealand farming including beef cattle breeding, stud and commercial sheep farming and Cashmere fibre production from goat farming.

We have a swimming pool and river fishing, golf, tennis and squash are available in Dipton.

Our central location is advantageous to those travellers wishing to experience the magnificent panoramic south — Milford Sound, Te Anau, Manapouri, Queenstown, Invercargill and Stewart Island are all within a day's return trip.

Directions: *Brices Road is signposted beside the Dipton Fire Station. Our home is 3 km from Dipton and 2 km past the golf course. Our name is at our entrance. If required we may be able to provide a pick-up service from Dipton.*

Waikaka

Farmhouse
Address: Blackhills, RD3 Gore, Southland
Name: Dorothy and Tom Affleck
Telephone: (020) 22-865
Beds: 2 Single (1 bedrooms)
Tariff: B&B Double $50, Single $30, Children under 13 half price;
Dinner $12
Nearest Town: Waikaka township, Gore

We are a family of six with four teenage children. Our fifty-year-old home, recently renovated to give generous comfortable living area, is situated on our 360 ha intensive sheep farm on a ridge above Waikaka River.
The guest room has two single beds (other beds may be available). The driveway is suitable for campervans to park close to the house and use our facilities.
You may have dinner with us or if you prefer only bed and breakfast. Our interests include family, farm, church, Masonic Lodge, sport and music. A warm welcome to couples and families.
Venture off the main road and enjoy warm hospitality, superb views and the refreshment of a quiet rural visit.
Directions: *Turn off State Highway 1 at McNab, onto State Highway 90. Turn left at Waikaka Valley corner, marked by church and windmill, follow signposts to Waikaka until T corner (approx 10 km). At T corner turn left, then first right onto metal Nth Chatton Road. Proceed 4 km veering right at each intersection. We live on Robertson Road, the last kilometre a steep hill — 20 minutes from State Highway 1.*

Ferndale, Gore

Farmhouse
Address: Ferndale, RD2, Gore
Name: Lorna and Colin Dickie
Telephone: (0203) 8335
Beds: 1 Double, 1 Twin Room
Tariff: B&B Double $55, Single $35; Dinner $15
Nearest Town: Mataura 7 km

Our home is 2,000 square feet, 10 years old, has large lounge-dining room and a pool room.
We are a middle-aged, semi-retired couple living on a 100-acre farmlet. We have sheep and thoroughbred horses.
We have a motorboat and are keen on camping and fishing. We are only abut 4 km from Mataura river, one of the world's greatest fishing rivers.
Our house is situated in a very quiet and peaceful area.

Directions: *Coming south, turn off State Highway 1 at Clinton Hotel, proceed south 37 km towards Mataura. Going north, turn through Mataura, past paper mills, 7 km up Ferndale Road.*

Tokanui

Farmhouse
Address: Progress Valley, RD1 Tokanui, Southland
Name: June and Murray Stratford
Telephone: (021398) 843 Tokanui
Beds: 1 Double, 2 Single (2 bedrooms)
Tariff: B&B Double $50, Single $25, Special rate for children; Dinner $15
Nearest Town: Invercargill 80 km, Dunedin 2½ hours' drive

Welcome to our place, just off the southern scenic route of State Highway 92. We are ideally situated to spend a few days exploring this unique area of the Catlins.
There are many unspoilt beaches, petrified forest, yellow-eyed penguins, waterfalls, bushwalks and caves all within 20 minutes' drive from our home. Nearby is an excellent craft shed and museum.
Our home is centrally-heated throughout and has an open fire in the lounge. All beds have electric blankets.
The youngest of our family, a keen rugby player, is at boarding school in Invercargill and comes home at the weekends.
When we are not working on our farm with the sheep, cattle and deer we like to play tennis or enjoy our many interests.
Visitors are invited to join in our community activities or they may prefer to go horseriding. We can arrange a 4 wheel drive trip to the more remote parts of the Catlins.
We have a power point in our garden for campervans.
Directions: *Please phone (meal times or after 6 pm is best).*

Tussock Creek, Invercargill

Farmhouse
Address: Sherwood Farm, Tussock Creek, No. 6 R.D., Invercargill
Name: Pat and Derek Turnbull
Telephone: (021) 397-270
Beds: 4 Single (2 bedrooms, guest bathroom)
Tariff: B&B $25 per person ($20 if more than one night); Dinner $15;
Campervans $20

*If you are looking for an interesting stay in a spacious residence, in a
peaceful setting — if you want to hear the bellbirds sing, hear the frogs
croak and watch the wood pigeons feed — or take a walk in our native
reserve — then this is it.*

*We have a grown up family and farm 600 acres of river flat with sheep
and cattle. Our interests include veteran athletics, tramping, gardening, C.W.I., and genealogy. We have travelled extensively.*

*We are suitable for a base as all southern tourist attractions are within
easy daily reach.*

*Having another 400-acre farm at Stewart Island enables us to arrange
connections and accommodation there if required.*

Directions: *Coming from either Invercargill or Queenstown/Te Anau
Highway, turn into Tussock Creek Road from Wilsons Crossing and
proceed east for 11½ km on bitumen and. Cross Makarewa River and
our gateway is by the bridge. Proceed towards the Reserve entrance
and turn right.*

Rimu, Invercargill

Farmhouse
Address: Rimu,
No. 7 R.D., Invercargill
Name: Margaret and
Alan Thomson
Telephone: (021) 304-798
Beds: 4 Single (2 bedrooms)
Tariff: B&B Double $55, Single $35; Dinner $20
Nearest Town: Invercargill 13 km

*Our home is approximately 30 years old, warm and comfortable with a
sunny aspect, all rooms overlooking a colourful garden, with the farm
beyond.*

*We run breeding ewes, a few very quiet Angora goats, and also have a
licensed meat processing factory on our property. The beautiful city of
Invercargill is only 13 km away and the choice of trips·by sea or air
easily arranged to wonderful Stewart Island. Te Anau, Queenstown
and Dunedin only 2½ hours' travel away.*

*You may have dinner with us and share an evening of relaxation and
friendship or if you prefer only bed and breakfast. We can provide the*

breakfast of your choice with all home grown products. Stay as many nights as you wish, a 'welcome' is always assured.
Directions: *Take State Highway 1, travel approximately 8 km from Invercargill P.O. (towards Dunedin), turn right (towards large green building with red roof), turn left, then right over railway line. Travel straight ahead for 4 km, we are on your left, A. J. Thomson on the mail box. Travelling from Dunedin on State Highway 1 take Rimu turnoff on left, turn right at crossroads, we are 1 km from there, on your right.*

NZ phone numbers are being changed. Ring 018 for directory.

Underwood, Invercargill

Homestay
Address: Underwood, No 4 RD, Invercargill
Name: Carol and Adrian Hunting
Telephone: (021) 358-252
Beds: 1 Double, 2 Single (2 bedrooms)
Tariff: B&B Double $50, Single $30, Children half price;
Dinner $15
Nearest Town: Invercargill

We are a young family of three living in a spacious, turn-of-the-century house on 20 acres situated on the southern scenic route. We grow our own fruit and vegetables, keep poultry and run a few sheep.
We have two guest bedrooms — one double room and one twin with a tiny turret room which is great for children. Extra beds are available if required. Both rooms have a cheerful aspect over the garden and front paddocks.
The lounge and dining room are warm and spacious with a glass enclosed porch off the dining room which gets a lot of sun.
Guests are welcome to have dinner with us or use our barbecue facilities if they wish. We offer a hearty cooked breakfast or Continental — whichever you prefer.
Directions: *From Invercargill — 1 km from start of State Highway 99. We're on the left hand side. From Te Anau/Riverton — 2 km after Wallacetown on the right hand side. For guests arriving in Invercargill by train, plane or bus we will be happy to meet you.*

Invercargill

Farmhouse + Self-Contained Accommodation
Address: "Lorneville Lodge", 11 R.D., Lorneville, Invercargill
Name: Bill and Pauline Schuck
Telephone: (021) 358-031, 358-762
Beds: 2 Single, 2 Double, 1 child's cot (2 bedrooms, guest bathroom)
Tariff: B&B Double $70, Single $35; Dinner $16.50 to $22;
Children under 13 half price; Campervans $7.50 per person;
Self-contained cottage $55 (up to 4 people, must be pre-booked and
for a minimum of 4 days), $12.50 (each extra person)
Nearest Town: Invercargill 14 km

*We are situated 3½ km from the main highway which takes you to
Queenstown and Te Anau.*
*We are a family who have moved out of town to enjoy the "good life" on
a 17½-acre farmlet. Our main interest is goat farming.*
We have sheep, hens, two cats, a dog and a pet opossum.
*Our home has had extensive renovations so that we can provide the
most comfortable accommodation possible. All beds have Sleep Well
matresses, electric blankets and sheepskin overlays. You have a private
bathroom if requested.*
*You may wish to spend time with us helping with chores and walking
around the paddocks or perhaps you want to sit and relax to take time
out from your busy itinerary.*
Safe playing area for children.
*Pauline is a newly-addicted patchworker and will be pleased to
arrange a meeting with local members of the Southern Patchworkers
and Quilters Circle.*
Babysitting, local tours, hunting and fishing trips by arrangement.
If you are travelling by bus or plane we are happy to meet you.
*You may have a family dinner with us or if you prefer only bed and
breakfast. All meals are prepared from farm fresh produce and our
vegetables come from our own organic garden. I enjoy cooking and can
promise you a delightful meal.*
*Invercargill has a beautiful park, interesting shops and friendly people.
Boat and plane leave Invercargill for Stewart Island.*
Directions: *Travel north on State Highway 6 from Invercargill for
10 km. Turn right at Lorneville garage on to Lorneville–Dacre
highway, proceed for 3½ km.*

Invercargill

Private Hotel
Address: 240 Spey Street, Invercargill
Name: Montecillo Travel Lodge
Telephone: (021) 82-503, Fax (021) 82-506
Beds: 3 bedrooms
Tariff: B&B Double $64, Single $39; Dinner $19; Campervans $20

We are Aileen and James Horn. Our Bed and Breakfast Hotel is in a quiet street and close to the centre of Invercargill (10 minutes walk to all shopping).

The main building is some 90 years old and we are returning it to its original state of large rooms and ensuite facilities, providing the best in beds and bedding.

We provide a full cooked breakfast — for the early starters or late sleepers — up to 9 am. A home-style three course roast dinner is available at 6 pm.

You can walk to the park and museum in five minutes. A golf course is ten minutes walk, as well as a number of historic buildings.

Your comfort and a restful stay in Invercargill is our business.

We can arrange trips to Stewart Island and ensure that your next stop is booked and suitable.

Our guests recommend a two-night stay to at least find out about Invercargill, Bluff and Stewart Island. Four nights to see it all well, and have a well-deserved rest.

Index

ORDER FORM

The New Zealand Bed and Breakfast Book and *The Australian Bed and Breakfast Book* are attractive and interesting guides that give details of homes and private hotels where you can be sure of feeling at home immediately. In the United States they are available at better bookstores or can be ordered directly from Pelican.

_____New Zealand Bed and Breakfast Book @ $9.95
_____Australian Bed and Breakfast Book @ $9.95

Subtotal_____
* Shipping and Handling_____
** Sales Tax_____
Total enclosed_____

Visa Mastercard   Card number:_____

exp. date:_____

signature:_____

*Add $1.50 postage and handling, plus 25 cents for each additional book ordered.
**Jefferson Parish residents, add 8% sales tax, all other Louisiana residents add 4% sales tax. *Prices subject to change without notice.*

Name _____
Address _____
City, State, Zip _____

. . . .

OVERSEAS ORDERS:

_____New Zealand Bed and Breakfast Book $16.95 US funds
_____Australian Bed and Breakfast Book $16.95 US funds

Total enclosed_____

Visa Mastercard Card number:_____

exp. date:_____

signature:_____

All payments must be made in International Money orders or charged to Visa or Mastercard. Payment for overseas orders includes airmail postage. *Prices subject to change without notice.*

To: PELICAN PUBLISHING COMPANY
P.O. Box 189
Gretna, LA 70054

Name _____
Address _____
City, State, Zip _____

The New Zealand Bed and Breakfast Book

Comment Form

In order to maintain our high standard of hospitality we welcome your comments and suggestions.

Did you stay at any B&B's especially deserving of praise?

Do you have any comments?

continued over

Did you stay at any Bed and Breakfasts where the hospitality or amenities were less than you expected?

Do you have any comments?

Where did you get your *New Zealand Bed and Breakfast Book*?

How many of our Bed and Breakfasts have you stayed at?

May we quote your comments?

Name ....

Address ....

....

Post to: Pelican Publishing Company, Inc., P.O. Box 189
1101 Monroe Street, Gretna, Louisiana 70053

NOTES

NOTES

NOTES

NOTES